INVENTIONS *of the* IMAGINATION

INVENTIONS OF THE IMAGINATION

ROMANTICISM AND BEYOND

EDITED BY
Richard T. Gray
Nicholas Halmi
Gary J. Handwerk
Michael A. Rosenthal
and *Klaus Vieweg*

A ROBERT B. HEILMAN BOOK

UNIVERSITY OF WASHINGTON PRESS
Seattle and London

Inventions of the Imagination: Romanticism and Beyond is published with support from a generous bequest established by Robert B. Heilman, distinguished scholar and chair of the University of Washington English Department from 1948 to 1971. The Heilman Book Fund assists in the publication of books in the humanities. This book also received support from the Byron W. and Alice L. Lockwood Foundation and the Walter Chapin Simpson Center for the Humanities, University of Washington.

© 2011 by the University of Washington Press
Printed and bound in the United States of America
Design by Thomas Eykemans
Composed in Warnock Pro, typeface designed by Robert Slimbach.
Display type set in Memphis, designed by Rudolf Wolf.
16 15 14 13 12 11   5 4 3 2 1

UNIVERSITY OF WASHINGTON PRESS
PO Box 50096, Seattle, WA 98145, USA
www.washington.edu/uwpress

LIBRARY OF CONGRESS CATALOGING-IN-PUBLICATION DATA
Inventions of the imagination : Romanticism and beyond /
edited by Richard T. Gray . . . [et al.].
       p. cm.
"A Robert B. Heilman Book."
Includes bibliographical references and index.
ISBN 978-0-295-99099-6 (pbk. : alk. paper) —
ISBN 978-0-295-99098-9 (cloth : alk. paper)
1. Imagination (Philosophy)—History. I. Gray, Richard T.
BH301.I53I58 2011
111'.85—dc22   2010054345

The paper used in this publication is acid-free and 90 percent recycled from at least 50 percent post-consumer waste. It meets the minimum requirements of American National Standard for Information Sciences—Permanence of Paper for Printed Library Materials, ANSI Z39.48–1984.

FRONTISPIECE: Francisco de Goya y Lucientes (Spanish, 1746–1828), "The Sleep of Reason Produces Monsters" (1799), pl. 43 of *The Caprices (Los Caprichos)*. Etching, aquatint, drypoint, and burin; 8 7/16 × 5 7/8 in.

Contents

INVENTIONS *of the* IMAGINATION

Introduction

Richard T. Gray

THE title of this volume, *Inventions of the Imagination,* contains several ambiguities. Most prominent among these is the undecidable status of the preposition "of," which can function either as an objective or as a subjective instance of the genitive case. According to the first reading, the faculty of the imagination itself would be the object of numerous inventions and reinventions, subject to persistent reconceptualizations over the course of history. This insistent retheorization of the imagination as a distinct human faculty is especially prominent during the Romantic period, and this constitutes one of the central themes pursued in the essays in this collection. In some instances, specific connections are drawn to the continuity of this problematic in literary and philosophical Modernism.

In the second reading, it is the faculty of the imagination itself that is, as "subject," the creative force responsible for diverse inventions. For the Romantics and post-Romantics, this productive energy of the imaginative capacity expresses itself in the privileged areas of art in general, of course, and in literature more specifically. Indeed, for the Romantics and their modern heirs, theories of the imagination and theories of art and literary production are so closely intertwined as to be virtually inseparable. One might think of the execution machine in Franz Kafka's short story "In the Penal Colony" as an especially visceral example of how these subjective and objective dimensions of the modern imagination converge; for the penal machine in Kafka's tale is not only an especially brutal (objective) invention of the imagination—one that fortunately has, to the best of our knowledge, remained purely imaginary (although at this writing it has significant competition), but simultaneously represents, as writing machine, the subjective process by which the imagination generates its own (written) artifacts (Kafka 206–9).

This collection of essays is conceived in such a way that its explorations of the imagination can proceed along both archaeological and genealogical paths. The essays represented here investigate, on the one hand, how the imagination was theorized and enacted by different individuals at various historical junctures. A majority of the essays focus on Romantic and post-Romantic European thinkers from the end of the eighteenth to the mid-nineteenth centuries, a period when theories of the imagination were prominent on the agenda of intellectual endeavors. By the end of the eighteenth century, an insistence on reason as the predominant human faculty had run its course and the imagination began to emerge as another force whose contributions to human intellectual existence and productivity had to be newly calculated and constantly recalibrated. This leads to the second larger aim of this volume, namely to chronicle some of the vicissitudes in the conceptualization and evaluation of the imagination and its products that occur across time and in a variety of intellectual disciplines, in particular in philosophy and literary studies.

The Romantics had already conceived of the imagination in the plural. The anonymous author of the so-called "Oldest Systematic Program of German Idealism"—variously attributed to the philosophers Georg Wilhelm Friedrich Hegel, Friedrich Wilhelm Schelling, and even to the poet Friedrich Hölderlin—wrote, for example: "What is needed today is a monotheism of reason and the heart, polytheism of the imagination and of art" (Hegel 235–36). It seems plausible to hypothesize that precisely this two-sided program, the attempt to establish a singularly operative and universal form of reason, on the one hand, alongside a plurality of imaginative capacities, on the other, exactly describes the ideological program of modernism from the end of the eighteenth century through perhaps to the present day. Are these two drives actually compatible with one another? Can a universal and monolithic form of reason tolerate the play, flexibility, and unpredictability of imaginative creativity? Turning these questions around: Could the creative imagination, conceived as a kind of absolute freedom of thought and fantasy, view the rules and governing logic of rational thought as anything but shackles and impossible limitations? Perhaps it is significant that enlightened reason and Romantic imagination, despite their differences, at least share one central metaphorical and perceptual "prejudice": an insistence on the importance of sight, vision, and "image" as the proper domain of human thought and creativity. These are some of the broader questions the contributions to this volume address.

Among the German Romantics, Friedrich Schlegel deliberated in particular on the polyvalence of the imaginative faculty, distinguishing a "productive imagination" peculiar to mathematics, a "visual" imagination at home in the representational arts, and what he called "fantasy," which he aligned with music. For Schlegel, literature comes to be theorized as the supreme human endeavor precisely because it fuses and relies on all three of these imaginative modes (372), and his position is representative of a general tendency at this time to view literature as the privileged vehicle for imaginative expression.

In his influential *Essay on Genius* of 1774, Alexander Gerard sought to synthesize imagination and the lawfulness of reason, without, however, clipping the wings of a primary inventiveness. For Gerard, genius comes to be defined as precisely that condition of the intellect in which this synthesis occurs:

> [G]enius arises from the perfection and vigour of the *imagination*. However capricious and unaccountable this faculty may be often reckoned, yet it is subject to established laws; and is capable, not only of such extent as qualifies it for collecting ideas from all the parts of nature, but also of such regularity and correctness as is in a great measure sufficient for avoiding all improper ideas, for selecting such as are subordinate to the design, and for disposing them into a consistent plan, or a distinct method. It is the first author of all inventions, and has greater influence in carrying them to perfection, than we are ready to suspect. It forms what we properly call genius in every art, and in every science. (70)

Gerard was thus one of the first European thinkers to articulate the modern valorization of the creative imagination, a doctrine that, through works such as Kant's *Critique of Judgment*, helped shape the aesthetic categories of post-Enlightenment and Romantic art and literature throughout Europe.[1] Romanticism, of course, led the way and set the terms of this overweening celebration of the imagination and its pivotal role in artistic and literary creativity. Edgar Allen Poe, for instance, declared in his prose poem *Eureka* that "the *only* true thinkers" are the "generally-educated men [!] of ardent imagination" (219), and similar views were frequently voiced by the literary and artistic avant-garde of the nineteenth and early-twentieth centuries. For the poet Charles Baudelaire, for instance, the imagination represented the "queen" (Baudelaire's term!) "among the human faculties" (qtd. in Bark 6).

Other intellectual disciplines shared this largely positive view of the imagination and its inventions. One thinks, for example, of Freudian theory, in which imagined events and real occurrences are considered to be of equal significance and influence within the psychic economy of the individual.[2] The corollary to this in contemporary psychoanalytic and theoretical discussions is surely Jacques Lacan's "Imaginary," which is invested with the power to disrupt the stratified discourse of what Lacan calls the "Symbolic" order (Lacan 196–97). Similarly, since the end of the eighteenth century, the role of the imagination in the generation of economic value has constituted a little recognized theme in economic theory, where "imaginary" value comes to be associated with the infinite productivity of the "growth" economy.[3]

However, the imagination has not always been identified with this potential for creativity, productivity, and freedom—indeed, some might claim that this is the rare exception. Although the association of Romantic aesthetics with a valorization of the imagination is a popular commonplace, we should not forget that even the Romantics warned of the dark and more sinister side of an unchecked imagination. The hero of Eduard Mörike's novel *Maler Nolten* (Nolten the painter), for example, actually perishes as the result of an unbridled imagination, and the novel voices a concrete warning against the demonic aspects of imagination unbound (449). The common Romantic and post-Romantic association of unbridled imagination with various forms of insanity represents one of the peculiar flash points between the order of reason and the disorder of creative vision, and the modern history of the imagination displays a marked tendency to waffle between these positive and negative evaluations. In the areas of literature, art, and aesthetic theory the positive interpretation has tended to predominate. But as early as the seventeenth century, the French philosopher Nicolas Malebranche, in his *The Search After Truth* (1674), stigmatized the imaginative faculty due to its close relation to the realm of the senses, and he consequently viewed it as a source of error and disorder (87). Critics of the imagination have traditionally been suspicious in particular of this intimate connection with the realm of the sensual, and one prominent subset of this sensualist argument was an association of the deviancies of the imagination with the feminine, whereas "healthy" reason was identified, of course, as a male principle. As late as the nineteenth century the uterus was conceived in medical treatises as the physiological seat of the imagination and its attendant pathologies (Bark 30). More generally, in the early nineteenth century Auguste Comte sought to found a positivist science, along with its concomitant social order, on the principle that one assert a fundamental "preponderance of observation over imagination" (36). Even prominent imaginative poets such as Goethe joined in the struggle against the purported excesses of the imagination. In his notebooks from 1805 he insisted that one of the primary aims of education was to place governors on the unbridled power of the imagination, and he went so far as to attack imagination as the "most powerful enemy" of reason and as a form of primitivism that posed a threat to the entire edifice of human culture. "What good does it do to tame the senses and cultivate reason," he wrote here, "or even to assure that reason attains its proper dominance; imagination lurks as its most powerful enemy, it possesses by nature an overwhelming drive for the absurd, a drive that even has a powerful influence over educated human beings . . . " (784). In the domain of political economy, Karl Marx struck a similar chord in his theory of commodity fetishism. For Marx, fetishism explains the mystique of the commodity in terms of the *imaginative*, rather than the material, investments individuals make into the products of their own labor (86–87). More recently, the French Marxist Louis Althusser diagnosed the fundamental role of imagination in the constitution and functioning of ideological mechanisms in his celebrated definition of ideology as "the *imaginary* relationship of individuals to their *real* conditions of existence" (153, emphasis added). Imagination in this theory becomes the condition of possibility for ideological self-deception.

If it is true, as the German cultural theoreticians Hartmut and Gernot Böhme have claimed, that in the Enlightenment and post-Enlightenment period the imagination is reason's "Other"[4]—invoking the many implications associated with this notion today—then one aim of the present volume is to interrogate the dialectic between "reason" and "imagination" and explore diverse theories and evaluations of their relationship for Romantic and post-Romantic philosophy, science, and art. The collection opens with Wolfgang Welsch's general philosophical meditations on the character of imagination as an epistemological category. Taking as his point of departure specific empirical experiences made by the individual, Welsch demonstrates how this empirical data is transformed by the power of imagination into what he calls an "essential image." Such an essential image is not, strictly speaking, simply a memory impression; rather, it is a kind of composite pieced together in the mind on the basis of a collection of empirical data. Our essential image of a mountain range, for example, does not encompass only our sensual and emotional impressions of those mountains (say, the Alps), but also includes an awareness that they are not static monoliths but rather the (temporary) results of long-term geologic processes. Welsch's main point is that the common view of the imagination as the power to invent and create ideas ex nihilo, as it were, is in error. The true inventions of the imagination are not things, but relations and connections among things. Imagination does not entail, in other words, the invention of the hitherto unknown; rather it permits us to reshape what is familiar and known by placing these things into differing configurations. Welsch exemplifies this epistemological process of the imagination—which he ultimately brings into relation with reflection—using the example of Zen Buddhism and the ideas of the Pre-Socratic philosophers.

If Welsch's deliberations are based in part on imagination's role in reshaping our perception of a mountain range by infusing it with the processual character of its evolution over time, Georg Braungart's essay presents a historical instantiation of precisely this discovery of so-called "deep time" in the seventeenth and eighteenth centuries and the repercussions this imaginative discovery has had in other fields of intellectual endeavor, above all in the development of imaginative literature. Baron Cuvier's palaeontological reconstructions of fossils and his theories about geological evolution—above all his theory of "catastrophism"—revolutionized conceptions about the age of the earth and contributed to a marginalization of the human being. Parallel to the effects of the Copernican and Darwinian revolutions, his research entailed new insights into the vast scale of historical time and the discovery of hitherto unknown species. Both his geological theories and his palaeontological reconstructions presented tremendous challenges to the human imagination—challenges that were answered by a more intensive application of the imaginative powers themselves. As Braungart elucidates, in his reconstructions of long nonexistent creatures and their former lives on the basis of fossils and bone fragments, Cuvier enlists an imaginative capacity that displays close affinities with poetic productivity. The "stories" he develops about these creatures and their former lives, while passing as hard science, in fact read more like historical fictions or novels. Moreover, the principles by which he arrives at his reconstructions—functionality, proportion, continuity, and coherence—closely resemble aesthetic principles. In a final argument Braungart demonstrates how the theory of the ice age was first publicized in a work of creative literature—namely, in Goethe's novel *Wilhelm Meisters Wanderjahre* (Wilhelm Meister's time as journeyman). Scientific constructivism and literary creation thus prove to be founded on the same productive (that is, *poetic*) principle: the power of the imagination to project an image of a nonexistent totality and (re)construct this whole on the basis of desultory fragments.

What we might call "enabling fictions" similarly constitute the theme of Beth Lord's essay. Her point of departure is the paradoxical Romantic belief, expressed in exemplary fashion by Friedrich Schlegel, that systematic philosophy can arrive at completion only when it incorporates a form of thought that by definition remains incomplete, namely poetry. Lord traces the genealogy of this idea back to two significant precursors of the Romantics, Spinoza and Kant, in whose works she uncovers the idea that imaginative fictions are required by any philosophical system in order that it might achieve closure. For both Spinoza and Kant, these fictions are enabling in the sense that they allow for the construction of a systematic whole. However, both of these thinkers insist that one must take care not to attribute material, positive existence to these fictions, for when this occurs they cease being productive illusions and instead become potentially dangerous *delusions*. In short, in order for these fictions to function properly as instruments that solidify the philosophical system, their *imaginary* character must constantly be acknowledged.

Michael Forster is concerned with imagination's role not in knowledge production, but in its interpretive reception. Focusing on Johann Gottfried Herder's conception of language and the manner in which it counters and escapes the Fregean-Wittgensteinean attack on psychologism, Forster shows that Herder's central notion of *Einfühlung*, of feeling one's way into the position of the text or the person being interpreted, depends on an imaginary investment that seeks to recreate the perceptual or affective sensations of the interpreted object or individual. However, Herder's imaginative-interpretive reconstructions must be strictly distinguished from simple identities with the represented affects themselves or from identification with the affected person. Far from *having* the feelings the interpreter discovers in the interpreted object, he or she instead imaginatively *recaptures* them in a noncommitted manner. This interpretive distance, if we may call it that, avoids the moral dilemma that the interpreter must subscribe to the views or share the affects he or she merely seeks to understand. Imagination thus builds a bridge to the ideas or affects being interpreted, on the one hand, but also erects a wall that prevents committed identification with those ideas or affects, on the other.

Hazard Adams's reflections on William Blake's theory of the imagination introduce a series of essays that concentrate on the relationship between imagination and the visual field. As a visual artist in his own right, Blake, according to Adams, insists on the relationship of the imaginative faculty to sight and image. For Blake, imagination represents a mode of vision that fuses the domains of subject and object: it is always constituted as image-ination, as the production of images. The fundamental principle behind Blake's theory of imagination, in Adams's view, is synecdoche, or the union of the particular and the universal. In this regard imagination is intimately related with the Romantic notion of the symbol, as well as with the Romantic ideal of fusing general and particular, universal and individual: what Manfred Frank, in reference to Friedrich Schleiermacher, has called *Das individuelle Allgemeine*, the individual-universal. One of the requirements of such "visionary ideas," as Blake calls these imaginative fusions, however, is that they must remain imaginary and tentative, never giving way to something stable and material.

Wilhelm Voßkamp pursues a similar problematic in the aesthetic theories of Friedrich Schiller, arguing ultimately that the power of imagination (*Einbildungskraft*) is fundamentally related to Schiller's concept of a *Bildungstrieb*, a drive to (aesthetic) shaping, as well as to his teleological project of human education (*Bildung*). The aesthetic education of the human race, which is the cornerstone of Schiller's theory of art, is thereby revealed to be erected upon a foundation of creative imagination. The anchoring point of all three of these conceptions—imagination, shaping drive, and education—is the root word *Bildung*, which they all share, and which itself is derived from the German *Bild*, meaning picture or image. For Schiller, as Voßkamp demonstrates, the imagination is always closely associated with the idea of potentiality and, ultimately, with that of freedom. Schiller's political project consists in transferring this freedom of the imagination to the domain of statecraft. This occurs, as Voßkamp outlines, via his aesthetic notion of the play-drive (*Spieltrieb*), which itself is associated with the free play of the human imagination. Schiller's aesthetic State, as a political construct that realizes human freedom, is thus prefigured in the aesthetic state or sensibility of the individual, which itself instantiates the freedom of human imagination. For Schiller as for Blake, the imagination circumscribes that domain of individual universality in which the particular (the aesthetic state of mind) and the general (the aesthetic State as political entity) commune.

Klaus Vieweg brings a variation on this theme in his examination of the place and role of imagination in Hegel's system of mind. Several themes from Voßkamp's analysis of Schiller's conception of the imagination recur here, although in greatly modified form. Hegel is concerned with the issue of human freedom not so much in its ultimate realization in the political state, as is the case with Schiller, as in its instantiation in the autonomy of human *Geist*, of mind or spirit. In Hegel's system, imagination serves a function very similar to that in Schiller's aesthetic theory: it mediates between the first stage of human knowledge, which Hegel terms intuition (*Anschauung*), and the ultimate station of autonomous, self-determining *Geist*. As such, imagination builds the necessary bridge and transition between the spheres of the sensual and the intellectual, the concrete and the abstract. Moreover, it accomplishes this by performing an activity reminiscent of its function in Schiller's and Blake's aesthetics: by fusing the particular and the general, the individual and the universal. We thus witness in the productive dialogue manifest in this group of essays the way in which a certain set of themes recur in the theory of the imagination throughout the more widely conceived Romantic period, even to the extent of crossing national frontiers.

Hegel remains the subject of Robert Pippin's essay, but the focus shifts from a concentration on the faculty of the imagination as such to the role of imaginative literature in the development of Hegel's *Phenomenology of Spirit*. Pippin begins with the observation that Hegel ends the *Phenomenology* by citing—actually, by misquoting—the lines of a poem by Friedrich Schiller. This leads Pippin to deliberate on the traditionally accepted relationship between art (in particular literature) and philosophy in Hegel, which assumes, as Hegel expressed in his *Lectures on Aesthetics,* that art is historically superseded by the greater reflexivity of philosophy. Pippin ultimately argues for a reversal of this implied hierarchy, at least insofar as he suggests that conceptual philosophy does not so much go *beyond* art and imaginative literature as necessarily *incorporate* it into its own project. Pippin is at pains to demonstrate that Hegel's *Phenomenology* itself relies on what we might call the *performative* aspect of imaginative art, or what Hegel might term its "enlivening" of the universal. Just as literary or other forms of art instantiate or perform an idea or norm whose intentionality unfolds over time—in the act of interpretive reception, as it were—so, too, all human intentions emerge only historically through the public response to enacted deeds. The self-realization of *Geist* in the *Phenomenology,* in other words, takes on the character of a dramatic performance whose intentions can be recognized only after the fact, in their impact and reception. Literature comes to be the model for acts of philosophical performance, and in this regard it is fitting that the words of a poet are taken—if philosophically mis-taken—as the final word of Hegel's *Phenomenology.*

Tilottama Rajan undertakes a radical reinterpretation of Hegel by reading him through the lens of Schelling's later philosophy, in particular his *Ages of the World.* She begins by asking whether there might be, in effect, a kind of subversive imagination that haunts the entire philosophical project of German Romanticism, from the early "Oldest Systematic Program of German Idealism," whose manuscript is written in Hegel's hand, through to Schelling's radical idea, formulated in the 1815 version of *Ages of the World,* that history consists of a series of ceaseless revolutions that refuse Hegelian synthesis and progress. Such an outcome undermines the institutional stability not only of the Hegelian state, but also the teleology of Hegel's aesthetic theory. The corollary of Schelling's turbulent primal imagination, in which contradictions are not sublated but merely suspended in a fantasy of wholeness, is what Hegel, in the *Aesthetics,* calls Symbolic art. Viewed from this perspective, the entire Hegelian system, not only of history but also of aesthetics, contains the germ of its own deconstruction, a deconstruction realized, as it were, in Schelling's later philosophy, which exposes the subliminally present, chaotic subtext of Hegel's systematic thought.

Richard Block's piece on Schelling's *System of Transcendental Idealism* circles back to a set of issues addressed in earlier essays in this collection, namely to questions about the state, the nation, and the ideal future community that remained one of German Romanticism's obsessions. For Schelling, imaginative works of art play the central role of shaping the original form on which the emergence of this future social unity will rely. However, through a reading of the footnotes and revisions Schelling makes to this theory of art, Block shows that what was first intended to be a model of adequate representation proves instead to be what he calls an *Abglanz*, a deflection or divergence that insists on difference rather than unity. Reading Schelling's theory through the perspective of Hölderlin's poem "Andenken" (Remembrance) as well as in the context of Heidegger's sustained interpretation of this poem, Block comes to the conclusion that Schelling's imagined ideal community is actually grounded in a divergence (*Abglanz*) that disrupts human communal bonds, constantly configuring the would-be friend as the Other. The imagined ideal of Romantic community remains precisely that: an imaginary fantasy.

Christoph Bode's essay serves as a superb coda for this collection, as it interrogates the continuity in theories about the imagination from Romanticism through to the American Modernists. Using examples drawn from Blake, Keats, P. B. Shelley (the representatives of Romanticism), Frost, H. D. (Hilda Doolittle), and Wallace Stevens (representing Modernism), Bode shows that the true continuity linking the Romantic and Modernist views of imagination is the very contradictoriness of how it is defined. In both their poetic practices and poetic theories, the Romantics as well as the Modernists defend an autonomous imagination as the generator of reality. At the same time, neither group is able to completely abandon the belief that imagination responds to and embroiders upon something that is really given in the world. For if the latter, objectivist hypothesis does not hold, then it becomes impossible to make any kind of authoritative statements about the world, God, the universe, etc. According to Boda, both the Romantics and Modernists refused to jettison the possibility of such truth claims completely. Their solution was to have it both ways: namely, to create miniature imaginative, textual (poetic) worlds, but to attribute to these imagined and fictional worlds the force of verifiable fact. In what Bode calls a form of "poetic faith," they acknowledge that literature is nothing but an imaginative, subjective construction, yet take these constructs seriously as *objective* positions—as poetic "facts," we might say. In its literary concretization, imagination is thus both subjective and objective, fantasy and reality, actively constructed and passively discovered. Literature, in short, is valorized as a kind of paradoxical fusion, as what we might term the imaginary-real or the fictionally true. Imagination thereby becomes the agency that validates the truth function of literature.

I would like to close this introduction by expressing the collective gratitude of the editors of this volume to all those individuals and institutions that have been instrumental in ensuring that this endeavor became much more than just a figment of our collective imagination. This project began as a conference, with the same name, that was held on the University of Washington campus from May 18–20, 2007. Special thanks are due, first and foremost, to my colleagues on the local organizing committee for that conference: Gary Handwerk (English and Comparative Literature), Nicolas Halmi (English and Comparative Literature), and Michael Rosenthal (Philosophy). Our year-long collaboration preparing the conference took place in a spirit of genuine cooperation and mutual respect, and this interchange proved rewarding on both a personal and professional level for all of us. The primary local supporter of the conference was the Walter Chapin Simpson Center for the Humanities, which provided significant tangible and intangible resources for the realization of the conference program. Institutions are only as supportive as the individuals who run them, and on behalf of the organizing committee and the editors of this volume I want to express our deep debt of gratitude to the outstanding staff at the Simpson Center: director Kathy Woodward, who backed this project from the outset, program manager Lauren Fleming, and financial specialist Lynette McVey. The Simpson Center also provided a generous subsidy in support of the publication of this collection of essays.

Numerous other people and institutions at the University of Washington have contributed in primary ways to the realization of this conference and to this volume of selected papers. These include the Center for West European Studies, the College of Arts and Sciences, and the Departments of Comparative Literature, Germanics, and Philosophy, all of which committed financial and other resources in support of the colloquium. We feel especially privileged to have been able to invite so many international speakers as presenters and as contributors to this collection of essays, and this dimension of the program was realized through the major support of two institutions, the Max Kade Foundation in New York and the Alexander von Humboldt Foundation in Germany. Indeed, without the initial start-up support from the Humboldt Foundation, neither the conference nor this volume could ever have been conceived. In this regard, the present volume represents the culmination of a three-year research collaboration between myself and philosopher Dr. Klaus Vieweg of the University of Jena, based on a project that received significant financial support from the Transatlantic Cooperation initiative of the Humboldt Foundation. The matching funds required of the North American participant in the Transatlantic Cooperation awards, as well as financial support for the publication of this volume, came from the Byron W. and Alice L. Lockwood Foundation. The conditions for realizing the scholarly collaboration that produced the initial conference and publication of this volume were thus met only after I was named to one of the Lockwood professorships by the College of Arts and Sciences. I want to take this opportunity to publicly express my personal gratitude to the College for this recognition. In these days when support for scholarly initiatives in the humanities is dwindling, the editors feel especially fortunate and privileged to be the beneficiaries of these numerous foundations, institutions, and individuals. Finally, we wish to express our gratitude to the University of Washington Press for agreeing to publish this collection so that the ideas generated at the conference can attain wider circulation. Our thanks are due specifically to the Press's humanities acquisition editor, Jacqueline Ettinger, who shepherded the volume through the review process with great sensitivity, care, and commitment.

NOTES

1   On Kant's conception of the imagination and its influence on subsequent thinkers, see Homann's succinct summary.

2   Freud acknowledged the psychic importance and influence of what he termed "fantasies" early in his career, when he found himself forced to abandon the so-called "seduction theory" as the primary etiology of hysteria. He resolved this early crisis in psychoanalytic theory by promoting the idea that fantasized seductions play as equal a role in the psychic economy as do real ones. Freud is most articulate about the importance of this valorization of fantasy in his historical retrospective on the psychoanalytic movement, first published in 1914, "Zur Geschichte der psychoanalytischen Bewegung" (On the history of the psychoanalytic movement); see especially 55–56.

3   For an examination of the role the concept of imagination played in German economic theory at the end of the eighteenth century, see the chapter "Economics and the Imagination" in Gray, *Money Matters* (109–69, esp. 145–69).

4   See in particular the chapter "Der Kampf der Vernunft mit der Einbildungskraft" (The battle of reason with imagination) in their monumental study *Das Andere der Vernunft* (Reason's other) 233–74.

WORKS CITED

Althusser, Louis. "Ideology and Ideological State Apparatuses (Notes Toward an Investigation)." *Lenin and Philosophy and Other Essays*. Trans. Ben Brewster. London: New Left Books, 1971. 121–73.

Bark, Karlheinz. *Poesie und Imagination: Studien zu ihrer Reflexionsgeschichte zwischen Aufklärung und Moderne*. Stuttgart: Metzler, 1993.

Böhme, Hartmut, and Gernot Böhme. *Das Andere der Vernunft: Zur Entwicklung von Rationalitätsstrukturen am Beispiel Kants*. Frankfurt/Main: Suhrkamp, 1983.

Comte, Auguste. *Auguste Comte and Positivism: The Essential Writings*. Ed. Gertrud Lenzer. New York: Harper & Row, 1975.

Frank, Manfred. *Das individuelle Allgemeine: Textstrukturierung und Interpretation nach Schleiermacher*. Frankfurt/Main: Suhrkamp, 1977.

Freud, Sigmund. "Zur Geschichte der psychoanalytischen Bewegung." *Gesammelte Werke*. Ed. Anna Freud. 18 vols. London: Imago, 1940–1987. 10: 43–113.

Gerard, Alexander. *An Essay on Genius*. London: W. Strahan, 1774.

Goethe, Johann Wolfgang von. *Tag- und Jahreshefte. Gedenkausgabe der Werke, Briefe und Gespräche* (Artemis Ausgabe). Ed. Ernst Beutler. 26 vols. Zürich: Artemis, 1948–1964. 11: 615–956.

Gray, Richard T. *Money Matters: Economics and the German Cultural Imagination, 1770–1850*. Seattle: University of Washington Press, 2008.

Hegel, Georg Wilhelm Friedrich. "Das älteste Systemprogramm des deutschen Idealismus." *Werke in zwanzig Bänden: Theorie-Werkausgabe*. Eds. Eva Moldenhauer and Karl Markus Michel. 12 vols. Frankfurt/Main: Suhrkamp, 1971. 1: 234–36.

Homann, Karl. "Zum Begriff der Einbildungskraft nach Kant." *Archiv für Begriffsgeschichte* 14 (1970): 266–302.

Kafka, Franz. "In der Strafkolonie." *Drucke zu Lebzeiten: Kritische Ausgabe*. Eds. Wolf Kittler, Hans-Gerd Koch, and Gerhard Neumann. Frankfurt/Main: Fischer, 1994. 203–48.

Lacan, Jacques. *Écrits: A Selection*. Trans. Alan Sheridan. New York: Norton, 1977.

Malebranche, Nicolas. *The Search After Truth*. Trans. Thomas M. Lennon and Paul J. Olscamp. Cambridge: Cambridge University Press, 1997.

Marx, Karl. "Der Fetischcharakter der Ware und sein Geheimnis." *Das Kapital: Kritik der politischen Ökonomie*, vol. 1. Vol. 23 of *Karl Marx/Friedrich Engels Werke*. Berlin: Dietz, 1972. 85–98.

Mörike, Eduard. *Maler Nolten: Novelle in zwei Teilen*. Ed. Wolfgang Vogelmann. Frankfurt/Main: Insel, 1979.

Poe, Edgar Allen. *The Science Fiction of Edgar Allen Poe*. Ed. Harold Beaver. Harmondsworth: Penguin, 1976.

Schlegel, Friedrich. *Fragmente zur Poesie und Literatur: Zweiter Teil*. Vol. 17 of *Friedrich Schlegel: Kritische Ausgabe*. Ed. Ernst Behler. Paderborn: Schöningh, 1991.

1

Imagination on the Move

Wolfgang Welsch

WHAT I want to attempt in the following essay amounts to lining up different versions of imagining alongside one another. I will do this more or less systematically, and at the end should stand the outermost goal of imagination.

FROM THE SIGHT OF THE PACIFIC
TO THE ESSENTIAL IMAGE OF THE PACIFIC

Our imagining *something* must naturally stand at the beginning of this series of versions of imagination. To give an example: While sitting at my desk, I close my eyes and imagine the Pacific Coast in California. I recall a particular place I have often visited: a bay north of Point Año Nuevo. I see the sand and the sea, feel the wind and the sun. Then in my imagination I walk for kilometers along the coast, as I liked to do. Section by section the familiar cliffs and rocks appear, and time and time again the unforgettable sight of the rolling waves. In all of this, of course, I make use of my reproductive power of imagination.

Suddenly Robinson Jeffers, the great poet of the Pacific, comes to my mind. And now my imagination wanders to Big Sur, where Jeffers spent most of his time. I climb Hawk Tower at Tor House, which he built in Carmel. The Pacific here appears less majestic, somehow more swirling.

This brings me (still strolling on the tracks of the reproductive power of imagination) to recall other encounters of mine with the Pacific at other places: in Japan, in Chile, etc.

Eventually I begin to imagine the Pacific in a way I have never seen it in reality. I envision it from far out at sea, on a ship, so far out that all around one sees no land, but just the Pacific. That is how, I think, it must have been perceived by Magellan, who, impressed by the tranquillity of this ocean, gave it its name: the peaceful ocean.

Finally I concentrate (having in the meantime made the transition to the productive power of imagination) on my essential image of the Pacific. One might think such an essential image cannot exist. But I bear such an image within me. If you were to transport me to the coast of an ocean anywhere in the world, without my knowing which one it is, I am sure I would be able to recognize immediately whether it is the Pacific or not.

This inner image is not simply empirical (it could not be photographed anywhere); nonetheless it is based on experience, and it proves its value empirically everywhere.

So much for a first journey in the imagination: from memory images to the essential image.

"MOUNTAINS FLOW"

Secondly, I want to carry you off to the mountains, to the Alps or the Andes. Viewed from the valley, just as from the heights, the summits appear majestic. One can well understand why several authors have spoken of this experience as leaving an impression of eternity. The world of these mountains is a world of its own, a sovereign and unchanging world in contrast to the bustling world of humans. So much for the common perception and the usual view. But then, here too, I begin to become *imaginatively* aware of various types of movement.

Everyone can see that the glaciers move. It is quite rightly said that glaciers "flow." Indeed, in the Alps they flow between 30 and 150 meters per year toward the valley, and in the Himalayas even more than one kilometer.

As I contemplate a range of mountains, the delimitation between the individual mountains becomes questionable for me. The mountains have famous names (Eiger, Mönch, and Jungfrau). We are used to treating mountains as individuals. But is our division of the mountain range into single mountains really justified? Actually there is only the mountain range as a whole, not individual mountains. A single mountain cannot be separated off from the mountain range, either in reality or analytically, nor can it even be delimited from the next mountain in a convincing way. And the reason for this is clear: The mountain chain at one time came into being in a single process with the entire range (not individual mountains) rising up from the earth's floor.

Eventually temporal perspectives become altogether irresistible. If you look around, you see not only mountain peaks and glaciers, but also endless masses of scree. They are the products of erosion. Mountains (because of their particular height) are constantly exposed to erosion. That is why for thousands of years they have been getting constantly smaller. And suddenly you understand what these peaks that appear so impressive truly are: not the radiant testimony to the first day of their existence, but the relics remaining after the process of erosion. Mountain peaks are the remains of decomposition, momentary remnants. What once gave them a prouder height is now spread out before our eyes as scree and rubble.

And now the whole genealogical film runs before my imaginative eye: 130 million years ago these heights (the Alps) were pressed upwards out of the ground due to the movement of tectonic plates. At that time they acquired their original height. But since then it has all been decomposition and decay. Erosion has increasingly carried them away, and today they are nothing but shrunken forms of their erstwhile greatness. Yet we admire these transitory relics of decomposition as majestic peaks!

Meanwhile the whole perspective has changed. The view of eternity has turned into a cinema of evolution. What momentary perception reveals has been relativized. In the film of the imagination I see the original emergence and then the successive decomposition that followed it. Moreover, this film in the imagination is by no means fictive; it is realistic. It shows us not the image of another world, but the truth about this world of mountains. The current sight is just the momentary result of the processes that the imaginative film reveals. Imagination, not direct perception, provides the truth.

My contemplation of the mountains might appear unusual. Yet in other spheres we are actually very familiar with what it points to. In spring we see a flower growing, coming into bloom, and withering soon after. Or we see a tree growing over the course of many years, and another one dying off. We see children growing up, and we prepare ourselves for our death.

Very well, I have changed spheres. I have moved on to examples from the realm of the organic. There the perspective that everything is in motion, that everything evolves and decays, is familiar to us.

In the example of the mountains, however, something comparable has become clear to me in the imagination, within the realm of the supposed changelessness of inorganic matter, which represents the common counter-image to the organic. The Alps did not yet exist 150 million years ago, and in a few million years they will have disappeared. The inorganic is in motion just as is the organic, only over considerably longer periods of time. Even the cosmos is anything but stable; it came into being about 14 billion years ago, and some day it will perish or give way to another cosmos.

What I sought to urge you to do in this second journey was to become aware of the changeability and mobility of even those things that are apparently most stable and most persistent, and to bring to mind, at least imaginatively, their fluid character. In a third journey I will try to point out possible consequences.

THINGS BECOMING ALIKE

Imagination Suggests a Different Way of Seeing
and Shows Another Order of the World

I directed my imagination first to the Pacific, then to the mountains. In doing this it was seen not only that the ocean is constantly in motion, but that mountains too are in the process of moving. People often think that imagination is an ability to invent new, unaccustomed things. For me the imagination appears above all to be an ability to see familiar things in a new and sometimes very different way. Simple forms of the imagination merely vary things within established categories: snow is suddenly red, a man has a goat's head, or (but here it is already getting more difficult) a square is conceived as round. Imagination can, however, also go much further: it can transcend well-worn categories and show an unaccustomed order in the world. In my example, mountains, usually viewed as stable, are in motion. In their own way they too flow, just as the water of the ocean flows in its own way.

Likewise, however—I must add this now—the sea too can suddenly look quite different than it usually does. The ocean can appear rigid and solid, like a rock formation. When you drive along Highway One in California and catch a first glimpse of the Pacific through the hills, this can appear to you like a giant steel blue wall set into the earth. In its majestic breadth it has the effect of being completely unmoving, like a homogeneous dark wall. Of course, this is an image created by the imagination, not by perception.

Our usual perception says that the ocean is moving and the mountains are unmoving. But imagination leads us beyond this convention. We can imaginatively see mountains as flowing and the ocean as rigid.

An East Asian Parallel: Dogen

The ocean and mountains are more closely related in their nature than the common view assumes. Dogen (1200–1253), the first Japanese patriarch of Zen Buddhism, described this in detail in his main work, the *Shobogenzo*. In the chapter "Sansuikyo" (The Mountain and River Sutra), he explained that mountains "are always moving" (163), always "flowing" (169), whereas conversely water always remains the same in its essence and to this extent "does not flow" (170). Dogen's underlying thought is, of course, that mountains and rivers (just like all other phenomena) are manifestations of Buddha-nature and are to this extent also "detached" from their concrete form—hence everything is ultimately the same.[1]

In the West: The Pre-Socratics, Philosophers of the Imagination

So my journeys in the imagination also led me to discover the kinship between oceans and mountains. But how can this way of seeing things be justified? How could one make it plausible (without borrowing from Dogen) by drawing on motifs familiar in Western thought?

Our customary view of the world perceives multiplicity and difference everywhere. We grasp things as substances that are well delimited and distinct from each other. However, as I have described, imagination can lead us to a different experience, to a different order of the world: oppositions begin to become weaker, delimitations disappear, things become more related and more unitary, they merge into one another—and in the end everything seems to be alike.

The first Western philosophers, the Pre-Socratics, wandered on such paths of the imagination; they were, so to speak, the Dogens of the West. To begin with, the Ionian natural philosophers made considerable scientific discoveries. Thales, for example, was brilliant at geometry, navigation, and astronomy. He wrote an "Astronomy for Seafarers" and predicted an eclipse of the sun and an earthquake. Or take Anaximander, who invented gnomon instruments and drafted the first maps of the earth and sea. But we consider Thales and Anaximander to be philosophers because, beyond what can be known in this way, they imaginatively developed models of what the constitution of the *whole* might be like and how everything might have developed overall. Just think of the doctrine ascribed to Thales that everything arises from water and basically is water, or of Anaximander's explanation of the world with recourse to the *apeiron*. These were imaginative designs of how things stand as a whole. And today we are astonished to discover that several of these designs, acquired by means of the imagination, have in the meantime found scientific confirmation. This applies in much the same way to Anaxagoras, who was the first to develop the idea of the big bang, and similarly to Democritus: he had never seen atoms, but he conceived of them imaginatively as the constituents of the universe.

The same applies to Heraclitus, whose great insight, to which he gave the name *logos*, was likewise one produced by the imagination. Heraclitus realized that superficially dominant substances and oppositions are underpinned by a deeper relatedness and unity, just as their apparent stability is undermined by a deeper processuality. And both relationality and processuality are based on the deeper law of *logos* underlying everything. Only once one conceives of this notion, which only imagination can produce, can it finally become clear that everything is, despite the superficial appearance of multiplicity and opposition, basically one: *hen panta*, Heraclitus's famous phrase (*Fragmente der Vorsokratiker* 1: 161).

I have mentioned the Pre-Socratics for two reasons. First, I wanted to remind you of the extent to which these ancestral fathers of philosophy were imaginative thinkers. Second, I wanted to point out the great degree to which their teachings (particularly those of Heraclitus) converge with the conclusions to which my two journeys in the imagination have led. The world is basically characterized not by the superficial appearance of multiplicity, substances, and opposition, but by a deeper relationality, processuality, and unity.

UNITY—THINGS IMAGINATIVELY BECOMING ONE

These features, I presume, provide the key perspectives for an appropriate ontology. When we move from the foreground perspective of substantial being to the deeper one of processes we see the objects that surround us in a different way. Chains of events take the place of substances. You no longer see, for example, a dog, but a type, a series of generations, a species; and you see this in the sequence of other species. Or you see an old machine, for example, a grandfather clock, in the sequence of inventions of mechanical apparatuses. And in the same way you no longer see a work of art simply for itself, but in the sequence of productions of artistic paradigms. Your whole view becomes historical. That is one thing.

The second thing is that you increasingly perceive and understand things in their relations. In this way, too, their independence dissolves. An example: we often see how water evaporates. We are able to observe this at home on the stove or in nature where vapors rise over a lake. But in doing so our perception was being a bit narrow-minded. Water, we thought, evaporates into the air. We took water for itself, and air for itself, and then marvelled at the transition of the one into the other, as if the air had not already had its part in the substantiality of the water. Without the atmospheric pressure of the air, the water would not have been water, but instead vapor from the start. The air into which the water merely appears to evaporate had already previously co-formed the water. Water, vapor, and air stand in a holistic co-conditioning relationship. Yes, it's really like that: you do something in the kitchen, and the whole earth takes part in it.

And the third trait, unity: When you have made clear to yourself that processuality and relationality are the basic traits of the world, then the division of the world according to substances, elements, and the like increasingly dissolves. The things that appear to stand as independent before our eyes are everywhere multiply conditioned by, and related to, one another. They are all connected (more remotely or closely) with one another; they form a pervasive and unitary nexus. In the end it is indeed true: *hen panta*. Heraclitus proclaimed this by appealing to the *logos*. Dogen expressed it in his way, teaching that everything is Buddha-nature. And several mystics in the Occident (and in more recent times, some physicists) have reiterated this insight. Leibniz, for example, thought that every living creature is a mirror of the universe. Another common trope for this view reads: "The whole world is contained in a drop of water." The imagination has long been a good means for realizing this view of the world. Today scientific reflection is lining up behind it.

AND WHAT ABOUT CONSCIOUSNESS— THE PRODUCER OF IMAGINATION?

I come to a final question: Is it really the case that *everything* converges to form a unity? Isn't one thing excepted from this? Precisely that thing which is responsible for developing this way of seeing: the imagining (and reflecting) consciousness itself?

To be sure, our imagining consciousness is also processual. It goes from idea to idea, and in doing so can change its whole way of seeing things. But despite all the changes in its ideas, this consciousness as such still seems to remain the same, namely, *my* imagining consciousness. Is this really so?

The dissolution of the self-being of things does not stop short of the being of consciousness. In precisely the same way as the imagining consciousness, for instance, begins to interpret the mountain range that stands before one's eyes differently, namely as the momentary state of an ongoing process, consciousness, on its path toward a unitary interpretation of the world, will likewise be unable to avoid changing its interpretation of itself.

To begin with, consciousness is required in order to situate and explain its own constitution, position, and capacity in the context of the conception of the whole that is dawning on it. Consciousness must comprehend itself and its capacities within the whole. It cannot exclude itself from its view of the whole, for otherwise this view would not be a view of the whole.

But how can it comprehend itself as an aspect of the whole? Only by understanding itself as something made possible by the whole and as a form of actualization of the whole. Consciousness itself belongs to the constitution of the whole it imagines and upon which it reflects; it must be made possible by this whole as an entity that also brings to mind its own constitution.

But if it is a consciousness that belongs to the whole, can it then still straightforwardly be "my" consciousness? In any case, surely not in the sense of an ego standing opposed to the whole. That would immediately bring down its claim to comprehend the whole—the true whole would then be the "whole" plus the ego. Consciousness must therefore comprehend its I-ness in a non-egoistic way, in something other than an I-like manner.

Certainly, the consciousness that grasps the constitution of the whole remains personal, linked with the actualization of a person. But if it really lays claim to insight into the structure of the whole, it cannot straightforwardly understand itself as the contingent consciousness of a contingent individual person, but instead must comprehend itself as the actualization of a consciousness that, so to speak, looks at the world and itself with the eye of the world. In any other case it would be incoherent. Hegel is perhaps the philosopher who has shown most clearly how an individual consciousness can also be the world's consciousness.[2]

As we've seen, imagination can alter one's view of the world and of oneself. Its power reaches surprisingly far. To conclude, I'd just like to emphasize that this is true not of the banal imagination that takes pride in producing ever more fanciful images, but of an imagination that is in league with reflection. In this alliance both imagination and reflection seem to accomplish their best work.

NOTES

1   For a more detailed analysis, see my essay "Zur Rolle von Skepsis und Relativität bei Sextus, Hegel und Dogen."
2   For an alternative option arising today from the perspective of a strictly evolutionary thinking, see my essay "Absoluter Idealismus und Evolutionsdenken."

WORKS CITED

Dogen Zenji. "Sansuikyo." *Shobogenzo: The Eye and Treasury of the True Law.* 3 vols. Trans. Kosen Nishiyama and John Stevens. Tokyo: Nakayama Shob, 1977. 2: 163–70.

Die Fragmente der Vorsokratiker. Eds. Hermann Diels and Walter Kranz. 6th ed. 3 vols. Zürich: Weidmann, 1951.

Welsch, Wolfgang. "Absoluter Idealismus und Evolutionsdenken." *Hegels Phänomenologie des Geistes: Ein kooperativer Kommentar zu einem Schlüsselwerk der Moderne.* Eds. Klaus Vieweg and Wolfgang Welsch. Frankfurt/Main: Suhrkamp 2008. 655–88.

———. "Zur Rolle von Skepsis und Relativität bei Sextus, Hegel und Dogen." *Kritisches Jahrbuch der Philosophie* 10 (2005): 71–101.

2

The Poetics of Nature

LITERATURE AND CONSTRUCTIVE IMAGINATION
IN THE HISTORY OF GEOLOGY

Georg Braungart

IMAGINATION AND CONSTRUCTION:
GEOLOGY AND LITERATURE IN
A METHODOLOGICAL PERSPECTIVE

I N his renowned book about time concepts in geological theories, *Time's
Arrow—Time's Cycle: Myth and Metaphor in the Discovery of Geological
Time*, which treats theories of geological time from Thomas Burnet's
Sacred Theory of the Earth (1680–89) to Charles Lyell's *Principles of Geology* (1830–33), Stephen Jay Gould quotes Sigmund Freud's famous dictum
about the three mortifications or blows human narcissism had to suffer
throughout the last four centuries of research and discovery: "Humanity
has in the course of time had to endure from the hand of science two great
outrages upon its naive self-love. The first was when it realized that our

earth was not the center of the universe, but only a speck in a world-system of a magnitude hardly conceivable. . . . The second was when biological research robbed man of his particular privilege of having been specially created and relegated him to a descent from the animal world" (Gould 1). The third outrage Freud then mentions—a consequence of Schopenhauer's and Freud's own theories—is that the human being has had to accept that he does not even rule his own psyche, that he is not, in Freud's words, "even master in his own house" (Freud 11). And Gould continues:

> But Freud omitted one of the greatest steps from his list, the bridge between spatial limitation of human dominion (the Galilean revolution), and our physical union with all "lower" creatures (the Darwinian revolution). He neglected the great temporal limitation imposed by geology upon human importance—the discovery of "deep time." . . . What could be more comforting, what more convenient for human domination, than the traditional concept of a young earth, ruled by human will within days of its origin. How threatening, by contrast, the notion of an almost incomprehensible immensity, with human habitation restricted to a millimicrosecond at the very end! (Gould 1–2)

Geologists, mineralogists, and palaeontologists had discovered that the earth must have existed comfortably for vast spaces of time *without* human beings (the "rust on an ore-ball," as the German physicist Georg Christoph Lichtenberg once expressed the role humanity plays on the globe in the late eighteenth century, or the "skin disease" of the earth, as Nietzsche saw it). This "revelation" was not easy to accept in the decades before and after 1800, when the success story of anthropology placed the human race in the center of the standard worldview. Far into the eighteenth century and beyond, people had thought the world to be approximately six thousand years old, as Bishop James Usher had calculated in the middle of the seventeenth century, working within the framework of the Bible. The history of the earth and the history of humankind were naively identified. Only few reckoned that things could possibly be different, and only slowly did the gap between the two scales of time become larger. Yet even in our day it is difficult to imagine the immense amount of time that passed before humanity appeared on the stage. When comparing the time span of the history of humankind to the old definition of the English yard, that is, the distance between the tip of the King's nose and the end of his outstretched hand, John McPhee wrote: "One stroke with a nail file on his middle finger erases human history" (Gould 3). The emerging discipline of geology had exposed the "dark abyss of time" (a term coined by the famous French natural scientist Comte Buffon in the late eighteenth century), which dealt a fundamental blow to human self-confidence. This is something we can hardly imagine in the present day. Literature and poetry played a significant role in helping to overcome this injury to human subjectivity.[1]

Thus in the history of modern subjectivity—this is my first assumption—the time horizon of geology brings about an immense relativization and loss of importance for the human being and human culture. Ideas of the *cosmic* or *spatial* marginalization of humankind (the Copernican Revolution) and the biological challenge to it (the Darwinian Revolution) had to be supplemented by the *temporal* marginalization of humanity brought about by geology, a science that at first glance seems to pursue the inoffensive occupation of studying fossils, bones, and strata. In the very heart of historicism and anthropology rises a science that implicitly voices a radical challenge to the self-confidence and the historical self-conception of humanity.

This represented a great provocation to the human power of imagination, which found itself forced to try to fathom this inconceivable abyss of time that appears to the human mind when people begin digging in the ground, collecting fossils and bones, and reconstructing the creatures of a former world no one had ever experienced or could possibly have imagined. But this is not my main point. What I want to examine is a crucial juncture in my current research project, which has the working title "Poetics of Nature: Literature and Geology," and in which I try to examine parallels between the cultural development of geology and palaeontology, on the one hand, and developments in literature, especially German literature, on the other. My questions are: How can we describe the interrelation between science and literature beyond motif analysis and biographical research? And how can this be carried out in the case of mineralogy, palaeontology, and geology? Many contributions on the relation between knowledge and literature exist in intellectual history and other fields. For my context, one of the most relevant terms is Joseph Vogl's plea for a "poetics of knowledge" (in German he uses the neologism *Poetologie*, calling this direction a "poetology of knowledge"). Following Michel Foucault and Stephen Greenblatt, he argues that this notion might be able to describe how knowledge moves through different manners of utterance: a literary text; a scientific experiment; a rule of law; or just a sentence from everyday life.[2] Viewed in this manner, literature is not only a medium in which knowledge is gathered and represented, but also a genuine and self-contained cultural power that articulates knowledge in a somehow privileged way, dependent on a cultivated poetic licence that is lent prominence in specific cultural contexts. Thus literature might even operate as a "counter-discourse" in Foucault's sense. Very similar to this, Stephen Greenblatt uses the term "circulation of social energy" to describe the traffic of knowledge and meaning between different social spheres and the consequent metamorphosis they then undergo. In this context, the relation between literature and the sciences is described in terms of a "shared code" (Pethes 204),[3] where both, the sciences and the literary system, are seen as a wellspring and generator of knowledge and the literary text is not simply viewed as a transformation or reiteration of knowledge produced somewhere else.

For my purposes, the concept of "imagination" may serve as a methodological key that allows us to analyze the interrelations between science and literature. The history of geology and palaeontology shows that in both cultural subsystems, in science and literature a kind of imagination is at work, one that creatively reconstructs or even *con*structs knowledge and structure. The term *poetics* can serve as a lynchpin that connects science and literature. Its Greek meaning, *poesis* (from *poiein*, to produce), marks the fact that in both domains a kind of imagination is in operation that produces its objects in complex and intricate ways.

When Bruno Latour and Steve Woolgar developed a theory of modern scientific procedures in their book *Laboratory Life* (1979), they emphasized their role as anthropologists visiting the laboratory setting and paid special attention to the "construction of scientific facts" (this is the subtitle of their book). They sum up their position in the following way:

> It is not simply that phenomena *depend* on certain material instrumentation; rather, the phenomena *are thoroughly constituted* by the material setting of the laboratory. The artificial reality, which participants describe in terms of an objective entity, has in fact been constructed by the use of inscription devices. (64)

The constructivist view on the history of the natural sciences is an important if not dominant tendency in this discipline. In his concise and instructive overview *Making Natural Knowledge: Constructivism and the History of Science*, Jan Golinski traces a line from Thomas S. Kuhn and Ludwik Fleck to Bruno Latour. He refers to Ian Hacking, who "has talked of experiment as the business of 'creating' phenomena, stabilizing them, and making them reproducible. Phenomena, he suggests, should not be thought of as 'summer blackberries there just for the picking,' but as entities that are made by instrumental engagement with the material world" (Golinsky 32). In 1935 Ludwik Fleck assumed that scientific knowledge arises in the context of a "thought collective" (*Denkkollectiv*), "which sustains a distinctive mode of reasoning (its 'thought style' or *'Denkstil'*)" (Golinsky 32). In Fleck's own words: "A fact always occurs in the context of the history of thought and is always the result of a definite thought style" (qtd. in Golinsky 33).

"Construction" is not yet identical with "imagination." I now want to give plausibility to the notion that geologists and palaeontologists, especially in the so-called heroic age of geology (between Buffon and Charles Lyell, that is, between 1750 and 1830), needed a good deal of imagination or *Einbildungskraft* (the power to create an image of something) not only to seek the remains of former life forms, but also to guide them in piecing these petrified bones together, imagining them covered with flesh and skin, and even conceiving an entire biography or novel—if not an "epic"—about these fragments they dug out of the ground. Their reconstruction of these creatures' lives, their food, their manner of walking or creeping, their struggles for life, and their wars—indeed, their fate as a whole and their ultimate extinction—is perhaps one of the greatest novels ever written. I also want to show how literary imagination can contribute to scientific discourse in more than an illustrative way; my example in this context will be Goethe.

GEORGES CUVIER: IMAGINING GEOLOGICAL CATASTROPHES

Baron Georges Cuvier (1769–1832), the French zoologist and geologist, was one of the pioneers of the emerging science of geology. He was the most influential proponent of a geological theory called "catastrophism." As Peter Bowler and Ivan Rhys Morus write:

> Cuvier noticed that the boundaries between successive formations
> seemed abrupt, so that the transition from one fossil population to the
> next appeared to have been more or less instantaneous. In his *Dis-*

course on the Revolutions of the Surface of the Globe, first published in 1812 as the introduction to his survey of fossil vertebrates, he attributed the sudden extinction of species to catastrophic earth movements and tidal waves. There did seem to be a lot of evidence for a dramatic transformation of the landscape in the recent geological past. (115–16)

Cuvier's theory was fascinating and impressive. He influenced writers and artists such as the painter John Martin (1789–1854). Martin's spectacular painting "The Deluge" from 1834 was demonstrably painted under the influence of the catastrophist theory of Cuvier, who visited John Martin in that very year, saw a version of the motif, and, in Martin's words, "expressed himself highly pleased" about the concordance of their opinions (Johnstone 18).

Baron Cuvier was also famous for his work in comparative anatomy, which made him an authority in identifying and "reconstructing" extinct animals merely on the basis of examining only a single bone, preferably a vertebra (*Wirbelknochen*). In her thrilling book *The Dinosaur Hunters,* Deborah Cadbury describes how the researchers involved in the run on the giant bones found in southern England sought his advice and expertise.[4] Cuvier had great talent in drawing bones and recombining them, and his constructive imagination was well known. In reflecting on the methodological problems of constructing animals out of chaotic remains, he wrote, "It is . . . extremely rare to find a fairly complete fossil skeleton. Isolated bones, scattered higgledy-piggledy, and almost always broken and reduced to fragments, are all that our beds give us in this class [the quadrupeds], and are the naturalist's only resource" (Cuvier 217). Starting from these fragments, the scientist has to combine the letters of his "alphabet," according to the principles of functionality, proportion, continuity, and coherence—criteria that can also be considered to be *aesthetic* principles. Cuvier is aware that this is highly combinatory, but also exact, work. "Beginning with each of [these fragments] in isolation, he who possesses rationally the laws of organic economy would be able to reconstruct the whole animal" (219). Cuvier also uses the term "imagining" when he mentions theories about "a certain primitive state" of the earth (199), and he refers to a frequently used metaphor of palaeontological hermeneutics that views the researcher's task as a process of decoding an old scripture, much like the work of a philologist:

As a new species of antiquarian, I have had to learn to decipher and restore these monuments, and to recognize and reassemble in their original order the scattered and mutilated fragments of which they are composed; to reconstruct the ancient beings to which these fragments belonged; to reproduce them in their proportions and characters; and finally to compare them to those that live today at the earth's surface. *This is an almost unknown art.* (183, emphasis added)

GOETHE AND THE FIRST THEORY OF THE ICE AGE

Wolf von Engelhardt, the famous mineralogist and editor of Goethe's writings on natural science, published a wonderful book in 1999 about Goethe's life and work titled *Goethe im Gespräch mit der Erde* (Goethe in dialogue with the earth), which demonstrates that Goethe was the first to discover the ice age.[5] In his novel *Wilhelm Meisters Wanderjahre* (Wilhelm Meister's time as journeyman, 1829), the eponymous protagonist is led to a mountain festival and is listening to a discussion between miners and their guests that deals with recent and former geological hypotheses about the origin of the earth. Von Engelhardt writes:

[S]everal derive the present form of our earth from the gradual recession of the waters which covered the globe; others believe that fire which initially had heated and melted the surface of the earth had retreated into the depth from where it had nourished the volcanoes and built up the highest mountains, by ejecta and lava flows; still others maintain that large formations which were prepared in the depths of the earth had been extruded through the earth's crust, by irresistible elastic forces; another party asserts that many features of the earth's surface were produced by masses fallen from the sky. A last small group pleads, finally, for ice as geologic agent. ("Did Goethe Discover the Ice Age?" 123)

He then continues by appending to this quotation the following passage from Goethe's novel in English translation:

Finally two or three quiet guests invoked a period of fierce cold, when glaciers descended from the highest mountain ranges far into the land, forming in effect slides for ponderous masses of primeval rock, which were propelled farther and farther over the glassy track. In the subsequent period of thaw, these rocks had sunk deep into the ground, to remain forever locked in alien territory. In addition, the transport of huge blocks of stone from the north might have been made possible by moving ice floes. However, the somewhat cool views of these good people did not make much headway. The general opinion was that it was far more natural to have the world created with colossal crashes and upheavals, wild raging and fiery catapulting. And since the heat of the wine was now adding its strong effect, the glorious celebration might almost have ended in fatal clashes. (123–24)

First, we note that Goethe refers to scientific theories about the history of the earth, theories that were much discussed in his time and may be attributed with some precision to specific scholars in this discipline. Second, the last of these discussed theories never had been published before. This theory, proven to be correct a few years later, thus first appeared in print in Goethe's novel! As Wolf von Engelhardt demonstrates, some fifty years prior to this Goethe had already discussed with his friend Johann Karl Wilhelm Voigt the problem of granite boulders found in unexpected places. At that time Goethe had read Buffon's pioneering book *Les époques de la nature* (1778) and had toyed with the idea of writing a "novel about the universe." Goethe argued with those critics of Buffon's theory who objected to his projections about the oldness of the earth, saying that he could not tolerate their claim that Buffon's theory was just a novel, a piece of fiction. The Bible, especially the book of Genesis, could be called a novel with far more justification, he maintained (Engelhardt, *Goethe im Gespräch* 66). Thus Goethe was fully aware of the blurring boundaries between fact and fiction, or more precisely, between science and fiction. Just fifty years later he dared to make public his assumptions about boulders strewn in unexpected places, these so-called "foundlings," in his novel *Wilhelm Meisters Wanderjahre*. In this instance, then, literary imagination was the forerunner of scientific "reconstruction." The professional geologists Jean Louis Agassiz and Jean de Charpentier "confirmed in 1837 and 1841, respectively, that Johann Wolfgang von Goethe had expressed in his novel *Wilhelm Meisters Wanderjahre*, already in 1829, the theory that during a past epoch of grim cold, rock masses were transported by ice into northern Germany and the forelands of the Alps" (Engelhardt, "Did Goethe Discover the Ice Age?" 123).

CONCLUSION

From its very beginnings in the seventeenth century through to the twentieth century, the history of geology is a history of imaginative reconstructions: imaginations about the origins of the globe, about an earth without human beings, about an earth replete with catastrophes. In addition to this we can mention the purely imaginative fantasies about those animals that existed in prehistoric times and were never perceived by the human eye. Sir Arthur Conan Doyle's *Lost World* and Michael Crichton's *Jurassic Park*, as well as many other such works, imagine encounters with these beings. After Thomas Burnet developed his *Theory of the Earth* in the late seventeenth century, a third type of fantasy arose: The earth is in a state of old age, it is a ruin, and the time of its ultimate collapse is near. A variant of this imagined scenario is the idea of an earth without human beings, and that human beings, like the dinosaurs, will disappear from the face of the earth. What were the feelings of "The Last Man"? This, of course, is the title of a novel by Mary Shelley. The list could easily be extended. In popular science in the nineteenth century we find a vital culture bent on representing the scenes of deep time, and here the boundaries between fancy and science are constantly blurred.[6]

The history of geology is perhaps the best subject in which to study how construction and imagination cooperate in the field of the natural sciences. It is one of the most instructive areas for investigating the interaction between art and science.

NOTES

I want to thank Richard Gray and Geoffrey Cox for revising my English in the text of this article.

1   See in this regard especially Braungart, "Apokalypse in der Urzeit."

2   See Vogl's programmatic essay "Für eine Poetologie des Wissens" as well as the edited volume *Poetologien des Wissens um 1800*.

3   For a general survey on related methodological problems, see Braungart and Till.

4   See in particular chapters 1, 3, and 5.

5   See also Engelhardt's essay "Did Goethe Discover the Ice Age?"

6   See Martin Rudwick's *Scenes from Deep Time* as well as his recently published opus magnum, *Bursting the Limits of Time*.

WORKS CITED

Bowler, Peter J., and Iwan Rhys Morus. *Making Modern Science: A Historical Survey.* Chicago: University of Chicago Press, 2005.

Braungart, Georg. "Apokalypse in der Urzeit: Die Entdeckung der Tiefenzeit in der Geologie um 1800 und ihre literarischen Nachbeben." *Zeit—Zeitenwechsel—Endzeit.* Eds. Ulrich G. Leinsle and Jochen Mecke. Regensburg: Regensburg University Press, 2000. 107–20.

Braungart, Georg, and Dietmar Till. "Wissenschaft." *Handbuch Literaturwissenschaft: Gegenstände und Grundbegriffe.* Ed. Thomas Anz. 3 vols. Stuttgart: Metzler, 2007. 1: 407–19.

Cadbury, Deborah. *The Dinosaur Hunters: A True Story of Scientific Rivalry and the Discovery of the Prehistoric World.* London: Fourth Estate Books, 2000.

Cuvier, Georges. *Fossil Bones, and Geological Catastrophes.* Ed. Martin J. S. Rudwick. Chicago: University of Chicago Press, 1987.

Engelhardt, Wolf von. "Did Goethe Discover the Ice Age?" *Eclogae Geologicae Helvetiae* 92 (1999): 123–28.

———. *Goethe im Gespräch mit der Erde: Landschaft, Gesteine, Mineralien und Erdgeschichte in seinem Leben und Werk.* Weimar: Böhlau, 2003.

Freud, Sigmund. "Eine Schwierigkeit der Psychoanalyse." *Gesammelte Werke.* Ed. Anna Freud. 19 vols. London: Imago, 1940–87. 12: 3–12.

Golinsky, Jan. *Making Natural Knowledge: Constructivism and the History of Science.* Cambridge: Cambridge University Press, 1998.

Gould, Stephen Jay. *Time's Arrow—Time's Cycle: Myth and Metaphor in the Discovery of Geological Time.* Cambridge, MA: Harvard University Press, 1987.

Johnstone, Christopher. *John Martin.* London: Academy Editions, 1974.

Latour, Bruno, and Steve Woolgar. *Laboratory Life: The Construction of Scientific Facts.* Princeton: Princeton University Press, 1979.

McPhee, John. *Basin and Range.* New York: Farrar, Straus, Giroux, 1981.

Pethes, Nicolas. "Literatur und Wissenschaftsgeschichte: Ein Forschungsbericht." *Internationales Archiv für Sozialgeschichte der Literatur* 28 (2003): 181–231.

Rudwick, Martin J. S. *Bursting the Limits of Time. The Reconstruction of Geohistory in the Age of Revolution.* Chicago: University of Chicago Press, 2005.

———. *Scenes From Deep Time. Early Pictorial Representations of the Prehistoric World.* Chicago: University of Chicago Press, 1992.

Vogl, Joseph. "Für eine Poetologie des Wissens." *Die Literatur und die Wissenschaften 1770–1930.* Eds. Karl Richter, Jörg Schönert, and Michael Titzmann. Stuttgart: Metzler, 1997. 107–27.

———, ed. *Poetologien des Wissens um 1800.* Munich: Fink, 1998.

3

Between Imagination and Reason

KANT AND SPINOZA ON FICTIONS

Beth Lord

THE early German Romantics found Spinoza and Kant exemplary of the kind of philosophy that isolates itself from poetry.[1] For the Romantics, philosophy can complete itself only *as* poetry, where poetry is defined as the infinitely uncompleted, that which is "forever becoming and never perfected" (AF 116). Attempts to build isolated philosophical systems necessarily end in the incompletion of not having achieved the "final synthesis" with poetry; that is, such philosophy has not completed itself because it has not yet become that which is forever incomplete (AF 451). In the view of the authors of the *Athenaeum*, neither Spinoza nor Kant had achieved this paradoxical completion, meaning that the systems of both thinkers had to be overcome. Yet as the opponents of early German Romanticism, Spinoza and Kant are also among its most prominent sources. It is widely acknowledged that the idea of the necessary incompleteness of systematic philosophy was a Kantian theme before it was extended by the Romantics. It is equally well known that Spinoza (or late eighteenth-century Spinozism, at least) had a profound influence on the immediate post-Kantians.[2] Does this central idea of early German Romanticism—that systematic philosophy can complete itself only as poetry—have its roots in both Kant and Spinoza?

In this essay I will suggest that the idea that systematic philosophy is incomplete, and the further idea that philosophy can be completed only by incorporating into it that which is radically *in*complete, can be traced to both thinkers. Furthermore, this idea emerges in both Kant's and Spinoza's texts through their similar use of "fictions" for the purpose of systematic philosophy. Both Spinoza and Kant make use of the term "fictions" to name ideas produced by the imagination that are neither true nor false, but that are important as problems to which reason can generate solutions. While neither Spinozist nor Kantian "fictions" (Spinoza's *fictio* or Kant's *Dichten*) are equivalent to Romantic "poetry" (Schlegel's *Poesie*), they fulfill a similarly fragmentary role in relation to the system. For both Kant and Spinoza, these anti-systematic fictions are systematically necessary for understanding the whole, and are therefore necessary for the practice of philosophy. In the first section of this chapter I will discuss how fictions are important to Spinoza's sense of organized knowledge and organized societies and show that fictions are a requirement of the systematic unity of the *Ethics*. In the second section I turn to Kant's use of fictions, arguing that they have a similarly important role for systematic understanding and rational progress.

SPINOZA

To understand the role of fictions in Spinoza's philosophy, we must briefly survey his theory of knowledge. In a famous passage of the *Ethics*, Spinoza sets out three types of knowledge (E IIP40S2).[3] The first is knowledge through imagination, where we know things from experience, memory, and hearsay. The second is knowledge through reason, where we know things truly according to their essences. The third and rarest kind is knowledge through intuition, where we can deduce true knowledge of things from true knowledge of the essence of God.

The first type of knowledge, imagination, covers most kinds of perceptual and empirical knowledge. Imagination includes the knowledge we gain from such disparate mental activities as sensing, experiencing, remembering, predicting, hypothesizing, and dreaming, and from such disparate sources as objects, signs, symbols, and written and spoken language. What connects all these ways of knowing, and what makes them all species of imagination, is their reliance on the *image*. For Spinoza, an image is the inadequate idea produced when one body physically affects another (E IIP17S). The bodies of external things leave physical traces on our bodies, which are the physical images we retain in the brain. The process of image-formation is experience itself, and these images are the source of memory and are used to anticipate, to predict, and to hypothesize. Images are the partial, inadequate ideas of external things. My image of the table on which I work, for example, includes all the properties accessible to my senses, but does not include its intrinsic, essential properties. The image also includes the affectedness of my senses. My image of the table is therefore not equivalent to the true idea of the table; my image is partially true, a fragment of the true idea of the table, which is confused with the partial idea of how my senses are affected. That image, partial and confused as it is, will go on to be the basis of my memory of the table, of the associations I draw from it, of my theorizing about this table and my speculations about tables in general. That is, images form the basis of a vast amount of what we consider knowledge, including all knowledge from experience and memory.

Images are inadequate ideas, partial or confused truths. By contrast, an adequate idea is the true conceiving of a thing in its essence. Adequate ideas are not representations or pictures in the mind; rather, adequate ideas are the activity of thought, the *true active conceiving* of a thing (E IIP43S). Spinoza's God has only adequate ideas and understands all things truly, as they are in their essence. Furthermore, God understands things clearly and distinctly—God understands the table's essence as being distinct from my essence, in a way which I cannot when I'm being affected by it. Now, an inadequate idea is not the opposite of an adequate one, but rather its fragmentation. An inadequate idea is simply an adequate idea that is partial, fragmented, or confused. As we have seen, God with his infinite intellect has an adequate idea of the table before me, and conceives it truly, in its essence. But my perception of the table is partial, and confused with my perception of my own sensory affectedness. In other words, I can never have an adequate idea of the table or conceive it truly in its *essence* because I can access the table only through my senses. As Spinoza says, "the ideas which we have of external bodies indicate the condition of our own body more than the nature of the external bodies" (E IIP16C2). We can never access the essence of external bodies, and our knowledge of them is always inadequate. Most of our knowledge is therefore through imagination; it involves some truth, but its truth is always partial and confused. For this reason, most knowledge from experience, and some of our scientific knowledge, is open to doubt, falsification, and revision.

We do, however, have some true knowledge, and we can gain more of it through reason, knowledge of the second kind. When we know through reason, we access adequate ideas, and we know things fully and truly. There are limits on what we can know through reason. As we have seen, I can never have an adequate idea of the table or any other external thing because my idea of it will always be mixed up with the idea of my own body, through which I access it. But I *do* have adequate ideas of some aspects of *my own* essence. Through this route I can have an adequate idea of *some aspects* of the table's essence, too: those aspects that the table's essence shares with my own essence. This is Spinoza's doctrine of the common notions (E IIP37-P40). For example, my essence involves an adequate idea of extension which I understand truly. The table, as an extended thing, also involves the adequate idea of extension. My knowledge of the table is therefore not strictly limited to what my senses tell me. I *know with certainty* that the table is extended, and this knowledge is not subject to doubt. That is because, on Spinoza's account, the adequate idea of extension in me is reinforced by the adequate idea of extension in the table. Amidst the confused images I have of the table, *some* true ideas shine through: those that are basic to the essences of all extended beings (E IIP40S1).[4]

As a result, when I lean on the table, I do not need to doubt whether it really exists or worry that it will suddenly disappear. That certainty does not come from experience or imagination; it comes from reason, or knowledge "from the fact that we have common notions and adequate ideas of the properties of things" (E IIP40S2). From my true knowledge of the extendedness of the table, I can deduce further true knowledge about its properties: that it is material, that it is subject to motion and rest, that it is subject to certain physical laws, etc. Reason includes knowledge through deductive inference. Through gaining more rational knowledge, we can understand the world and the universe better and better, but more importantly, we can learn more about ourselves. Spinoza's goal in the *Ethics* is to help us develop our reason so that we can truly understand our own essence and can "deduce" from our own essence what follows necessarily from it.

Knowledge through reason alone, however, is not possible as long as we are finite human beings, for we are always encountering other things in the world and being affected by them. We are constantly amassing and reorganizing images. Thus for finite human beings, knowledge involves *both* imagination and reason, and our knowledge can be represented on a continuum that involves proportions of both. In fact, our capacity to think rationally relies on our capacity to imagine. This is the case for two reasons. First, it is only by exposing ourselves to more and more experiences that we will discover what things have in common with us, and thus reinforce the adequate ideas that we share with them. Second, and similarly, knowledge through deductive inference (from the laws of physics, for example) can get off the ground only once some knowledge has been ascertained through experiment. Experience and experiments are acts of imagination that can lead us to discover and develop true ideas which can be known rationally. Spinoza therefore advocates a wide variety of experiential encounters and experiments to help us become more rational (see, for example, E IVP45S). A Spinozist's life is "a long affair of experimentation" (Deleuze 125). This means that imagination, while it is inadequate and partial knowledge, is absolutely necessary to our gaining true, adequate knowledge. Imagination is not an inferior form of knowledge to be overcome but the necessary structure of our experience, within which we seek opportunities to perfect our thinking and to make our ideas more adequate.

This project of perfecting our thinking is the explicit aim of Spinoza's *Treatise on the Emendation of the Intellect*, written seven years before the *Ethics* but never completed. In this work, Spinoza introduces a tool that helps us to use our imagination to increase our reason: this is our ability to produce *fictions*. Fictions are products of the imagination, normally made up of combined images of things that are not immediately present to perception. Typical fictions include a winged horse, the character Don Quixote, string theory, and my thoughts about what's going on in the next room. We can see why it might be useful or pleasurable to engage in fiction, or even how it might come naturally to us to do so. More importantly, however, this activity helps us to develop our rational understanding (Gatens and Lloyd 34–36).

What distinguishes fictions from other kinds of images is that fictions are concerned with what is *possible*, not with what is impossible or necessary (TIE 52–53).[5] That is, fictions are those images whose existence does not involve a contradiction, but neither does their nonexistence. Strictly speaking, of course, Spinoza does not admit possibility into his system: everything that is actual is also necessary, as it unfolds from the necessity of the divine nature (E IP29). Wherever he uses the term "possibility," Spinoza refers to that which, from God's perspective, is either impossible or necessary, but which from our human perspective we cannot be certain of one way or the other (E IP33S1). Thus "God cannot engage in any fiction" because God has adequate knowledge of everything (TIE 54). Furthermore, it is the essence of reason to understand things in terms of their necessity (E IIP44). That is, reason is driven to understand things as they follow necessarily from God's nature. Insofar as we are rational, we are motivated to experiment with images and to produce fictions in order to hold them up and determine whether they are necessary or impossible. Human beings engage in fiction because their adequate knowledge is limited, but fictioning is not the idle activity of an inadequate intellect. It is, rather, a productive activity that creates ordered sequences of our abundance of images and passes them on to be either accepted as necessary or rejected as impossible. Since seeking to understand necessity is a rational pursuit, the person who is more rational will have less of his mind taken up with passively amassing random images and more of it occupied by the production of organized fictions.

The activity of fictioning (or feigning) involves holding up certain ideas for scrutiny and critique until the truth becomes clear. Spinoza gives us a number of examples, including the fiction that his friend Peter is coming to visit and the fiction that the earth is a hemisphere (TIE 52, 56). The fiction that Peter is coming to visit may arise on the basis of evidence (Peter said he might drop by) and be entertained for pragmatic reasons (Benedict should get some wine ready in case he does). If Peter does visit, the necessity of that visit will have been confirmed; if he doesn't, its impossibility will be certain. Our inadequate knowledge of the future, combined with our need to anticipate it, means that we must—and constantly do—entertain fictions of this kind. The fiction that the earth is a hemisphere is one that we can entertain only as long as we do not see its impossibility. Spinoza suggests that we might do this for educational reasons, to help someone to develop their own reasoning about the shape of the earth (TIE 56).

As a third example we might consider the fiction—understood to be neither necessary nor impossible in Spinoza's day—that celestial movements are caused by gravitational force. This is a hypothesis that Spinoza says becomes a fiction only if we claim that it is *true* of heavenly bodies

(TIE 52n). There is a problem if we draw an inference about the nature of the heavens without being certain of its necessity, "for one may conceive many other causes to explain these movements" (TIE 57n). In this case we might uphold the fiction that celestial movements are caused by gravitational force either for the purpose of scrutinizing this idea or for the purpose of taking scientific investigation further. In these cases we pretend to believe something "for the sake of argument." Where the limitations of our experience prevent our attaining adequate knowledge of the true nature of the planets, we may well need to uphold such fictions in order to have a coherent explanatory framework for the universe.

Producing fictions, then, enables us to plan for the future, to develop the reasoning ability of others, and to provide speculative cosmological explanations that provide a framework for scientific investigation. Fictions contribute to the coherence and systematicity of our experience insofar as we do not yet understand that its true coherence is in God. One of the chief ways that fictions are useful is therefore in creating the systems in and by which people conduct their lives: religion and politics. When people are largely irrational, their knowledge governed by imagination, they do not know that their lives are truly explained through the necessity of God's nature and their virtue determined through their own essence. Instead, they are liable to look to image-systems for organized models of how to live.

Spinoza advocates the control of irrational populations through political and religious systems that, although fictional, are likely to lead people to more rational knowledge (E IVP37S1&2). Where these fictional systems are grounded in what is common to human essences (the common notions again), they will be good for human society. Useful fictions are those that promote tolerance and community, such as the story of Jesus Christ and the legal and constitutional systems of the democratic state: both are organized systems of images used to manage the behavior of people who are not fully rational. However, where organizing systems are devised by those who lack rational knowledge of human essence—ideologues, religious zealots, and dictators—the danger to society is very great. In these cases individuals are kept irrational by being encouraged or forced to believe in malevolent fictions, a condition in which they are easily controlled, oppressed, and enslaved.[6] Fictions prove dangerously useful in providing explanatory structures and power relations for individuals and societies. Spinoza's firm view is that we ought to make use of benevolent religious and political fictions until people live exclusively according to reason, where neither state nor civil laws would be required. According to Spinoza's epistemology, of course, human knowledge and action will never be purely rational, so some fictional organizing structure will always be needed.

Fictions, for Spinoza, lend systematicity and coherence to our experience, given that we are finite modes with limited understanding of our place in God or nature. This is perfectly illustrated in a rare instance in the *Ethics* where Spinoza uses the term "fiction," which is otherwise found largely in the *Treatise on the Emendation of the Intellect*. There is one part of the *Ethics* where Spinoza *needs* to make use of a fiction: Part V, where Spinoza writes about the mind in its eternal form reaching the third kind of knowledge (Gatens and Lloyd 38–39). This is knowledge through intuition; if we reach this kind of knowledge, we know in the way that God knows, starting with perfect knowledge of God's attributes and proceeding to know the essences of things in their eternal form.

This is one of the most contested parts of the *Ethics*. One problem is how Spinoza can say anything at all about the third kind of knowledge, given that he writes from the perspective of the *second* kind of knowledge, that is, reason (Deleuze 57).[7] Spinoza himself is eminently rational, but he nevertheless exists as a finite mode that lacks intuitive knowledge. In the *Ethics* Spinoza in fact makes no claims to *know* through the third kind of knowledge; he claims only to know rationally that the human mind is capable of such knowledge and that that is its greatest striving and virtue (E VP25). This much can be deduced from what Spinoza has already determined the mind to be. At a certain point, however, Spinoza must describe what it is like for the mind to know intuitively and to be eternally. Intuitive knowledge and eternal being are fundamental to our essence, and thus are eternally and necessarily what we are; but our discovery of that fact can be represented only as a leap out of reason and into intuition. That is, in our rational thinking about intuitive knowledge and eternity, we must represent to ourselves a situation where we leap into intuition and begin to be eternal.

This story of the leap into eternity, of the mind *beginning* to be eternal, is Spinoza's fiction. As Spinoza says, the temporal terminology of beginnings is inadequate when it comes to eternity (E VP31S); so too is the notion that the eternal, infinite, intellectual love of God "comes to be" (E VP33S). In fact, the mind already *is* eternal, but we are unable to understand our eternal being adequately until we actually *have* intuitive knowledge. Since neither Spinoza nor the reader has that intuitive knowledge, we must stop at the limits of rational knowledge and use a fiction that makes our eternal being and intuitive knowledge explicable to us, who understand only through reason:

> Although we are already certain that the mind is eternal . . . , nevertheless, for an easier explanation and better understanding of the things we wish to show, we shall consider it as if it were now beginning to be, and were now beginning to understand things under a species of eternity, as we have done up to this point. We may do this without danger of error, provided we are careful to draw our conclusions only from evident premises. (E VP31S)

The last line makes clear the connection to the fictions of the *Treatise*. Just as we were able to uphold fictions where the limitations of our experience prevented our attaining adequate knowledge of the true nature of the planets, we are able to use fictions where the limitations of rational knowledge prevent our true understanding of our own eternal being. Spinoza explicitly calls this move "feigning" and its product a "fiction" in the Scholium to Proposition 33. The fiction of the mind beginning to be eternal (E VP31S) and the related fiction that this knowledge gives rise to the intellectual love of God (E VP32C, VP33S) are problems for reason to scrutinize. They will be resolved only once the mind has that intuitive knowledge and truly understands the necessity of the mind's eternity (see also Lloyd 135–38).

Like all fictions, Spinoza's fiction of the leap into the eternal gives coherence to a system. The system to which it gives coherence is that of the *Ethics* itself. Spinoza's fiction occurs very near the end of the text, at the juncture between the explanation of the capabilities of a maximally rational being—such as Spinoza himself—and the presentation of what is beyond that rational life and fundamentally unpresentable. The fiction enables Spinoza to transcend his own capabilities and the capacities of representation, and thereby to complete the system of the *Ethics*. This fiction is systematically required not only for our understanding but also for the *Ethics* to posit what goes beyond those things the text is able to describe.

Fictions are essential not only for pragmatic speculations, scientific progress, and social organization, but also for the progress and possibility of philosophy as a system. Spinoza's rational system depends for its closure on a product of imagination; the presentation of the whole necessarily includes the fragment. This is the sense in which Spinoza is a precursor to the Romantics: he recognizes that his rational system can be completed only through the incorporation into it of something that is profoundly alien to it, the imaginative fiction. The system of the *Ethics* would be incomplete, presenting only a fragment of reality, if it did not include the fragmentary fiction that makes it whole. The representation of Spinoza's philosophy *as a system* requires the inclusion of the anti-systematic, the non-rational, the non-philosophical; it can be represented as a whole only when completed by something that will never be whole or complete itself.

The lineage for early German Romanticism in Spinoza includes the centrality of fictions to systematic philosophy: the idea that the system is completed by something that is forever fragmentary and incomplete. Friedrich Schlegel characterizes Spinoza as "the ideal of the species" of the systematic, universal philosopher (*Ideas* 137, AF 346).[8] This kind of philosophy can never achieve completion without poetry:

> Universality is the successive satiation of all forms and substances. Universality can attain harmony only through the conjunction of poetry and philosophy; and even the greatest, most universal works of isolated poetry and philosophy seem to lack this final synthesis. They come to a stop, still imperfect but close to the goal of harmony. (AF 451)

The inability to achieve completion characterizes universal philosophy. Yet it is also the primary criterion of Romantic poetry itself (AF 116). Furthermore, since Romantic poetry strives to reveal the infinite in the finite, Spinoza's philosophy—which claims that infinite substance is expressed through its finite modes—is its basis (Beiser, *German Idealism*, 448–50). The attempt to know or reveal the infinite is as problematic as Spinoza's attempt to represent eternity. Indeed, Schlegel claims in his lectures on transcendental philosophy that the poet's feeling for the infinite is a *fiction* in Spinoza's sense: something that is neither true nor false, but that must be imagined and critically examined (Beiser, *German Idealism*, 457).

In this sense, the universal philosopher who abjures poetry may be practising Romantic poetry nonetheless. In the fragment preceding the one quoted above, Schlegel remarks that Spinoza is an enemy of poetry "because he demonstrates how far one can get with philosophy and morality unaided by poetry" (AF 450). But unlike Plato and Epicurus, who are true enemies of art because they isolate poetry from philosophy, "it is very much in the spirit of [Spinoza's] system not to isolate poetry." Perhaps what Schlegel indicates here is that for Spinoza, poetry and art are not differentiated from the mass of texts and objects that contribute little to rational understanding. In that sense Spinoza is the enemy of poetry because he does not deem it useful to philosophy. But to invert this idea, since poetry is not isolated in its own closed realm, cut off from the philosophical system, it is everywhere immanent to the philosophical system. Poetry is within philosophy as the imaginative fictions that reason needs in order to complete the philosophical system. Not only that; reason needs fictions in order to complete the *representation* of the philosophical system in the text of the *Ethics*. Spinoza's text, which will always be incomplete in its attempt to present the unpresentable, is supremely "poetic" in the Romantic sense.

KANT

Early German Romanticism's debt to Kant's theory of imagination has been well documented (see, for instance, Lacoue-Labarthe and Nancy 27–58 and Gasché vii-xxxii). From the role of imagination in transcendental apperception and image-formation in the first *Critique* to the aesthetic ideas of the third, Romanticism has a clear lineage in the problems Kant sets. Kant's theory of imagination arises in the context of other seventeenth- and eighteenth-century accounts and shares with Spinoza's that imagination is essential to knowledge. Kant's imagination is a crucial part of knowledge-formation, enabling sense data to match up with concepts in a unified way through the rule-governed production of images (CPR A115–25, B151–52, A140–42/B179–81).[9] This procedure, represented as a unified, regular structure for each given concept, is not a fiction but a "schema." When the imagination engages in the same image-producing activity for ideas that have no objective validity, then the imagination enters the realm of fiction.

Kant's "fictions" are not drawn from Spinoza and do not fulfill exactly the same function.[10] For Kant, fictions are indeed products of imagination that are useful for reason, but they do not have the emendatory role for knowledge that they have for Spinoza. Quite the contrary, for in the *Critique of Pure Reason* fictions are characterized as the traps into which reason falls, lures to unfounded knowledge, making us think that we are capable of knowing beyond the limits of possible experience. Ultimately, though, both Kant and Spinoza use fictions speculatively to present what transcends the limits of human knowledge, arguing that such use is acceptable as long as we are careful to keep it under control. Not only are such controlled fictions acceptable for Kant; as for Spinoza, they are essential for the sake of positing experience and knowledge as systematic wholes.

Kant defines fictions as products of imagination based on the material of sensation (CJ 5: 243). This has both positive and negative connotations. In the *Critique of Judgment*, the productive imagination can generate creative reconfigurations of nature that entertain us and point toward ideas that cannot be presented in experience: "a poet ventures to give sensible expression to rational ideas of invisible beings, the realm of the blessed, the realm of hell, eternity, creation, and so on" (CJ 5: 314). The fictions generated by the imagination of the artistic genius similarly present aspects of experience with a "completeness" toward which reason strives but that is not found in experience itself. These fictions, or "aesthetic ideas," which give rational ideas "a semblance of objective reality," prompt reason to think more than what can be apprehended in the object itself (CJ 5: 314–15). Fictions, in the form of poems and paintings, give reason the opportunity to think these transcendent thoughts without the temptation to make knowledge claims about them.

The danger of granting the imagination the freedom to engage in fiction is that if it breaks free of its grounding in actual experience it may generate illusory objects, becoming fanatical in its claims for their existence. Fanaticism (*Schwärmerei*) is the flipside of genius, as Kant intimates when he warns that artistic genius must be subjected to rules (CJ 5: 309–11). The worry is averted as long as the imagination, in breaking free of nature, does not actually attempt to present a supersensible object. Kant advocates what we might call "fictioning without fiction"; the imagination's pure activity of fictioning, free from all sensible boundaries, is to be encouraged, as long as it does not result in a "positive" fiction which claims objective reality (CJ 5: 274–75).[11] Fictioning in the "negative" sense enables the imagination to connect to ideas of morality and the infinite, and is superior to the fictioning that involves the mere reconfiguration of images from experience. Indeed, Kant is as sensitive as Spinoza (though not as disturbed by it) to the ways in which such images are used by political and religious authorities to keep people docile. Far better that individuals should discover religion through the "expansion of the soul" brought about by an imaginative meditation on the infinite, than that they are plied with a religion of "images and childish devices" designed to reduce them to passivity (CJ 5: 274–75). Producing positive fictions, on the other hand, is the attempt "to SEE something beyond all bounds of sensibility," which leads beyond rational religion to fanaticism and mania (CJ 5: 275).

These positive fictions can mislead us into believing in transcendent objects, and in the most extreme cases can lead to delusion. This is treated in Kant's 1766 essay "Dreams of a Spirit-Seer," in which he seeks a physical explanation for the spirit-seer's claim to perceive "illusions of the imagination" as having real existence in a specific space outside their bodies (Dreams 2: 343–44). Kant explains both perception and delusion here in terms of Newtonian optics. We can draw a series of lines from the optic nerve to the perceived object, which will converge on a *focus imaginarius* in the object. In the case of an imagined object, that focus will be in the mind. But in the case of delusion, that internal imaginary focus is displaced outside the mind, through lines externally extended and converging on a point in space (Dreams 2: 346–47). Deluded people believe in fictions through the illegitimate extension of an internal imaginary focus, but as long as that focus is kept within the imagination, such fictions are unproblematic.

In the *Critique of Pure Reason*, Kant uses the same optical explanation of converging lines as an analogy for the activity of reason. This occurs in the Appendix to the Transcendental Dialectic, where he discusses the regulative employment of the transcendental ideas. The transcendental ideas are ideas of unconditioned absolutes that reason necessarily generates in order to organize experiential knowledge and that have no corresponding objects in experience (CPR A326–27/B382–84). Ideas of unconditioned absolutes, such as the totality of appearances, are problematic and have to be treated carefully. Since their objects cannot be assumed, they cannot be used constitutively to determine objects of experience, but they do have a regulative use for organizing the concepts of the understanding. Regulative employment of the transcendental ideas involves

> directing the understanding towards a certain goal upon which the
> routes marked out by all its rules converge, as upon their point of
> intersection. This point is indeed a mere idea, a *focus imaginarius*,
> from which, since it lies quite outside the bounds of possible experi-
> ence, the concepts of the understanding do not in reality proceed;
> nonetheless it serves to give to these concepts the greatest possible
> unity combined with the greatest possible extension. Hence arises the
> illusion that the lines have their source in a real object lying outside
> the field of empirically possible knowledge—just as objects reflected

in a mirror are seen as behind it. Nevertheless this illusion . . . is indispensably necessary if we are to direct the understanding beyond every given experience (as part of the sum of possible experience), and thereby to secure its greatest possible extension, just as, in the case of mirror-vision, the illusion involved is indispensably necessary if, besides the objects which lie before our eyes, we are also able to see those which lie at a distance behind our back. (CPR A644–45/ B672–73)

If the concepts of the understanding are extended, they converge upon an imaginary point that lies outside the bounds of possible experience. We cannot say that concepts actually proceed from this point, just as we cannot say that optical lines actually proceed from an imaginary object, but this *focus imaginarius* gives the concepts of understanding the unity and extension that are needed to make sense of them on a larger scale.

The *focus imaginarius* is useful—indeed, it is indispensable—in building systematic knowledge. This is particularly true when it comes to nature, where we need big concepts of nature's unity and homogeneity in order to organize our experiential concepts. The danger of the *focus imaginarius* is the danger of delusion: we easily displace the focus outside the field of possible experience and believe there are direct lines from the object to our concepts of understanding. For example, reason is entitled to entertain the idea of an *ens realissimum* in a regulative capacity so as to guide our understanding of the ultimate ground of experience, but it must guard against the assumption that it is an objectively given thing that determines actual beings, at which point the idea becomes "a mere fiction" (CPR A580/ B608). As a fiction in the positive sense, this reified idea can lead reason to "fictitious knowledge," delusion, and fanaticism (CPR A702/B730). But Kant believes these fictions are inevitably generated by reason when it seeks systematic knowledge. Just as using a mirror to see the bigger scene behind us involves the illusion that the reflected objects are behind the mirror, using the transcendental ideas of reason to gain systematic understanding necessarily involves the illusion that the ideas have a real object. The trick is to encourage the fictioning activity but to suppress the fiction generated by it in order to enhance science, morality, and religion.

This fictioning activity that we use to present systems is the same as the "fictioning without fiction" that Kant advocates to present ideas aesthetically in the *Critique of Judgment*. Indeed, aesthetic ideas are the "counterpart" of rational ideas, since an aesthetic idea is an imaginative presentation to which no determinate concept is adequate, and a rational idea is a concept to which no imaginative presentation is adequate (CJ 5: 314). Rather than believing in the fiction that the rational idea of the *ens realissimum* has objective existence, we should allow the imagination to devise images and narratives that prompt our thought about a supreme being but that do not tempt us to connect those thoughts to concepts of possible experience. This is the value of the symbol, which connects sense data to a concept indirectly; that is, it schematizes by analogy (CJ 5: 351–54). In this way we can usefully hold on to the thought of a supersensible supreme being— which we must do if we are to understand nature and morality as a system—without falling into the trap of assuming that it is objectively given.

Art, and especially poetry, are therefore important for building our understanding of reality as a whole as systematic:

> Poetry fortifies the mind: for it lets the mind feel its ability . . . to contemplate and judge phenomenal nature as having aspects that nature does not on its own offer in experience either to sense or to the understanding, and hence poetry lets the mind feel its ability to use nature on behalf of and, as it were, as a schema of the supersensible. Poetry plays with illusion, which it produces at will, and yet without using illusion to deceive us. (CJ 5: 326)

Poetry encourages us to think about nature's supersensible ground while holding us back from claiming to have knowledge of the supersensible. It does this through the imagination's activity of "fictioning without fiction" or, as Kant puts it here, playing with illusion without deceiving. The imagination brings ideas to presence without attempting to give them objective reality. Systematic understanding is therefore generated through a process of imaginative fictioning that is incomplete because it is prevented from arriving at the end product of its activity, the positive fiction. The fictioning process, which gives presence to ideas of the supersensible, is fragmentary and forever incomplete. As Gasché interprets Kant, the presentation of ideas "produces only fragments." Fragmentation "represents the *positive* mode in which presentation of the whole occurs" (Gasché xxvii). Poetry, in presenting ideas, brings completion to the system through fragmentation.

With his analogies of the converging lines and the mirror, Kant suggests that transcendental illusions are endemic to reason, just as optical illusions are endemic to perception. Fictions are the inevitable by-product of reason's attempt to think the whole systematically, and they are inevitable in both philosophy and science. But these fictions can be significantly avoided through poetry, which enables us to think the whole without succumbing to transcendental illusion. Poetry therefore enables philosophy and science to be complete as systems, and it does this through the incompleteness of its own activity. "Fictioning without fiction," poetry indefinitely forestalls the completion of its presentational process in a positive fiction. That forestalling prevents reason from falling victim to transcendental illusion in its construction of systematic wholes.

Romanticism's fascination with this idea—of the completion of the system of philosophy through what is incomplete—has its roots in Kant, but also in Spinoza. In both Kant and Spinoza this idea crystallizes around the anti-systematic fictions that are crucial for the presentation of reality and philosophy as systematic wholes. Kant argues that when philosophy seeks completion by representing what transcends experience, we are at risk of believing in fictions; Spinoza counters that philosophy *must* complete itself, and must use fictions to represent what transcends experience. According to *Athenaeum Fragment* 168, where Schlegel ranks highest that form of philosophy that does not inhibit a leap into the supersensible, Spinoza is closer to the Romantic vision. Yet it is Kant who suggests that poetry, as infinitely uncompleted presentational activity, is philosophically important for the systematic whole. The Romantic insistence on the fusion of the fragmentary with systematic philosophy has a complex genealogy. Let me suggest that it includes both Spinoza's and Kant's ideas of the imaginative fictions that support the systematic whole. Caught between imagination and reason, fictions are also between philosophy and poetry, neither of which is complete on its own.

NOTES

I would like to thank the organizers at the University of Washington for inviting me to present a version of this paper at the 2007 conference "Inventions of the Imagination." The financial assistance of the British Academy in the form of an Overseas Conference Grant is gratefully acknowledged.

1   See, for example, Friedrich Schlegel's remarks on Spinoza in *Athenaeum Fragments* (hereafter AF, with references to fragment number) 346, 450, and 451, and

Ideas 137; and his remarks on Kant in AF 107, 220, 298, 322, and 388. See also Lacoue-Labarthe and Nancy 27–58.

2   The gulf between "Spinoza" and "Spinozism" is considerable throughout the eighteenth century and becomes even more complicated in its final two decades. Most thinkers after 1785 were less familiar with Spinoza than with the influential interpretations of Spinoza by Jacobi and Herder, each with its own problems and philosophical-religious agenda. See Beiser, *The Fate of Reason*, 44–91 and di Giovanni 417–41. For a longer study of Kant's place in this story, see Lord, *Kant and Spinozism*.

3   References to Spinoza's *Ethics* are to Curley's translation and follow his method of citation: E for Ethics, Part I-V, and Proposition number (P), followed, where needed, by Corollary number (C) or Scholium number (S). Thus E IIP40S2 is *Ethics* Part II, Proposition 40, Scholium 2. More detailed studies of Spinoza's theories of knowledge and imagination can be found in Hampshire, De Deugd, and Gatens and Lloyd.

4   Note that in E IIP40S1, Spinoza distinguishes these "common notions" from "transcendental" concepts such as Being and Thing, and also from "universal" concepts such as Man and Horse. Transcendental and universal concepts are based on the generalization of images (and are therefore fictitious), whereas common notions are based on what individuals in their essence have in common. A helpful interpretation of Spinoza's common notions can be found in Deleuze 54–58.

5   Spinoza's *Treatise on the Emendation of the Intellect* is abbreviated TIE, and accompanying references are to its marginal paragraph numbers.

6   Spinoza's argument against this kind of enslavement is developed in his *Theological-Political Treatise*, which was banned upon its publication in 1670. The implications of Spinozist political fictions have been extensively taken up by contemporary thinkers including Balibar, Negri, and Gatens and Lloyd. For a commentary on imagination in the *Theological-Political Treatise*, see De Deugd 137–88.

7   That Spinoza writes from the perspective of the second, and not the third, kind of knowledge is by no means accepted by all commentators. This is part of a wider debate concerning the possibility of attaining the third kind of knowledge during our finite existence. For discussion, see Lloyd 105–47.

8   For an overview of Schlegel's reflections on and contributions to philosophy, including his reliance on Spinoza, see Beiser, *German Idealism*, 435–61.

9   Kant's texts are abbreviated CJ (*Critique of Judgment*), CPR (*Critique of Pure Reason*), and Dreams ("Dreams of a Spirit-Seer Elucidated by Dreams of Metaphysics"). References to Kant are to the *Akademie* volume number and pagination. In the case of CPR, references are to the A and B editions of the text, as is standard. For an overview of the role of imagination in Kant's philosophy, see Makkreel or Young.

10 Kant probably never read Spinoza directly, though he was familiar with Jacobi's book on Spinoza. Of course, Spinoza is not the only philosopher of the time to make use of the concept of fictions. It is likely that Hume is a source of Kant's use of this term.

11 This "fictioning without fiction" is advocated in slightly different terms in the

Critique of Pure Reason. Kant explains that scientific hypothesizing is a variant of fictioning that avoids fanaticism by staying closely tied to what is actually given in experience (CPR A769–70/B797–98).

WORKS CITED

Balibar, Etienne. *Spinoza and Politics.* London: Verso, 1998.

Beiser, Frederick C. *The Fate of Reason.* Cambridge, MA: Harvard University Press, 1987.

———. *German Idealism.* Cambridge, MA: Harvard University Press, 2002.

De Deugd, C. *The Significance of Spinoza's First Kind of Knowledge.* Assen: Van Gorcum, 1966.

Deleuze, Gilles. *Spinoza: Practical Philosophy.* Trans. Robert Hurley. San Francisco: City Lights, 1988.

di Giovanni, George. "The First Twenty Years of Critique: The Spinoza Connection." *The Cambridge Companion to Kant.* Ed. Paul Guyer. Cambridge: Cambridge University Press, 1992. 417–47.

Gasché, Rodolphe. "Ideality in Fragmentation." Foreword to Schlegel, *Philosophical Fragments.* vii-xxxii.

Gatens, Moira, and Genevieve Lloyd. *Collective Imaginings: Spinoza, Past and Present.* London: Routledge, 1999.

Hampshire, Stuart. *Spinoza and Spinozism.* Oxford: Oxford University Press, 2005.

Kant, Immanuel. *Critique of Judgment.* Trans. Werner S. Pluhar. Indianapolis: Hackett, 1987.

———. *Critique of Pure Reason.* Trans. Norman Kemp Smith. London: Macmillan, 1929.

———. "Dreams of a Spirit-Seer Elucidated by Dreams of Metaphysics." *Theoretical Philosophy 1755–1770.* Trans. and ed. David Walford and Ralf Meerbote. Cambridge: Cambridge University Press, 1992. 301–60.

Lacoue-Labarthe, Philippe, and Jean-Luc Nancy. *The Literary Absolute.* Trans. Philip Barnard and Cheryl Lester. Albany: SUNY Press, 1988.

Lloyd, Genevieve. *Part of Nature: Self-Knowledge in Spinoza's Ethics.* Ithaca: Cornell University Press, 1994.

Lord, Beth. *Kant and Spinozism: Transcendental Idealism and Immanence from Jacobi to Deleuze.* Basingstoke: Palgrave Macmillan, 2010.

Makkreel, Rudolf A. *Imagination and Interpretation in Kant.* Chicago: University of Chicago Press, 1990.

Negri, Antonio. *The Savage Anomaly: The Power of Spinoza's Metaphysics and Politics.* Trans. Michael Hardt. Minneapolis: University of Minnesota Press, 1991.

Schlegel, Friedrich. *Philosophical Fragments.* Trans. Peter Firchow. Minneapolis: University of Minnesota Press, 1991.

Spinoza, Benedict de [Baruch]. *Complete Works.* Trans. Samuel Shirley. Ed. Michael L. Morgan. Indianapolis: Hackett, 2002.

———. *A Spinoza Reader: The Ethics and Other Works.* Ed. and trans. Edwin Curley. Princeton: Princeton University Press, 1994.

Young, J. Michael. "Kant's View of Imagination." *Kant-Studien* 79 (1988), 140–64.

4

Herder on Interpretation and Imagination

Michael N. Forster

THE idea that imagination plays an essential role in understanding one's own concepts and in interpreting, that is, in coming to understand, other people's concepts, has a long history. To mention some examples: Aristotle already in *De Interpretatione* and *De Anima* treats the imagination's preservation of images that share the same form as real features of the world, which we encounter through the senses, as an essential aspect of our understanding of general concepts (*De Interpretatione* 16a; *De Anima* 432a; cf. 427b-29a). Hume, in the course of his famous discussion of abstract ideas in *A Treatise of Human Nature*, explains our grasp of general concepts in terms of the imagination's associating together a fund of particular images related to one another by resemblance—a fund that can be called on in order to see whether or not particular images resemble some new case encountered, and therefore whether or not that new case falls under the concept in question (Hume 67–71). Kant's project in the Schematism chapter of the *Critique of Pure Reason* sets out from that Humean account (Kant likewise ascribes our ability to possess empirical concepts to the imagination's provision of a fund of images), and then attempts to extend it further in order to cover a class of concepts that Hume had not envisaged, namely a priori concepts (*Critique of Pure Reason*, A137–42/B176–81).

In this article I would like to make some observations about what seems to me an especially interesting specific version of the generic theory that imagination plays an essential role in the possession and interpretation of concepts: Herder's version. The essay proceeds as follows: the first section describes the philosophy of language that underpins Herder's whole position and offers some defense of the part of it that is most important for our topic. The second section sketches the theory of the role of the imagination in interpretation that Herder bases on his philosophy of language, and offers some defense of this as well. Finally, the third part discusses some potentially fruitful consequences of Herder's position in connection with the solution of philosophical puzzles concerning interpretation.

HERDER'S PHILOSOPHY OF LANGUAGE

Let me begin by briefly sketching Herder's philosophy of language generally, including the part of it most relevant to our topic. Already by the mid-1760s, in *On Diligence in Several Learned Languages* (1764) and *Fragments on Recent German Literature* (1767–68), Herder advanced two revolutionary doctrines that essentially founded the modern philosophy of language as we have known it since: (1) Thought is essentially dependent on, and bounded in its scope by, language. That is to say: one can think only if one has a language, and one can think only what one can express linguistically. (2) Meanings, or concepts, are identical with *word-usages*.[1] They are not identical, as many philosophers both before and even since have supposed, with such items in principle independent of language as objects to which reference is made, Platonic forms, or Empiricist mental ideas (à la Locke or Hume).

Herder's two doctrines strikingly anticipate positions held by the most important twentieth-century philosopher of language: the later Wittgenstein. This is not accidental; Herder (and Hamann) influenced Wittgenstein via Fritz Mauthner.[2]

A case can be made that Herder's philosophy of language is actually superior to Wittgenstein's in at least one important respect, though. Herder also embraces a *third* doctrine in the philosophy of language: (3) a quasi-empiricist doctrine to the effect that meanings or concepts must, by their very nature, be anchored in perceptual or affective *sensations*. Unlike cruder traditional versions of such a doctrine, for instance Hume's, Herder's incorporates two important qualifications (hence the "quasi-"). These qualifications are (a) that the dependence goes both ways, that is, that the sensations of a concept-using human being also depend for their specific character on his concepts (it is not, as Hume supposed, simply a matter of a person's first having, say, the sensation of blue and then on that basis developing the concept of blue, but rather, acquiring the concept affects the very nature of the sensation); and (b) that the dependence is loose enough to permit *metaphorical* extensions (so that, for example, the sensuous "in" found in a statement like "The dog is in his kennel" becomes the non-sensuous, or at least the less directly sensuous, "in" found in a statement like "Smith is in legal trouble").[3]

At first hearing, such a doctrine is likely to strike modern philosophical ears as misguided (it used to strike mine that way). This is mainly because of the intervening strong influence of Frege's and Wittgenstein's anti-psychologism concerning meaning, or (precisely) *exclusion* of mental items such as sensations and images from any essential involvement in meaning and understanding. However, I want to suggest that Herder is probably correct here. The following are five points in defense of his doctrine.

(i) One's confidence in Fregean-Wittgensteinian anti-psychologism should be at least a little undermined by recalling another of Wittgenstein's doctrines: his very plausible doctrine that such concepts as "meaning" are in their pre-philosophical state vague and fluid.[4] This doctrine makes it seem rather unlikely that our commonsense concept of meaning carries any such sharp partitioning of meaning from sensations and images as Fregean-Wittgensteinian anti-psychologism advocates. Indeed, Wittgenstein himself occasionally concedes that in excluding psychological items from meaning in this way, his conception of meaning as use departs from the ordinary meaning of the term "meaning," selectively accentuating one strand of it to the neglect of others.[5]

(ii) Herder's quasi-empiricist doctrine might seem incompatible with his own and Wittgenstein's broadly shared identification of meaning with *word-usage.* Now, it is true that in Wittgenstein's version of such an identification the notion of "word-usage" refers strictly to a pattern of linguistic competence that excludes any essential role for sensations or images. But this need not be true of *any* doctrine that meaning is word-usage. After all, a *usage* is of its very nature a usage in relation to some *context* or other, and there is no obvious reason why the context in question might not essentially include *sensations* or *images*. So there is after all no real incompatibility here.

(iii) Frege's anti-psychologism is based on a dubious Platonist ontology (the "third realm"). Wittgenstein's instead appeals, somewhat more plausibly, to arguments concerning the criteria we use for ascribing conceptual understanding to people: Wittgenstein argues that what is decisive here is linguistic competence, not whatever sensations or images a person may happen to have. However, there are two sides to Wittgenstein's case, which seem to me very different in their levels of plausibility. On the one hand, Wittgenstein argues that linguistic competence is *necessary* for understanding—and this seems entirely plausible. On the other hand, he argues that linguistic competence is *sufficient* for understanding, and in particular that understanding doesn't require any psychological process, such as having sensations or images. But this seems much less plausible. Suppose, for instance, that someone had never had a sensation of redness and could not generate images of redness (say, because he was congenitally blind or color-blind), but that we managed to teach him to make all of the right intralinguistic statements about redness—for example, concerning its position in the color spectrum, its being a brighter color than gray, and so on—and that in addition we managed, by implanting some sort of fancy electronic device in his brain, to enable him to apply the word "red" when and only when presented with something red (despite, let it be stipulated, still not having sensations or images of redness).[6] Would we in such a case want to say that he fully understood the word "red"? It seems at least very plausible to say that we would *not.*

(iv) Another reason why Herder's doctrine might seem misguided is because, as Wittgenstein tirelessly and correctly points out, it is never necessary that one *currently* have appropriate sensations or images in order to understand a concept. This point certainly cuts against theories held by some of Herder's predecessors (for example, Aristotle). But Herder's own theory can easily accommodate them by emphasizing a person's *having had* relevant sensations or having the *ability* to generate relevant images.

(v) In the light of these considerations, someone might perhaps concede, pace Frege and Wittgenstein, that sensations or images are *sometimes* internal to concept-possession, but still remain skeptical that they *always* are, as Herder's doctrine asserts. Candidate counterexamples which are likely to seem attractive here include concepts such as "chiliagon" and "God." But these seem easy to cope with by means of a traditional empiricist strategy of conceptual analysis. Other candidate counterexamples are the logical connectives, such as "and" and "not."[7] However, these do not in fact constitute convincing counterexamples to Herder's doctrine at all. For whenever one observes a certain state of affairs added to another (for example, a chair being red and [then] having a cat sitting on it as well), one has a sensory illustration of "and"; and whenever one observes a certain state of affairs ceasing to obtain (for example, the cat initially being on the chair but then jumping off it), one has a sensory illustration of "not."[8]

In sum, I would suggest that Herder's third doctrine is at least very plausible, and that his philosophy of language may therefore in an important respect actually be superior to Wittgenstein's.

HERDER'S THEORY OF INTERPRETATION

Herder's philosophy of language carries a number of important implications for his theory of interpretation (that is, his theory of how to arrive at an understanding of what other people have said or written). Doctrine (1) carries the reassuring implication that in a certain and significant sense an author's language cannot be fundamentally inadequate or distorting as an expression of his thought. While an author may indeed on occasion fail to express his thoughts exactly, he cannot be *incapable* of expressing them exactly.[9] Doctrine (2) carries the implication that interpretation is fundamentally (though not necessarily exclusively) a matter of identifying an author's *word-usages*, and thereby his meanings. Finally (and for our purposes here, most importantly), doctrine (3) carries the implication that interpretation must somehow recapture the (perceptual or affective) *sensations* that are internal to an author's meanings.

This last implication is a central component of Herder's famous position that interpretation should employ a method of *Einfühlung* (literally, "feeling one's way into [the standpoint of the person being interpreted]"). This position in fact has several different components, not all of which are immediately relevant here.[10] For example, one component is a principle that interpretation commonly confronts a mental distance between the interpreted author and the interpreter, which the latter needs to overcome by means of laborious historical and philological work (that there is, as it were, an "in" there into which he needs to feel his way by such means). Another component is a principle that sound interpretation requires a measure of sympathy, or at least open-mindedness, toward the interpreted author.[11] But the component of Herder's ideal of *Einfühlung* that is most relevant here derives from his quasi-empiricism about meanings or concepts: because all meaning essentially involves an aspect of (perceptual or affective) sensation, in order to understand an author's meanings it is always essential that the interpreter grasp the relevant sensations ("feel his way into them").[12]

Aristotle had already implied something a bit similar to this in *De Interpretatione* 16a: "Spoken words are the symbols of mental experiences and written words are the symbols of spoken words. Just as all men have not the same writing, so all men have not the same speech sounds, but the mental experiences, which these directly symbolize, are the same for all, as are also those things of which our experiences are the images." Herder's position, however, differs from Aristotle's in at least three significant and attractive ways: First, whereas Aristotle had strongly privileged vision over the other senses as a source of relevant perceptual sensations (cf. *De Anima* 429a), Herder does not.[13] Second, whereas Aristotle's position is restricted to perceptual sensations, Herder's also includes affective ones (note that the verb *fühlen* and its cognates readily cover both cases).[14] Third, whereas Aristotle believes that people's relevant sensations are basically the same at all times and places, Herder believes that both perceptual and affective sensations vary markedly in their character between different historical periods and cultures, and indeed often even between different individuals within a single period and culture.[15] This makes the interpreter's task in this area far more challenging than Aristotle had supposed.

Herder's commitment to the essential importance of *Einfühlung* in interpretation comes out in numerous passages. For example, concerning the interpretation of other historical periods and cultures, he writes in *This Too a Philosophy of History* (1774):

One would have first to *sympathize* with the nation, in order to feel a *single one* of its *inclinations* or *actions all together*, one would have to *find* a single word, to *imagine* everything in its fullness—or one reads—*a word!*. . . . The *whole nature* of the soul, which *rules* through everything, which *models* all other inclinations and forces of the soul *in accordance with itself,* and in addition *colors* the most indifferent actions—in order to share in feeling this, do not answer on the basis of the word but go into the age, into the clime, the whole history, feel yourself into everything—only now are you on the way towards understanding the word. (Herder, *Philosophical Writings* 292)[16]

Accordingly, in connection with perceptual sensation specifically, he argues in the *Fragments on Recent German Literature* that in order really to understand the Greeks we need to learn to see like them (*Werke* 1: 559). And in connection with affective sensation specifically, he argues in *On the First Documents* (1769) that because people's concepts of happiness and pleasure are based on their distinctive "temperament," "feeling nature," "sense for rapture," in order really to understand the ancient orientals' versions of those concepts we must imaginatively recapture these affective states of theirs (*Werke* 5: 74–75).

Similarly, Herder represents *Einfühlung* (in the relevant sense) as essential for the interpretation of *individual* authors (whether they are historically/culturally distant from the interpreter or not). For example, in a section of *On the Cognition and Sensation of the Human Soul* (1778) titled "Our thought depends on sensation," he writes:

The deepest basis of our existence is individual, both in sensations and in thoughts. . . . One ought to be able to regard every book as the offprint of a living human soul. . . . The more modest wise man . . . seeks to read more in the spirit of the author than in the book. . . . Every poem . . . is a . . . betrayer of its author. . . . One sees in the poem not only, for instance, . . . the man's poetic talents, one also sees which senses and inclinations governed in him, by what paths and how he received images, how he ordered and adjusted them and the chaos of his impressions, the favorite sides of his heart. . . . To be sure, not every soul from the gutter is worthy of such a study; but of a soul from the gutter one would also need no offprints, neither in writings nor in deeds. Where it is worth the effort, this *living reading*, this divination into the author's soul, is the *only* reading, and the deepest means of education. It becomes a sort of enthusiasm, intimacy, and friendship which is often most instructive and pleasant for us where we do not think and feel in the same way. (*Philosophical Writings* 217–18; cf. 291)

Much of Herder's own interpretive work focuses heavily on precisely this task of recapturing the distinctive perceptual and affective sensations of a period/culture or individual. A good example of this in connection with periods/cultures is *This Too a Philosophy of History*; a good example of it in connection with the individual is *On Thomas Abbt's Writings* (1768).

The exact techniques that Herder uses in order to accomplish the task in question are fairly complicated and would merit further investigation. One that is especially important, though, is the following. As can be seen from the methodological remarks in *This Too a Philosophy of History* (quoted above) as well as from Herder's actual practice when interpreting historical periods and cultures within the work, he believes that a *holistic* approach is required: an approach that takes note of a historical period or culture's distinctive environment, historical situation, activities, art objects, values, statements, etc., together, as an essential prerequisite for accurately identifying the nature of even a single one of its relevant sensations. Herder espouses this sort of holism in connection with interpreting individuals as well.

Herder's position concerning the importance of *Einfühlung* in interpretation, as just described, can easily seem misguided today. For example, the widespread acceptance in contemporary philosophy of anti-psychologism concerning meaning may make it seem misguided. But, as I have already suggested, such anti-psychologism itself seems quite dubious on reflection. So it should not stand in the way of an acceptance of Herder's position.

Herder's position can also seem misguided because it may appear that he makes it a condition of understanding that the interpreter *share* the (perceptual or affective) feelings of the period/culture or individual interpreted—which would have absurd and even dangerous consequences. For example, it would imply that in order to understand Hitler's anti-Semitic effusions in *Mein Kampf,* one needs to have anti-Semitic feelings oneself. However, Herder is *not* in fact committed to any such foolish view. In *The Spirit of Hebrew Poetry* (1782–83) he argues that feeling one's way into the standpoint of (say) David's psalms in order to understand them does not require that the interpreter actually share David's hatreds and joys; that this should not be the interpreter's goal; and that the interpreter's recapturing of David's feelings should instead take a different, imaginative form: "David had his affects and worries as a refugee and as a king. We are neither, and hence may neither curse enemies that we do not have nor exult over them as victors. But we must learn to understand and appreciate these feelings" (*Werke* 5: 1194). Herder's idea is therefore that a sort of imaginative recapturing of relevant sensations is possible which does not require actually *having* or *having had* them, and that it is only *this* that is strictly required for understanding.[17]

This seems quite plausible. For, (1) it seems true that one can achieve a kind of imaginative grasp of perceptual or affective sensations which, while being more than a mere knowledge of them by description, is also less than a full-blooded possession of them (and that this is indeed a routine feature of such processes as reading and understanding literature, for example). Moreover, (2) it seems true that some sort of recapturing of sensations is necessary for interpretation. This is certainly supported by Herder's case for quasi-empiricism, or the internal role of sensations in meaning. But it also accords well with, and indeed helps to explain, our general experience in interpretation. For example, compare the sort of relentlessly "external" account of ancient Greek religion that one finds in a book such as Walter Burkert's *Greek Religion* with the sort of, by contrast, sensation-rich account of it that one finds in Walter Otto's books on the subject.[18] Despite the extraordinary sophistication and detail of Burkert's account, it does seem that we only really begin to understand the ancient Greeks' religious conceptions when we complement it with a sensation-rich account more like Otto's. And finally, (3) recourse to the possibility of an imaginative recapturing of sensations that does not involve the actual possession of them does justice to those considerations while also avoiding the sorts of absurdities discussed in the previous paragraph.

THE RELEVANCE OF HERDER'S THEORY TODAY

Herder's position affords resources for solving certain important problems concerning interpretation that have been raised by more recent philosophers. Let me give two examples.

First, Hans-Georg Gadamer (appropriating and historicizing a position of Martin Heidegger's) has argued that understanding essentially rests on "pre-understanding," a system of pre-cognitive perspectives on and attitudes toward the world, but that pre-understanding varies historically, so that, since one is restricted to one's own age's form of pre-understanding (or at least to a residue of it that remains even after one has modified it in various ways), one can never exactly reproduce another age's understanding of its own discourse.[19]

A Fregean-Wittgensteinian anti-psychologist would probably reject Heidegger's and Gadamer's assumption that understanding essentially rests on pre-understanding on the ground that this amounts to a form of psychologism. But for reasons sketched earlier, I think that one should be quite skeptical about such a reaction, and that such a dismissal of Gadamer's problem would therefore be too quick; in some version or other the idea that understanding essentially rests on pre-understanding is probably correct.[20] Nor does it seem plausible to attempt to forestall Gadamer's problem by questioning his thesis of the historical variability of forms of pre-understanding (and hence of forms of understanding); this too seems right.

Instead, I would suggest that a better way of forestalling Gadamer's skeptical conclusion that an exact understanding of historical Others is impossible lies in Herder's insight that a type of imaginative access to another person's (perceptual and affective) sensations is possible that falls short of the sort of *committed possession* of them that normally underlies our understanding of our own concepts, but which is nonetheless sufficient to support understanding. If all pre-understanding capable of supporting understanding had to have the character of committed possession, then a version of Gadamer's skepticism would indeed be inevitable, since one cannot simultaneously be in committed possession of one's own form of pre-understanding and of different, incompatible forms of pre-understanding. But since a merely imaginative, non-committed sort of pre-understanding is in fact sufficient to support understanding, Gadamer's skepticism can be avoided.[21]

Second, Anne Eaton has drawn attention to the following very interesting problem in connection with the interpretation of works of art: Understanding these often seems to require having affective sensations of a certain sort, but the affective sensations in question may in certain cases be morally reprehensible ones, so that the requirements of understanding and those of morality come into conflict. For example, it seems arguable that Titian's *Rape of Europa* essentially expresses certain (by our lights) morally reprehensible feelings about rape that were typical of the period and culture to which Titian belonged, in particular a certain sort of male erotic titillation at and disdain for the victim of rape, so that in order fully to understand the work one would need to participate in such feelings. How, if at all, is this problem to be solved?

Here again, an anti-psychologist will no doubt see the solution as lying in his sharp separation of understanding from feeling. But, for reasons already indicated, such a solution seems dubious.

However, Herder's position once again makes a more plausible and attractive solution possible: What is required for understanding does indeed include recapturing feelings, but not necessarily in the form of actually *having* them, since an imaginative, noncommitted recapturing of them is also possible and is sufficient to support understanding. And, unlike actually *having* an affective feeling, the imaginative, noncommitted reproduction of it is motivationally inert, and hence morally unproblematic.[22]

———◆———

NOTES

1   For more details concerning doctrines (1) and (2), including textual evidence, see Forster, "Herder's Philosophy of Language, Interpretation, and Translation" (324–51).
2   Concerning this influence, see Forster, "Herder's Philosophy of Language" (356, note 116).
3   For more details about doctrine (3), including textual evidence, see Forster, "Herder's Philosophy of Language" (351–56).
4   See Forster, *Wittgenstein on the Arbitrariness of Grammar* (137ff.).
5   See especially *Wittgenstein's Lectures* (44, 47–48, 121).
6   The stipulation that he applies the term correctly but still lacks the sensation might be questioned on the ground that applying the term correctly is *sufficient* for having the sensation. However, I think that a little further reflection shows that this is not in fact true.
7   Logic requires no more than these two.
8   To forestall an objection that is likely to seem tempting here: Recall that, unlike cruder versions of a doctrine of concept-empiricism, Herder's version is not committed to claiming that such observations could be made *without* the concepts in question.
9   The interpreter need not, therefore, take seriously the suggestion—implied by Plato's self-description in the Seventh Letter, for example—that an author may be entertaining ineffable or less than fully effable thoughts.
10 For a fuller list of the components in question, see the editor's introduction in Herder, *Philosophical Writings* (xvii-xviii).
11 "Open-mindedness" is the more accurate description of Herder's ideal, for just

as he rejects negative prejudice as detrimental to sound interpretation, so too he rejects excessive sympathy (see, for example, Herder, *Werke* 5: 1194).

12   August Wilhelm Schlegel, who took over Herder's interpretive ideal of *Einfühlung*, points out that in principle it would be possible to, for example, master the Greeks' use of a certain word "grammatically" but still not understand the word due to a failure to grasp the "intuitions" that underlay its use. See Huyssen 69ff., 89.

13   See especially Herder, *Philosophical Writings* 204. This move is closely connected with Herder's tendency, in comparison to other thinkers, to demote vision in importance relative to the other senses, especially hearing (see, for example, Herder, *Philosophical Writings* 97–99, 106–11).

14   Indeed, in *Treatise on the Origin of Language* (1772), Herder holds that it is part of our original animal nature to *fuse* perceptual sensation with affective sensation (albeit that *qua* human beings we in a way manage to detach the former from the latter by means of language/reflection). See Herder, *Philosophical Writings* 88–89, 101–3, 137–38. Similarly, in *On the Cognition and Sensation of the Human Soul* (1778), Herder maintains that the only healthy state for a human soul is one in which cognition includes affect, and that any attempt to abstract cognition from affect amounts to a sort of pathology. See Herder, *Philosophical Writings* 226–29.

15   See Herder, *Philosophical Writings* 114–15, 203–5, 217–23, 249–53, 291.

16   In translating this passage I have retained Herder's liberal and rather distracting use of emphasis.

17   Aristotle had held something rather similar about perceptual imagination. However, he had held that this at least required *having had* the relevant sensations, whereas Herder does not strictly seem to require even that. Moreover, Herder generalizes the point to cover affective sensations as well.

18   See especially Otto's four books *Die Götter Griechenlands, Dionysos, Die Manen,* and *Die Musen.*

19   See Gadamer's *Truth and Method*, especially the section dealing with Heidegger's hermeneutic circle and the historicity of understanding.

20   Heidegger and Gadamer would of course be loath to equate pre-understanding with a subject's perceptual and affective sensations. They instead envisage it as something more "primordial" than either the subject-object distinction or the distinction between the theoretical and the practical. However, what is plausible in their position seems to me not badly (re)cast in such terms.

21   In qualifiedly endorsing Gadamer's notion of "pre-understanding" here, I mean to endorse his idea that it is a *necessary condition* of understanding, not the implication that the "pre- [*Vor-*]" sometimes seems to carry for him (though not for Heidegger) that it is something that takes place, or at least can take place, temporally *prior* to understanding. Herder's picture, which seems right to me, is that the sensations that support conceptual understanding are *inter*dependent with it: Not only are the concepts in question essentially infused with the sensations in question, but *also vice versa.* This point should deter one from thinking of the sort of imaginative, noncommitted grasp of another person's sensations that is being described here as a sort of *tool* for effecting understanding of the person's

concepts, as though one could get hold of the tool first and then employ it to produce that result afterwards. The two things are too intimately connected to stand in such a relation, though the former remains a necessary condition of the latter. That consequence might sound disappointing. But if so, then the same point also carries a happier consequence. The account discussed here naturally invites questions (or perhaps challenges): How can an imaginative grasp of a historical/cultural or individual Other's different sensations be achieved? How can it be judged to have taken place correctly rather than incorrectly? The point just made suggests at least part of an answer to such questions: The interpreter can be guided toward a correct grasp of the Other's sensations by determining the extra-sensational aspects of the Other's usage of words, and to that extent the Other's concepts— which, since they are internal to the character of the Other's sensations, at least constrain viable intuitions concerning the character of the Other's sensations. And one can judge an interpreter's intuitions for correctness or incorrectness by seeing whether the extra-sensational aspects of his associated usage of words match up with those of the historical/cultural or individual Other whose sensations he is attempting to access, since their failure to do so will be enough to show that he has fallen short in the attempt (even if their success in doing so may not be enough to show that he has succeeded in the attempt).

22 Cf. *De Anima* 427b, where Aristotle makes a similar point about the motivational inertness of perceptual imagination as contrasted with perceptual sensation.

WORKS CITED

Aristotle. *De Anima Interpretatione.* In *The Basic Works of Aristotle*, ed. Richard McKeon. New York: Random House, 1941.

———. *De Anima.* In *The Basic Works of Aristotle*, ed. Richard McKeon.

Eaton, Anne Wescott. *Titian's "Rape of Europa": The Intersection of Ethics and Aesthetics.* Dissertation, University of Chicago, 2003.

Forster, Michael N. "Herder's Philosophy of Language, Interpretation, and Translation: Three Fundamental Principles." *The Review of Metaphysics* 56 (2002): 324–51.

———. *Wittgenstein on the Arbitrariness of Grammar.* Princeton: Princeton University Press, 2004.

Gadamer, Hans-Georg. *Truth and Method.* New York: Continuum, 2002.

Herder, Johann Gottfried. *Philosophical Writings.* Ed. and trans. Michael N. Forster. Cambridge: Cambridge University Press, 2002.

———. *Werke.* Ed. Ulrich Gaier, et al., 10 vols. Frankfurt/Main: Deutscher Klassiker Verlag, 1985.

Hume, David. *A Treatise of Human Nature.* Harmondsworth: Penguin Books, 1969.

Huyssen, Andreas. *Die frühromantische Konzeption von Übersetzung und Aneignung.* Zürich and Freiburg: Atlantis, 1969.

Kant, Immanuel. *Critique of Pure Reason.* Trans. Norman Kemp Smith. London: Macmillan, 1933.

Otto, Walter. *Dionysos: Mythos und Kultus.* Frankfurt/Main: Klostermann, 1933.

———. *Die Götter Griechenlands: Das Bild des Göttlichen im Spiegel des griechischen Geistes.* Frankfurt/Main: Schulte-Bumke, 1947.

———. *Die Manen: Von den Urformen des Totenglaubens.* 2nd ed. Darmstadt: Wissenschaftliche Buchgesellschaft, 1958.

———. *Die Musen und der göttliche Ursprung des Singens und Sagens.* 3rd ed. Darmstadt: Wissenschaftliche Buchgesellschaft, 1961.

Wittgenstein, Ludwig. *Wittgenstein's Lectures: Cambridge 1932–1935.* Chicago: University of Chicago Press, 1982.

5

William Blake

IMAGINATION, VISION,
INSPIRATION, INTELLECT

Hazard Adams

IN 1897, W. B. Yeats published two essays on Blake. One was entitled
"William Blake and the Imagination" and the other "William Blake and
His Illustrations to the Divine Comedy."[1] In juxtaposition, though Yeats
did not emphasize the point, the two titles indicate something important
about Blake's notion of imagination that separates him from the so-called
English Romantics who used the word: rigorous insistence on the relation
of imagination to sight and to visual art.

At the outset of a discussion of this matter, I should mention three
things: First, Blake belonged in many of his tastes and attitudes to an
intellectual and artistic generation prior to that of the English Romantic
poets. Some have called that generation, at the end of which came Blake,
the "Pre-Romantics," but as Northrop Frye wryly remarked a half-century
ago, he knew of no group of poets who thought of themselves as merely

precursors of a later, more important movement (*Fables of Identity* 130). Born in 1757, Blake was thirteen years Wordsworth's senior, fifteen years older than Coleridge, thirty-one older than Byron, thirty-five than Shelley, thirty-eight than Keats. Among the poets whose work he illustrated and knew well were Young (born 1683), Blair (born 1699), and Gray (born 1716). He spoke well of Macpherson, Cowper, and Smart. These were all poets of a style appealing to a taste different from that of the Romantics. In Blake's extant writings, only Wordsworth and Byron, among the Romantics, are mentioned. Blake's annotations to Wordsworth's *Poems* and *The Excursion* could not have been written before 1814, and his dedication of *The Ghost of Abel* to "Lord Byron in the wilderness" is of about 1820, when Blake was 63.

Second, Blake was a professional engraver and visual artist, and most of his mentions of imagination have to do with visual art, especially painting and engraving. Blake's was a painter's and engraver's imagination, and for him imagination was connected literally to sight. But "sight" was not an adequate word for what he had in mind. His word was "vision."

Third, in his long poems, Blake was a maker of chains of metaphor that, if followed out, imply the identification of all things with each other. This characteristic of his poetry has a limited parallel in his critical writings, where imagination implies vision, vision implies inspiration, inspiration implies intellect, and intellect implies imagination. These are all words that Blake frequently employed.

To say, however, that Blake's notion of imagination was grounded in sight requires that we understand just what he meant by vision. It may be well to remind ourselves now that his generation and the poets he read had more spatially oriented imaginations than did the Romantics. The notions of imitation and *ut pictura poeisis* still had life in criticism. The first thing to observe is just how literally connected with seeing Blake's notion of vision was and how important for him "image" was in the word "imagination."

In a letter of August 23, 1799, Blake wrote to the Reverend Dr. Trusler,

> This World Is a World of Imagination & Vision I see Every thing I paint
> In This World, but Every body does not see alike. . . . Some See Nature
> all Ridicule & Deformity & by these I shall not regulate my proportions,
> & Some Scarce see Nature at all But to the Eyes of the Man of Imagina-
> tion Nature is Imagination itself. As a man is So he Sees. This world is
> all One continued Vision of Fancy or Imagination. (702)[2]

Over the next decade or more, Blake seems to have refined slightly the language of this statement; nevertheless, it presents, when clearly understood, a view that Blake held all of his life.

The fundamental way to consider Blake's statement is epistemologically. In his poem *Milton*, Blake has Milton say that he has come "to caste off Bacon, Locke, & Newton from Albions covering / To take off his filthy garments, & clothe him with Imagination" (142). This is to reject the epistemology of subject and object and introduce a way of seeing that frees the mind from the abstract fiction of an object lacking the so-called secondary qualities of perception. It isolates those qualities from the real. Blake identifies nature with this dull objectivity. Nature is the deluding product of a faith solely in what Blake calls "general knowledge," and it is rare when Blake uses "nature" in any other way. In his late years, Blake annotated Wordsworth's *Poems* and remarked that natural objects "Weaken deaden & obliterate Imagination in Me" (665), and he saw in Wordsworth "the Natural Man rising up against the Spiritual Man Continually" (665). "Spiritual" meant for Blake the appropriate way of seeing, literally of vision. It had little, if anything, to do with mysticism as we usually think of it. Nature was for him the external world, unreal when regarded as apart from man; it was constructed by the dominant philosophy of the time and projected as an other. This is the nature that is the "Ridicule & Deformity" of Blake's letter.

It is also the product of a mistaken view of what it is to see. For Blake the material eye as a source of vision is a delusion. We do not see passively with it. Our minds see through it in two senses: see through it if one is still to speak *as if* there were a material body separate from mind; see through it if one can recognize it as a delusion of matter. The truth is that when the so-called outer world is seen, it is the projection of an active intellect. Imagination is intellectual. That act is an act of imaging. In the same letter to Trusler, Blake refers to what he calls "Spiritual Sensation" (703), a phrase I think he would not have used later because of sensation's connections to the notion of passive reception of sense data. Spirit is intellectual.

But all people do not imagine the world in the same way. Some people have weak imaginations. The "greatest of all blessings," Blake remarks, is "a strong imagination, a clear idea, and a determinate vision" (693). Some minds see more intensely and therefore more clearly than others, but even equally strong imaginations will see things differently. In a description of his "Last Judgment," Blake writes, "its Vision is seen by the Imaginative Eye of Every one according to the situation he holds" (554; Blake deleted "Imaginative Eye," because for him it is the mind that sees). Great artists see alike, that is, intellectually and actively rather than copying or recording a passive response of sense; yet their visions will be individual, different, though metaphorically related. Art does not improve; situations vary and change; genius can be equaled but not surpassed.

Seeing, or vision, as I shall call it from now on, is grounded for Blake on clarity, which is achieved by intense concentration. There should be nothing mysterious about it. Blake rarely uses "mystery" in an honorific sense. He usually thought of mystery as something imposed by a priesthood or an elite in order to maintain power, and religion should be devoid of it. For him, the most important thing in art is outline and "attention to minute particulars."

> A Spirit and a Vision are not, as the modern philosophy supposes, A cloudy vapour or a nothing: they are organized and minutely articulated beyond all that the mortal and perishing nature can produce. He who does not imagine in stronger and better lineaments, and in stronger and better light than his perishing mortal eye can see does not imagine at all. (541)

The passage implies remarkable intensity of vision that seems to have been characteristic of Blake's activity when he drew what are called his "visionary heads." Allan Cunningham, one of Blake's earliest biographers, tells a story, perhaps somewhat embellished, about Blake that informs us about his practice:

> He was requested to draw the likeness of William Wallace—the eye of Blake sparkled, for he admired heroes. "William Wallace!" he exclaimed, "I see him now, there, there, how noble he looks—reach me my things!" Having drawn for some time, with the same care of hand and steadiness of eyes, as if a living sitter had been before him, Blake stopped suddenly and said, "I cannot finish him—Edward the First has stepped between him and me."[3]

This passage suggests a discipline of creative vision that required projection of an image (as on a blank wall) and then the drawing of it. When Blake said he copied imagination I think he meant something like this. If another visual idea gets in the way, the vision is suspended. (Blake was having some fun here, in that Wallace was the frustrating Scottish foe of Edward I.)

All of Blake's likes and dislikes in painting, and they are vigorously expressed, arise from his emphasis on intensity and clarity of vision. (We can notice that a professional engraver might very well emphasize the importance of outline.) "Nature has no Outline: but Imagination has" (270); and if there is no "determinate and bounding form" (550) there is no "idea in the artist's mind" (550). Copying nature ends up with only what the material eye can see. Rubens as an influence is an "outrageous demon" (547) who leads followers to "blotting and blurring" (546). Chiaroscuro is an "infernal machine" (547). The mortal eye, with which these styles work, is caught up in the flux of time and cannot seize intellectually on anything and fix it clearly in vision. Over and over, Blake's long poems emphasize proper vision. In *Jerusalem*, for example, Blake views time as a huge visual pattern, and elsewhere he chastises historians for reasoning on events. They should present acts for all to visualize, not theories about acts (544). Acts alone are real, and anything that is not an action is not worth reading (544).

Blake presents his own version of what Sir Philip Sidney treated as a poetic improvement on nature. One difference is that Sidney thinks of beautification, while Blake thinks of clarification. The latter is a different sort of improvement in that it is composed of inventions of "intellectual vision" (704) that can go beyond what the mortal eye can see. Thus Blake complains that what he calls the corporeal eye, separated from imagination, sees not only passively but also dully:

> What it will be Questiond When the Sun rises do you not see a round
> Disk of fire somewhat like a Guinea O no no I see an Innumerable
> company of the Heavenly Host crying Holy Holy Holy is the Lord God
> Almighty I question not my Corporeal or Vegetative Eye any more
> than I would Question a Window concerning a Sight. (565–66)

In a description of an illustration he made to Milton's "L'Allegro," Blake speaks of "The youthful Poet sleeping on a bank by the Haunted Stream by Sun Set [who] sees in his Dream the more bright Sun of Imagination" (684). But one does not have to dream to imagine; one can do it consciously looking through the eyes. Indeed, the imagination is not a state of mind that one turns on and off; Blake remarks, "it is the Human Existence itself" (132); and he holds in his annotations to Berkeley's *Siris*, "Jesus considerd Imagination to be the Real Man" (663). The sun of the passages I have offered is not an allegorical image standing for an abstract idea. It is a visionary idea, not a substitute for a Platonic one. It is what it is and refers only to itself. As such it communicates vision to the reader who makes identification with it, something impossible with an object. Writing about his "Last Judgment," Blake remarks:

> If the Spectator could Enter into these Images in his Imagination approaching them on the Fiery Chariot of his Contemplative Thought if he could Enter into Noahs Rainbow or into his bosom or could make a Friend & Companion of one of these Images of wonder which always entreats him to leave mortal things as he must know then would he arise from his Grave then would he meet the Lord in the Air & then he would be happy[.] General Knowledge is Remote Knowledge it is in Particulars that Wisdom consists & Happiness too. (560)

Blake makes an important distinction between what he calls the daughters of imagination and the daughters of memory. They are the true and false muses respectively. Inspired by the daughters of memory, a painter is "confined to the sordid drudgery of facsimile representations of merely mortal and perishing substances" (541). "Walking in another man's style, or speaking or looking in another man's style and manner" (547) is the same. An art based on memory cannot create, only copy and mirror the false knowledge of the passive subject.

More than an improvement on nature, indeed a denial of it, vision at its greatest intensity sees potentially into the infinite in a thing. But Blake's infinite is not a Platonic realm without image; it is the "regions of my imagination" (705). Every moment, like every so-called piece of matter, is a window into it. The fundamental principle of imagination is the synecdoche:

> To see a World in a Grain of Sand
> And a Heaven in a Wild Flower
> Hold Infinity in the palm of your hand
> And Eternity in an hour. (493)

These are by no means casual lines. Infinity is the largest and the infinitesimal is the smallest of things, and they are identical. Synecdoche supports Blake's notion of the individuality and yet communality (by that trope) of what imagination creates. "This world of Imagination [with its attention to the 'minute particular'] is the World of Eternity" (555). In the religion of imagination or the proper imagining of religion, the Savior *is* the human imagination; and the human imagination is the Savior. It is what saves us from a living death in the world of vegetable nature. Jesus is the spirit of imagination in man, no more, no less: There is "no other Gospel than the liberty both of body & mind to exercise the Divine Arts of Imagination" (231).

Every artistic imagination produces according to its own individuality what "Eternally Exists" (554). A string of metaphorical identities relates all things. In *Jerusalem* there is described a receptacle of all that can be imagined and can occur:

> All things acted on Earth are seen in the bright Sculptures of
> Los's Halls & every Age renews its powers from these Works
> With every pathetic story possible to happen from Hate or
> Wayward Love & every sorrow & distress is carved here
> Every Affinity of Parents Marriages & Friendships are here
> In all their various combinations wrought with wondrous Art
> All that can happen to Man in his pilgrimage of seventy years[.] (161)

This is the collective imagination of all art, a synecdoche to which belongs every visionary act in all of time. The apocalyptic act in *Jersusalem* is a vision: "All Human Forms identified even Tree Metal Earth & Stone" (258).

Blake held Chaucer in high regard, and he describes Chaucer's pilgrims as "Visions of . . . eternal principles or characters of human life" that "appear to poets, in all ages" (536). Blake remarks that Gray's vision of eternal characters can be seen "in the person of his Bard on Snowdon" (543). Every great artist enters in vision into this place, which is seen according to his or her situation. To enter it does not require servile allegiance to prior models, but to one's own individuality. (This is not to say that an artist need not learn the techniques of his craft.) Beyond these images, metaphorically unique but also identical (just as two sides of a metaphor include both sameness and difference), art does not, cannot, and need not go.

But there is always danger if these humanly made images are erected into gods, or even one God, and given divine names. As such they become destructive to humanity, for properly "All deities reside in the human breast" (38). Objectified, they are no better and probably worse than kings. Thus, for Blake, Jesus is and must remain an imaginative creation, supremely human. But it is a misfortune that, as Blake says,

The Nature of Visionary Fancy or Imagination is very little Known &
the Eternal nature & permanence of its ever Existent Images is considerd as less permanent than the things of Vegetative & Generative
Nature. (555)

The imaginative expression of vision is for Blake a continuum that cannot be divided into invention that is then executed in some external form.
The execution *is* the invention, a process of creation and discovery. At the
beginning of *Milton*, Blake connects the brain and the hand in poetic and
artistic creation when he asks his muses to

. . . Come into my hand
By your mild power; descending down the Nerves of my right arm
From out the Portals of my Brain. (96)

The idea comes into being in the execution just as a reality comes into
being in imagination. The two, which are one, cannot be divided by an
"idiot Reasoner" who "laughs at the Man of Imagination" (131) and might
say, if he were trying to be an artist, "I have these wonderful ideas but somehow can't express them." This is a true dissociation, both of sensibility and
of imagination.

Yeats made some mistakes about Blake in his essays. He called him a
mystic, neglecting to declare just what he meant by that word, the vague-
ness of which in common usage goes against all that Blake required of art.
Yeats said that Blake was unfortunate in being an artist who had to invent
his own symbols. But for Blake, all artists have always had to do that. If they
have borrowed or stolen, they have had to make the symbols their own in
the contexts they have created. Yeats said of Blake that he was a "too literal
realist of imagination" ("Essays and Introductions" 119). For a chapter title
in his *Fearful Symmetry: A Study of William Blake*, Northrop Frye short-
ened the phrase, leaving out the "too" (85–107). He was right to do so. Frye
was writing a book of literary criticism, and he was right to have argued
elsewhere that "literal" ought to have something to do with the literary
rather than with its opposite (*Fables of Identity* 130). If that is the case, then
a poet cannot be too literal, and the real is what the imagination literally
envisions, intellectually and spiritually; and it is always an image.

NOTES

Some paragraphs of this essay are drawn from Professor Adams's book *Blake's Margins: An Interpretive Study of the Annotations*, © 2009 Hazard Adams, by permission of McFarland & Company, Inc., Box 611, Jefferson NC 28640 www.mcfarlandpub.com.

1   See Yeats, "Ideas of Good and Evil" (1896–1903).
2   All quotations from Blake are from *The Complete Poetry and Prose of William Blake* and given parenthetically in the text.
3   Allan Cunningham, *Lives of the Most Eminent British Painters* (rev. ed., 1830), as quoted by Wilson (271).

WORKS CITED

Blake, William. *The Complete Poetry and Prose of William Blake.* Newly revised edition. Ed. David V. Erdman. Garden City: Anchor Press/Doubleday, 1982.

Frye, Northrop. *Fables of Identity: Studies in Poetic Mythology.* New York: Harcourt, Brace & World, 1963.

Frye, Northrop. *Fearful Symmetry: A Study of William Blake.* Princeton: Princeton University Press, 1947.

Wilson, Mona. *The Life of William Blake.* London: Rupert Hart-Davis, 1948.

Yeats, William Butler. "Ideas of Good and Evil." *Essays and Introductions.* London: Macmillan & Co., 1961. 111–45.

6

Imaginative Power as Prerequisite for an Aesthetics of Freedom in Friedrich Schiller's Works

Wilhelm Voßkamp

SCHILLER'S CONCEPT OF IMAGINATIVE POWER IN THE LITERARY TRADITION

FOR Friedrich Schiller, imagination is a central category for the concept of beauty and, in turn, part of an aesthetics that encompasses not only the general principles of art but the historico-philosophical function of art for politics as well.[1] In contrast to Kant's epistemological definition of imagination, Schiller's focus is a theory of beauty in which the sensual plays a primary role. The sensual, however, does not mean for Schiller what it signifies in the medical-anthropological tradition, which is oriented exclusively around the body or the corporeal and in which, in the eighteenth century, the concept of beauty had played a role since antiquity, as made manifest, for example, in the thought of Nicolas Malebranche. In his "Kallias" letters, Schiller gets to the heart of his aesthetic agenda by emphasizing that he neither wants to explain beauty "in a sensual-subjective manner (like Burke et al.), nor in a subjective-rational manner (like Kant), nor in a rational-objective way (like Baumgarten, Mendelssohn and the whole parade of perfection enthusiasts) . . . ," but instead "in a sensual-objective way" ("Kallias" 394).

These distinctions, drawn in contradistinction to—in simple terms—the empirical tradition, on the one hand, and the rationalistic tradition, on the other hand, reveal the following. Schiller's undertaking is nothing other than a philosophically ambitious attempt to formulate his concept of "imagination as inventive power" within the context of a general (and universally valid) theory of beauty. The primary medium here is poetry, in which the field of perception is correlated with imagination and the field of concepts is correlated with language: "Language places everything before reason and the poet must place (represent [*darstellen*]) everything before imagination; poetry wants intuition, language merely gives concepts" ("Kallias" 432). This, again, conveys that Schiller's notion of imagination is—unlike in the prevailing debate in the eighteenth century—less concerned with a capacity for subject formation and the designing of individual life stories than with the fundamental concept of aesthetics.

In what follows, this will be illustrated in two steps: First, a specific poetological characterization of Schiller's concept of "imagination as inventive power" will be outlined; then, in a second step, the role of imagination in Schiller's aesthetics will be explicated from a functional perspective.

POETOLOGICAL CHARACTERIZATIONS
OF SCHILLER'S IMAGINATIVE POWER

In all theoretical texts in which Schiller deals with the concept of imaginative power—these are, in addition to the "Kallias" letters, the "Zerstreute Betrachtungen über verschiedene ästhetische Gegenstände" (Scattered reflections on various aesthetic objects), the treatise "Über Matthissons Gedichte" (On Matthisson's poems), and, above all, *Über die ästhetische*

Erziehung des Menschen in einer Reihe von Briefen (On the aesthetic education of humanity in a series of letters). In all of these treatises, Schiller continually emphasizes the spontaneous, the arbitrary-indeterminate character of imagination and its freedom: "As is well-known, imagination and its freedom only follow the law of association of ideas, which has as its original basis the accidental correlation of perceptions in time, or, in effect, something completely empirical." The poet achieves "his purpose by freely evoking the action of our imagination" ("Über Matthissons Gedichte" 994).

Schiller constantly characterizes the "freedom" of imagination as the "absence of determination" or its "unlimited determinability," or generally as the concept of possibility. The realm of the visual is repeatedly referred to as the medial element here: images are opposed to concepts, and Schiller explicitly addresses the "pictography of sentiments [*Bilderschrift der Empfindungen*]" (*Über Anmut und Würde* 434). In its limitless freedom, spontaneity can achieve "its purpose" only through an "autonomous action" of the artist and the image-producing imagination, an "intuitive business [*intuitives Geschäft*]" ("Zerstreute Betrachtungen" 559), which is nothing less than the creative principle as such. Thus Martin Heidegger, in his *Übungen für Anfänger: Schillers Briefe über die Erziehung des Menschen*, a seminar held in 1936–37, characterized Schiller's concept of imagination as "the actual capacity of producing what is creative [*das eigentliche Vermögen der Produktion des Schöpferischen*]" (74).

Taking this point into account, it becomes immediately evident that the determinable, the visual, or the intuitive-creative do not yet present the conditions of possibility for the general aesthetics after which Schiller is striving. That this is so comes to light particularly clearly in the two aims that motivate the emphasis Schiller places on the power of the imagination. The first aim is the desired progression or elevation of the individual for the benefit of humankind. Its crux is the possibility of actions that affect the whole human race. "In order to be certain that he [the poet] addresses pure humanity, he must have overcome the individual in himself and elevated himself to the level of the entire species. [Only] by feeling as a human being can he be sure that the species will feel along with him" ("Über Matthissons Gedichte" 995–96). At least, it is only under these conditions that such empathetic reception could be expected.

Even more important than this argument about an aesthetics of reception is the demand (based on Kant) that what is intuitive, and as such wholly indeterminate, be connected with the principle of the universal, with the "idea of the absolute." "What is required of imagination is that it summons its complete potential of comprehension for depicting the idea of the absolute, toward which reason relentlessly pulls. If the imagination is inactive and dull, or if the psyche tends toward concepts rather than toward perceptions, the most sublime object will merely remain an object of logic and will not be called before the aesthetic forum" ("Zerstreute Betrachtungen" 565). What is being invoked here, of course, is nothing less than the difference between aesthetics and epistemology.

As much as his imaginative contemplations, then, which constitute the poet's sine qua non, his structuring powers ("potential of comprehension") likewise have to be activated in order for beauty to emerge. In a letter to his friend Gottfried Körner dated 25 October 1794, Schiller emphasizes this in a precise and vivid manner, pointing out that imagination "[tries to] provide all its representations with sensual completeness, material totality. Reason, however, does not need all the manifold parts of the imagination's representation. Thus, reason is given more than it needs by the imagination, and in just this way, beauty is created. All its ideas are completely determined, and this complete determination is superfluous to reason" (qtd. in Bolten 108).

Here Schiller not only emphasizes the overwhelming features of intuitive imagination, he also insists on the necessity of its surplus character of "superfluity" for a theory of art concerned precisely with achieving a balance between these imaginative intuitions and the human being's superior capacity for reason. Yet this also points to the extraordinarily difficult task Schiller's aesthetics face with regard to the issue of integrating imaginative power. It is not by chance that at exactly this point in his letter to Körner Schiller speaks of beauty as an "imperative."

IMAGINATIVE POWER AND ITS FUNCTION
IN THE CONTEXT OF SCHILLER'S AESTHETICS

Discussing the (transcendental) question of the conditions of possibility for the beautiful as aesthetics, Schiller characteristically first conceives of imagination in *Über die ästhetische Erziehung des Menschen* (1795) as a "luxuriating imagination." As in his criticisms of the aftereffects of the French Revolution, Schiller rejects an imagination without function ("luxuriating") as vehemently as he does a cold "spirit of abstraction" that stifles the fire "at which the heart should have warmed itself and the imagination been kindled" (*Über die ästhetische Erziehung* 583). Therefore, it is crucial "to restore through a higher art the totality of our nature, which the arts themselves [this refers to a specialized and one-sided culture of reason as civilization] have destroyed" (588).

At this point, we can recognize the teleological structure of Schiller's philosophy of history. Over the course of his theory of *Aesthetic Education*, Schiller tries in various ways to solve the problem he identifies for the (future) theory of beauty. Starting from a necessary interaction of the "drive toward matter" (*Stofftrieb*) and the "drive toward form" (*Formtrieb*), "capacity for feeling" and "capacity for reason,"[2] Schiller arrives at his peculiar notion of the "play-drive" (*Spieltrieb*). Its special capacity or quality is seen as its ability to find a way out of the boundless "determinability" underlying imagination, or its "complete absence of determination"; this allows it to bring about "the sublation of our unconditional determinability whereby we achieve determination" (*Über die ästhetische Erziehung* 627). Schiller calls this state of the "real and active determinability" the "aesthetic," and it is a state that henceforth knows "no limits, because it embraces all reality" (634). Elsewhere, the concept of the *whole* is taken up once more: "The aesthetic alone is a whole unto itself" (637).

Characteristically, Schiller consistently emphasizes the particular role of imagination, especially in the context of "a free association of images" that comprises "its entire charm": "From this play of feely associated ideas . . . the imagination, in its attempt at a free form, finally makes the leap to aesthetic play" (664). The metaphor of the "leap" always refers to the artist's creative act, and it stands in a theological tradition. With this derivation of the play-drive and its constitutive imaginative power, the aesthetic could attain fulfilment if Schiller did not emphasize beauty's imperative character. For Schiller, in the tradition of Kant, there must be a connection between the "play of imagination [and] the seriousness of [the human being's] conduct" for art to attain its appropriate historical-philosophical significance (594). Therefore, Schiller has to take a further step, which can be identified in the transition from the play-drive to the "shaping spirit [*Bildungstrieb*]" (657). The connection between the value of imagination and art's claim of an operational momentum in history only becomes comprehensible when this transitional step has been retraced.

Schiller's hypothesis is: "As soon as the play-drive emerges, which takes pleasure in semblance, a mimetic drive for shaping is activated, and it, in turn, treats semblance as something autonomous" (657). Schiller tries to consolidate this incipient independence of aesthetic semblance into the concept of "aesthetic education" (particularly in the final letters of *Über die ästhetische Erziehung*), establishing its essential function in the context of a historico-philosophical perspective that ennobles the character of human beings by means of art. This notion of "aesthetic education" has to be taken seriously if we want to solve the paradox of education *by means of* art and education *to* art that Hans-Georg Gadamer identified in Schiller's aesthetics (78–79). Beauty has to be recognized as a sine qua non for humankind in order for art to function as an "instrument" that steers the process of the individual's ennoblement and perfection.

These formulations explain why Schiller accords so much value to aesthetic semblance as a form of "determinability." Aesthetic semblance is the condition of possibility for what is called "humankind." "Beauty can become a means of leading humanity from matter to form, from a limited to an absolute existence" (*Über die ästhetische Erziehung* 628). Thus, beauty can be called "our second creatress" (636). Schiller's utopian emphasis can be explained only from this vantage point: "Here alone [in the aesthetic state] do we feel pulled out of time, and our human nature expresses itself with a purity and integrity, as though it has as yet suffered no foreshortening through the intervention of external forces" (637).

Yet the question remains whether the emphatic stress laid upon beauty with regard to the desired human perspective is also suitable for maxims having to do with a single individual's education. Schiller again follows an anthropological approach, characterizing the human being generally as an ever-changing creature with regard to the initial distinguishing drive of matter and the formal drive: "The human being must turn everything that is mere form into world and make all his potentialities fully manifest . . . , he must destroy everything in himself that is mere world and bring harmony into all his changes. In other words, he must externalize all that is within him and give form to all that is outside him" (603). The concepts of the "aesthetic state" (that is, the aesthetic *condition*) and the "aesthetic State" (in the political sense) make it clear that these maxims for the individual are also embedded in a general historico-philosophical conception. Both ideas are constitutive regarding Schiller's objective of attaining an aesthetic education as the consequence of a productive imagination.

If we follow Schiller's argument with regard to beauty's role as a possible condition for refining both the individual and humanity as a whole, his statements on the "aesthetic state" (in the sense of a condition of the mind) provide an extension of the main problem, which is to make the transition to an "aesthetic State" (in the political sense) plausible from this individual point of departure. In the aesthetic state, the human being can experience in advance, as a kind of anticipation, his possible perfection: "The division of labor and alienation seem abandoned, and a state of totality and integrity is accomplished" (Berghahn 163).

The concept of the "aesthetic state" is always—as the discussion of imagination has already shown—based on potentiality ("determinability"), which means a state of possibilities that should come into practice in the domain of political and social reality. The characterization of this transition has to be the aim of every effort to determine precise goals for an aesthetic education. It is crucial to get "from a freedom (made possible by the aesthetic state) to a freedom in public interaction." Thus beauty, as Schiller stated in his literary journal *Die Horen*, is an "imperative" (*Sämtliche Werke* 1132). Is it now possible, in the transition from potentiality to topicality, from individual to the public sphere, to make precise determinations about beauty's effects on politics?

Thus we arrive at the question of the "aesthetic State" as political entity. According to Schiller, the aesthetic State can be understood as the "object of free play. *To bestow freedom by means of freedom* is the fundamental law of this kingdom" (*Über die ästhetische Erziehung* 667). Unlike the constitution of rights and codified laws (Schiller speaks, respectively, of the "dynamic State" and the "ethical State"), this project is part of a long utopian tradition in which the consonance of the interests of the individual with the interests of society in general is paramount. Yet Schiller reacts to this utopia of mutual freedom in the tradition of Thomas More's *Utopia*, with a model of sociability ("social character" of society), on the one hand, and, on the other hand, with specific references to the contemporary political situation.

The concept of sociability focuses on tolerance: "Preserve the freedom of others—Show freedom yourself." Moreover, it likewise appeals to those forms of ideal society in which the individuals engage in an untroubled, open-ended dialogue. It is thus with good reason that Jürgen Habermas sees in Schiller a theoretical position that foreshadows his concept of an ideal communicative society (Habermas 59–64). It is characteristic that, for Schiller, there is no picture more appropriate for "the ideal of good sociability [*das Ideal des schönen Umgangs*]" (*Über die ästhetische Erziehung* 667) than a well-performed English dance, where each person seems to be following only his own lead and yet never steps on anyone else's toes.

Considering the "few select circles [*auserlesene Zirkel*]" (669) Schiller speaks of, scholars have rightly pointed to Winckelmann's idea of the Greek "polis," but also—obviously—to contemporary freemason circles, clubs and salons, and actors' troupes. With good reason, the parallel to Goethe's *Unterhaltungen deutscher Ausgewanderten* (Conversations of German emigrants) has also frequently been mentioned in the discussion of the ideal of the good sociability distinguished by exquisite taste. Art can be characterized as a "symbol of freedom [as well as] a school of freedom, as educational instrument for the republican, that is, for the human being capable of freedom" (Wölfel 196). This utopian republic of humankind can—at least partly—be seen as a "glance" toward examples of contemporary social culture.

Schiller does not stop, however, at pointing to the communicative sociability and communicative competence that can be developed by means of beauty; rather, he gets quite precise with reference to political conditions, criticising serfdom and speaking of the "ideal of equality" (*Über die ästhetische Erziehung* 669). His suggestive notes on a "pure Church" and a "pure Republic" are more difficult to interpret in the context of the "select circles" in which he projects their emergence. The concept of a "pure Republic" can probably be located in the discussion surrounding Rousseau's "social contract," which—immediately extending the discussion of utopian traditions—addresses questions about how the needs of the individual can be brought into congruence with the necessities of society. The notion of the "pure Church" can be connected to Augustine's "doctrine of two realms." In his differentiation between *civitas dei* and *civitas terrena*, Augustine emphasized that the "State of God" was already incorporated in the "earthly State," and that there was no completely dichotomous separation between them.[3] The anticipatory function of the "pure State" in everyday political life can thus be found here in Schiller's works once again; for Schiller, it is a republicanism that must be developed beforehand, as it were, in the medium of art and beauty.

A trenchant summary of Schiller's intentions conveys a peculiar two-fold structure: on the one hand, Schiller sees art, at the horizon of imagination, as the only medium capable of comprehending the development of the individual as a process that anticipates the history of humankind; on the other hand, the aesthetic *state* (as human condition) is not a fulfilment, an end in itself, but instead forms the transition to the conception of an aesthetic State as *political* entity. This conveys the political connections Schiller envisions in his theory of art and imagination. This ambiguity regarding art and politics helps explain the frequent ambivalences and seeming contradictions in Schiller's works. The "borderline between aesthetics and politics" is continuously crossed (Wölfel 191). This is precisely why Schiller's insistence on the power of imagination helps us illuminate his lifelong efforts to lend these different poles, the aesthetic and the political, critical and instrumental weight in his entire work—and ultimately to bring them into connection with one another.

NOTES

1   On the concept of imagination in general, see Schulte-Sasse's essay in the lexicon *Ästhetische Grundbegriffe* (88–120). For more recent research on Schiller's *Aesthetic Education,* see Carsten Zelle's entry on this text in Luserke-Jaqui, *Schiller-Handbuch* (409–45), which includes an extensive bibliography.
2   See especially the twelfth and thirteenth letters of *Ästhetische Erziehung* (604–11).
3   For a neo-Marxist perspective on this issue, see in particular Hardt and Negri's *Empire.*

WORKS CITED

Berghahn, Klaus. "Ästhetische Reflexion als Utopie des Ästhetischen: Am Beispiel Schillers." *Utopieforschung: Interdisziplinäre Studien zur neuzeitlichen Utopie.* Ed. Wilhelm Voßkamp. 3 vols. Stuttgart: Metzler, 1982. 3: 146–71.
Bolten, Jürgen, ed. *Schillers Briefe über die Ästhetische Erziehung.* Suhrkamp Taschenbuch Materialien 2037. Frankfurt/Main: Suhrkamp, 1984.
Gadamer, Hans-Georg. *Wahrheit und Methode: Grundzüge einer philosophischen Hermeneutik.* 4th ed. Tübingen: Mohr, 1975.
Habermas, Jürgen. *Der philosophische Diskurs der Moderne: Zwölf Vorlesungen.* Frankfurt/Main: Suhrkamp, 1985.
Hardt, Michael, and Antonio Negri. *Empire.* Cambridge, MA: Harvard University Press, 2000.
Heidegger, Martin. *Übungen für Anfänger: Schillers Briefe über die ästhetische Erziehung des Menschen. Wintersemester 1936/37.* Seminar-Mitschrift von Wilhelm Hallwachs. Ed. Ulrich von Bülow. Marbach: Deutsche Schillergesellschaft, 2005.
Luserke-Jaqui, Matthias, ed. *Schiller-Handbuch. Leben—Werk—Wirkung.* Stuttgart/Weimar: Metzler, 2005.
Schiller, Friedrich von. "Kallias oder über die Schönheit. Briefe an Gottfried Körner." Schiller, *Sämtliche Werke.* 5: 394–433.
———. *On the Aesthetic Education of Man: In a Series of Letters.* Ed. and trans. Elizabeth Wilkinson and L. A. Willoughby. Oxford: Clarendon, 1967.

———. *Sämtliche Werke*. Eds. Gerhard Fricke and Herbert G. Göpfert. 5 vols. Munich: Hanser, 1959.

———. *Über Anmut und Würde*. Schiller, *Sämtliche Werke*. 5: 433–88.

———. *Über die ästhetische Erziehung des Menschen in einer Reihe von Briefen*. Schiller, *Sämtliche Werke*. 5: 570–669.

———. "Über Matthissons Gedichte." Schiller, *Sämtliche Werke*. 5: 992–1011.

———. "Zerstreute Betrachtungen über verschiedene ästhetische Gegenstände." Schiller, *Sämtliche Werke*. 5: 543–69.

Schulte-Sasse, Jochen. "Einbildungskraft/Imagination." *Ästhetische Grundbegriffe: Historisches Wörterbuch in sieben Bänden*. Ed. Karlheinz Barck, Martin Fontius, Dieter Schlenstedt, Burkhart Steinwachs, and Friedrich Wolfzettel. 7 vols. Stuttgart: Metzler, 2000. 2: 88–120.

Wölfel, Kurt. "Prophetische Erinnerung: Der klassische Republikanismus in der deutschen Literatur des 18. Jahrhunderts als utopische Gesinnung." *Utopieforschung: Interdisziplinäre Studien zur neuzeitlichen Utopie*. Ed. Wilhelm Voßkamp. 3 vols. Stuttgart: Metzler, 1982. 3: 191–217.

7

The Gentle Force over Pictures

HEGEL'S PHILOSOPHICAL CONCEPTION OF THE IMAGINATION

Klaus Vieweg

OR Hegel, Aristotle's thoughts on mind and knowledge, especially in his work *On the Soul*, are "still to this day the most distinguished and unique work of speculative interest on this subject" (Hegel, *Enzyklopädie* 10: 11).[1] Accordingly, the purpose of a philosophy of mind (*Geist*) can only be to introduce the *concept* (*Begriff*) into the knowledge of mind. Hegel's effusive praise of a philosophy that is more than two thousand years old, and his massive insistence on the concept, on the *logos* of knowledge, may appear oddly anachronistic in view of current theories of knowledge. But what might at first look like a dusty attic will soon reveal extensive and unfamiliar treasures and offer the cornerstone for a modern philosophy of knowledge and aesthetics. Hegel's theory provides an Ariadne's thread leading out of the labyrinth of conflicting opinions about the nature and role of the imagination. One can speak of a new founding of a modern theory of imagination, one that, of course, connects up with *individual* ideas presented by other modern philosophers (Hume, Kant, and Schelling, for example) but nevertheless outlines the fundamental positions of a wholly independent, original conception of the imagination that has not been superceded even today. Here, however, I will only be able to point out a few of the basic outlines of Hegel's logic of knowledge.

IMAGINATION AND MIND (*GEIST*)

The Hegelian conception of imagination has a particular advantage due to the fact that it is embedded in a holistic theory of the mind. For textual support, the section "Philosophical Psychology" in Hegel's *Encyclopedia of Philosophical Science* provides the most succinct summary of Hegel's theory. His primary arguments can be broken down into the following three points.

a) The imagination is held to be a particular formation or developmental phase of *Geist*. The German term *Geist* denotes a philosophical, metaphysical principle that cannot be adequately translated by "mind" or "spirit." To grasp *Geist*, one must understand it as the stages in a process of self-production. This self-generation means self-determination or autonomy, the self-determination of mind as self-liberation. The formal essence of mind consists in freedom and can be grasped as a process of "freeing itself to itself," as the realization of the concept of its freedom. In this way, *Geist* makes itself free from everything that does not correspond to its concept, *free from every form that is not adequate to it.* To be free does not mean to exist independently alongside something other, but to come to oneself in a process of self-realization.

b) This self-realization or self-relation as active self-production is conceived of as a logically based, step-by-step development predicated on the activity of *Geist*. From the lower, abstract determinations, the higher, concrete determinations are deductively generated according to the necessity of logic. In this way the previous determinations then appear as moments in the higher stages, where they attain their partial validity. This logical process of grounding this progressive movement, as a return to the basis (*Grund*), avoids, for example, the often identified but mistaken view that the activity of knowledge is mere collection, a simple aggregate of capacities that should be identified, analyzed, and then brought into interconnection (see Düsing). In a clear dismissal of the empirical-psychological process of temporal sequences, this step-by-step process is concerned with the *self-development of Geist*. From the very beginning this movement is present as thought, as a form of thought that attains its justification by means of logic. The process of this ascension to a determined knowledge "is itself rational and involves a determined, necessary transition on the part of the concept from one determination of intelligible activity to another" (Hegel, *Enzyklopädie* [1827] 415). Hegel thereby can establish the contours of a *logic of knowledge*, of an epistemology in the strict sense, in clear distinction to a mere analytic or synthetic conception of mental capacities. In *Science of Logic* Hegel had demonstrated the relationships between the particular and the universal, between subjectivity and objectivity; these lie at the heart of the present argument and gain their practical confirmation through it.

c) The faculty of imagination (*Einbildungskraft*) belongs to the second level of theoretical mind (*Geist*), a level Hegel describes with the term "representation" (*Vorstellung*). Theoretical mind, or intellect, assumes a prominent place in the encyclopedic system. Within the sphere of subjective mind a change occurs in the stage of phenomenology, a move from the standpoint of consciousness to the standpoint of mind. Here we stand at the formal beginning of philosophizing—science must "presuppose the liberation from the opposition of consciousness" (Hegel, *Wissenschaft der Logik* 5: 45). In the preceding stage, phenomenology, the result is shown to be the one-sidedness of the *paradigm of consciousness* and the dualism of consciousness and object, of mind and world, of subject and object. The principle of identity common to each of these dualities makes itself manifest insofar as we are concerned not with external relations but rather with an internal relation, with *Geist* as a *self-relation*, as a *self-determining universal*. Everything about which we want to obtain knowledge, all that we want to know, must thus be taken as a *self-forming of Geist*; it must be understood as *Geist*—a core moment of *monistic idealism*.

This being-one implies, in Hegel's terms, the identity between the nature posited by the mind as its world, and the presupposing of the world as self-standing (*selbständiger*) nature, between the *posited* and the *pre-supposed* (*voraus-gesetzten*) world. It has to do with the identity of the determinations as inherent—existing in *Geist* and existing as constituted by *Geist*. Objectivity shows itself to be subjective and subjectivity shows itself to be objective. The path of knowledge as a logical transition, in stages, of theoretical mind, of subjective-intelligible innerness, of abstract self-determining in itself and its expression in the *language of knowledge*, contains three chief stations: *intuition, representation*, and *thought*—whereby fantasy occupies the middle ground, the seam between *aisthēsis* and *noēsis* (Fulda 326). The path in question is that from mere certainty to truth, to *justified* knowledge. From the form of the external-singular, of common subjective universality, the content—rational in itself—is raised to the form of a true identity between singularity and universality, which Hegel conceives of as determined knowledge. This intellectualizing of knowledge demonstrates the necessity of the translation of the true content from a *still insufficient form inadequate to mind* into the adequate form of the concept. The stage of representation, or the faculty of imagination, is presented as an indispensable transition or middle ground in the self-constitution of finite subjectivity (Düsing 311–12).

FROM INTUITION TO REPRESENTATION

In order to comprehend these initial stages in the self-determination of intellect, we must first briefly outline the chief characteristics of *intuition*. This is the irrevocable presupposition for understanding the faculty of imagination, and it has serious philosophical implications. On the basis of the paradigm of consciousness that has been overcome, intellect does not relate to its content as to an object, but rather is related *exclusively* to its own determinations. The separation of its determinations of the subjective and the objective is shown to be a merely apparent one.

The initial form of this logical structure is found in intuition, in which a given encountered *inner or outer sensation* (or affection) emerges as an identity of the subjective and the objective. A singular, particular content that reaches the object appears at the same time as posited by a singular, isolated subjectivity. A content that is supposedly only found and appears to be given in the sense of a sensation from the outside, a receiving of impressions, or the effect of external things, proves to be identical with what is posited subjectively, while at the same time the impression of what is objective reveals itself to be the expression of what is subjective—the act of finding turns out to be one of positing. "The myth of the given" remains an illusion (appearance) that, as such, must be analyzed and refuted, and this also holds for the opposing "myth of construction." In Hegel's view, intuition constitutes the immediate, most present form in which subjectivity relates to its determinations as to something supposedly given and encountered in the external world. Intuition is the *immediate presence*, the "presentation" of the singular ego (*Ich*), here and now—the identity of receptivity and activity in intuition (Hegel, *Vorlesungen über die Geschichte der Philosophie* 19: 205). We are dealing not with a panoply of duplicated intuitions but rather with the immediate unity of being that already exists, and being that is created (Hegel, *Phänomenologie* 231–32). The assertions "My vision is blue" and "There is a blue object" are identical; in intuition the effect of both propositions is posited as one.

The one that sees and the one seen, hearing and making sound, mind and world, are taken as identical. This reveals *the simple mind-structure* of intuition, its *logos-authorship* (see Welsch 140–52). Pure intuition (as well as pure representation) is mere appearance or semblance that proves itself to be such; intuition and the faculty of imagination are infected by thought from the very beginning. Intuition is sensual *and* intellectual, natural *and* rational at the same time. "That which produces and the product join together in a unity" (Schelling 528).[2] The proposition "Man is always a thinking being" finds its confirmation in a master of seeing and intuition, Paul Cézanne, who in a conversation with Joachim Gasquet expressed his awareness that visible nature, the nature that exists outside, and the nature that is perceived, the nature that exists inside, are concurrent texts, that they interpenetrate with each other (cited in Busch 324).

As the abstract orientation toward some thing that is self-identical, the attention required for sensation is related to a supposedly objective and self-standing being (what is to be paid attention to), which ultimately reveals itself, however, to be an abstract other-being of sensation itself. There is no content other than that of the intuited object, where intellect finds itself thus *apparently* determined from outside. In this way an initial knowledge of the thing is achieved. A complete active-knowledge, however, has not yet been attained, only an initial sight (*Sicht*) of the object, not yet an in-sight (*Ein-Sicht*) into it. The side of finding, the side of the given, presupposes that one be required to treat something that exists outside of the subject as the content of the affect. Hence the intuition necessarily projects this content into space and time (Hegel, *Enzyklopädie* 8: 83) and intuits it as a particular content manifest in these forms. This spatio-temporality is held to be the "first abstract externalization" (Hegel, *Enzyklopädie* [1827] 418). Intellect requires a formal milieu in which something is discretely and continuously contrasted with something else. These are indispensable coordinates for the epistemic determination of the contents of feeling (Rometsch 173).[3]

Schelling understands the present as a being-driven back to a moment, to a point of time to which in reality we cannot return: "In order to be able to intuit the object in general as object, the ego [*Ich*] must posit a past moment as the ground of the present. The past thus originates ever anew only through the action of intellect, and the past is only necessary to the extent that this going back of the ego is necessary" (Schelling 554). Here time and movement are lent fundamental importance, for it is an event, an occurrence in time, that is intuited. Space and time are, for Hegel, both subjective and objective forms: thus he argues against the one-sidedness both of objectivist concepts (space and time as forms existing in nature) and of the Kantian position (which holds time and space to be merely subjective forms of intuition). Reason thus has not only a regulative relation to knowledge but also a constitutive one.

Attention requires pure immersion in the object, the disregard of all other things and of oneself. This displacement into the thing in order to become aware of it is of fundamental relevance and remains indispensable for knowledge. What is at issue here is the total absorption in the thing, without reflection, and by means of a skeptical overcoming of our individuality and our vanity: we let the thing prevail over us. This amounts to surrender to the object. Thus Hegel polemically attacks the conventional notion of a good education, which dismisses the object in this sense as unnecessary. Opposed to this renunciation of all pre-judgments and purportedly secure knowledge, opposed to this *Pyrrhonian-Buddhist quietude* of being in oneself, opposed to this negation of one's own self-validation—a self-validation based on the cancellation of external time, a cancellation that, to be sure, also bears within it the danger of pausing and becoming unfree—there stands the self-validation of subjectivity. The content is also *mine, but not merely mine*, for subjectivity becomes objective, and objectivity is made subjective. The form of internality is transformed to the form of externality, and vice versa. In this inversion, this exchange, or this oscillation, intellect has ascended to the first level of its self-determination, to *formal self-determinateness*. The mere and simple particularity implies a common sort of subjective universality (a sort of commonality of intuiting; see Rometsch 173ff.) and the finitude of intuition.

With the movement into the inner, with the act of remembering, intuition becomes immediately sublated into representation—it is preserved, negated, and brought to a higher level—whereby its spatio-temporal determinateness is transformed. The approaching border-crossing is sketched by Hegel as follows: "The course of intellect in representations is to make immediacy likewise internal, to intuitively posit itself in itself, and also to sublate the subjectivity of internality and in itself to externalize itself from it and to be in itself in its own externality" (*Enzyklopädie* 10: 257).

REPRESENTATION

Remembrance

In the first step of representation, the immediacy necessary for intuition, Being is changed, insofar as it is something finite, into *something past*; but at the same time the intellect preserves the intuition as *inner, unconscious presence*. "As at first remembering the intuition, the intellect posits the content of feeling in its internality, in its *own* space and its *own* time" (*Enzyklopädie* 10: 258). Hegel refers to this content as a picture or image (*Bild*) that is freed from its initial immediacy and abstract singularity and taken up in the universality of the intellectual ego. It was in this sense that Friedrich Schlegel once spoke of the image as a counter-object, freed from the control of the object. Put in a Kantian manner, what is at issue is the capacity to represent an object without its presence in intuition. This unique space-time posited by intellect is valid as *universal* spatio-temporality, in which the content first gains permanence in distinction to past intuition (*Enzyklopädie* 10: 259). The space and time of intuition, by the same token, are particularities, bound to the immediate present of the object. This *external* space-time is resolved at the price of the original determinateness of the content, which can undergo arbitrary and contingent changes when transposed into the contours of my picture (image).

At this level—remembrance as the *first manner of representing*—intellect appears as the *unconscious, timeless* place for the preservation of pictures (images). Indeed, in an allusion to Aristotle, Hegel uses the metaphor, so treasured by Derrida, of the *"nocturnal, dark shaft"* in which a world of infinite pictures is preserved (*Enzyklopädie* 10: 260). Without inhabiting consciousness, these images sleep and are the inactive soul. A countless number of images and representations slumber in this shaft of internality, a powerful reservoir of images that remain hidden by the nocturnal darkness, a dark picture gallery of immeasurable expanse, comparable to the Parisian Louvre without light. These images are indeed the *property* of intellect. They bear the legal title of *inalienable opinions*, but are not yet in my actual possession; what is still lacking is the capacity to call up the sleeping images at will. There is lack of will, free power of disposal over this astonishing treasure chamber. All determinations exist merely in virtual possibility. They are contained in seed, but in an unconscious, dark spring, in the universal existence in which what is distinct is not yet posited as discrete (*Enzyklopädie* 10: 260).[4]

What is purely formless, chaotic, and indifferent, this shoreless ocean— *the dark side of intellect*—is a new form of the universality of intellect. It is like a great chest that I am certain contains a treasure, but in which I cannot distinguish what diverse jewels are preserved. The images no longer exist; they are no longer there in consciousness or in the past. They exist only "unconsciously," since it is only with their distinction, with the positing of difference in light of the present, that knowing can proceed. Thus we achieve the bridge from remembrance to the faculty of imagination, the transition to the second stage of representation, to *inner presencing, inner representation*, by positing *the inner present of the image*, the overcoming of the existent, the past. The inner is placed, presented, before the intellect, brought insistently before the inner eye. The waking of the sleeping picture, intellect awakening to itself, makes it possible to relate the picture to an intuition that has the same content. The initial creations of the faculty of imagination also appear as a world of spatio-temporally unformed shapes, shapes without mass, positings by which the unconscious picture can be thoroughly displaced. In principle there follows a subsuming, for example, the sensation "blue" or "sorrow" under a universal form—blueness, sorrowfulness. Kant, whom Hegel here follows to a certain extent, spoke of the active capacity of the synthesis of the manifold: "The imagination must bring the manifold of intuition into an *image*; it must therefore antecedently take up the impressions into its activity, so previously it must record the impressions in their activity, that is, apprehend them" (*Kritik der reinen Vernunft* 176). On the basis of the *apprehension*, the subsumption of the multiplicity under the unity of representation, intellect can take internal possession of its property (the images), externalize them, and provide them (in the internal) with the seal of the external. Intellect is able to place what is unique to it in an internal opposition to itself and thus to possess its existence (*Dasein*), to be by itself—internal presencing (*Vergegenwärtigung*) as the free subjectivity of internality.

Already, with this subsuming or reflecting as a power of the universal, representation proves itself to be the middle ground between the immediate finding of oneself as determined, and thinking as intellect in its perfect freedom. The pure faculty of imagination without thought that is often hypostatized, especially by artists, is a deception. The presentation is essentially infected and determined by thought. It positions itself in the intermundane world of intuition and thinking as the hinge, as the universalization of the sensual, that is, the particular, and as the sensualization or particularization of the universal, the universality of intuition and the making-intuitive of the universal.

Following this prologue, which was necessary for the comprehension of what follows, we now come to our topic: the faculty of imagination, fantasy as that which *determines the images*, the actual transition from finding to inventing, from passive to active finding. Here lies the cornerstone of Hegel's theory of symbolic forms, his logic of signs, which elevated him, according to Derrida, to the status of founder of modern semiology.

Imagination

In Hegel's theory we can find three stages of imagination:

a) First Stage: Reproductive Imagination

Images are (as discussed above) internally re-presented. Intellect places these before itself in a new space-time in which the original spatio-temporal concretion is dissolved. On the basis of this abstraction and the coming-to-be of universal representations, there occurs a contingent and arbitrary reproduction of the content. This supposed occurrence in succession, the coordination between similar images, remains an act accomplished by intellect itself, which subordinates singular intuitions under the internally constituted picture and thus gives itself universality, presenting the universal as something common, re-presenting it (Hegel, *Enzyklopädie* 10: 266). Intellect either elevates a particular quality of a thing to the status of the universal, or it lends fixed form to a concrete universal.

b) Second Stage: The Productive, Associative Imagination—Fantasy

With the association of images, the relating of images to one another, the intellect ascends a step further, to the stage of fantasy. This involves the activity of freely joining, synthesizing, or combining pictures and representations, the inventive inner presentation itself of created representations, a freely willed production of new images. This creative imagination, the imagined synthesis, is responsible for the uncreative sensualization, for making the content into an intuition without a concrete example. In consequence of the transition from an objective connection to an innovative subjective bond, *internal-imaginative* existence is conferred upon a self-constituting content originating from the intellect itself, whereby the self-intuition of the intellect is perfected—the power of forming images for itself.

Taken in anticipation, the intellect emerges as a single, concrete subjectivity determined in itself and with its own content, and it demonstrates here the already present universality of thinking, whose justification is at play from the very outset. The representations are anticipations of a concept that is yet to be constructed. The intellect demonstrates its sovereignty over the stock of images and representations belonging to it, fantasy as the gentle power over pictures (images; Hume 58).

In fantasy we now have, consciously posited in arbitrary freedom by the intellect, a *new, second present*, a higher identity of universal and singular. What is found and what belongs to the intellect are completely posited in a unity, with fantasy being the capacity of plastic construction, and the images of fantasy presenting the unification of what is inner or mental and what is intuitive. In this the intellect demonstrates its power over images, raising itself to the level of *the soul of images* and seeking thereby to give itself validity and objectivity, as well as to manifest and preserve itself in its own creations. Hegel sees the identity of singularity and universality at this higher stage as subsisting in the intellect, now constituted as a singularity in the form of a concrete subjectivity in which the self-relation—the basic structure of the mind—is determined as being and as universality by means of the intuition of the universal and the universalization of the intuition (*Enzyklopädie* 10: 268).

The intellect creates novel inner worlds, a cosmos of the coming-into-being and the passing-away of possibilities, numerous inner word-images. It appears as unbridled picture-giving power, as the untiring and active inner picture-maker, as free play with possibilities. There is (writes Hume) nothing more worthy of wonder than the readiness with which the imagination assembles its representations, "hurrying from one end of the universe to the other to assemble the representations that belong to the object" (Hume 38). Kant sees in this the disclosure of an "unpredictable field of related representations" in which the content, a determined concept, could "be aesthetically extended in an unlimited way" (*Kritik der Urteilskraft* 251). Thus the creative imagination is able to promulgate itself inexhaustibly in its own products. According to Hegel, this play of fantasy constitutes the universal foundation of art, its formal aspect, presenting the true universal in the form of the singular image (*Enzyklopädie* 10: 267).

But the play of fantasy has a double aspect: being restless and without rules, the form of representation implies an indifferent external arrangement of the multiform images with their many meanings. Creativity, activity, and restlessness always remain ambivalent qualities; they do not in themselves guarantee a successful product. Non-creativity, tranquility, passivity, and simple letting-be are by no means to be devalued from the outset, for they are the very foundation of the faculty of imagination. Fantasy is able to create the human and the inhuman, to build heaven and hell, and thus to demonstrate its power as well as its deficiency. It can darken the present with shadows culled from the past as well as with those derived from a projected future (Schelling). This play is capable—like the faculty of understanding—of revealing monstrosities of all kinds. According to Hegel, in this synthesis of the faculty of imagination we are concerned only with formal reason, for imagination presents neither the highest capacity of free being nor completely successful making-present.[5] The content as such is indifferent to fantasy, for thought has not yet attained the form appropriate to the content. It is *only in thought*, which conceptualizes, tests, and verifies, that universality and singularity are completely identical; only here can content and conceptual form coincide.

Fantasy and Appearance (Schein)

When *phainesthai* is taken in a substantive way, *phantasia* has the meaning of appearing. We thereby unintentionally come upon the domain of Pyrrhonian skepticism, the true champion of appearances. Its criterion is what appears, the *phaenomenon*, which we are to understand as the image, *phantasia*, and the subjective aspect of my imaging, that is, the appearance as subjectively holding something to be true. As enduring positions of skepticism, negativity, subjectivity, relativity, and *ataraxia* come to expression in the language of appearance. Fantasy has the function of a necessary transition point on the path to knowing and, like skepticism, presents a Janus-face: one free and the other unfree, one steadfast and the other negative, one tranquil and the other restless, one happy and the other unhappy. For the countenance of imagination is an amalgamation of the phenomenal and the logical, of image and concept.[6]

As is well known, art that has its formal source in fantasy is considered to be *free play with appearance*, or a world of semblance. Schiller describes such activity of fantasy as an *idealization*. According to Humboldt, art, as a *facultas fingendi*, creates a non-reality, a picture and appearance that surpass all reality. Imagination or fantasy can thus also be understood as *ideation*. In its images, in its thoroughly ambivalent imaginings, fantasy is freer than nature. The spheres of the external and internal empirical worlds, the lights of the world and the firing of the neurons, are not worlds of true reality but, in the yet stronger sense used in art, mere appearance, semblance of being, though also bearing the stamp of contingency and arbitrary will. Only art based on *beautiful* fantasy provides appearances with a "higher reality born of *Geist*" (Hegel, *Vorlesungen über die Ästhetik* 13: 22). Hence, far from being mere illusion (*Schein*), the appearances of art—and not those of common reality—can be characterized as the higher reality and the truer existence, for they constitute the manner in which the universal is made present. They are monograms of the absolute (Schelling), though not its highest mode of being presented.

c) Third Stage: Sign-Making Fantasy

The creations of fantasy initially remain only internal and subjective, for their images are particular and only subjectively capable of intuition. Still absent is the moment of being, the externalization, creating the present in the external, external neo-representation as a step toward objectification. What is perfected in inner self-intuition, the mere synthesis of concept and intuition, the merely internal and subjective, must be determined as being and be made into an external object. In this activity, in externalizing, intellect produces new intuitions and thus, at this higher level, we return to the point of departure of "intuition." In the sign (*Zeichen*) actual vividness (*Anschaulichkeit*) is added to the self-constituted representation. The intellect makes itself, as Hegel puts it, into a thing, into an object in which merely singularized subjectivity is transgressed. It becomes *sign-making fantasy*. In this passage the basic features of Hegel's semiology make themselves evident, including his philosophical concept of language, of linguistic signs. Here Hegel appears as one of the founders of the modern philosophical understanding of language.

Since at the level of fantasy the intellect relates to itself in arbitrary freedom and identity, it has already turned back to immediacy and so must establish what it has itself created, its pictures and representations, as existing and objectified, and thereby fulfill the mind-structure in a higher way. The sign-making fantasy constitutes a unity of self-created, self-standing representations and an intuition—again a higher identity of subjectivity and objectivity. An alien meaning is attributed to an arbitrarily chosen external object. In consequence of this arbitrary attribution, the immediate and characteristic content of intuition disappears and another content is given to the intuition for its inner soul, for its meaning: Ernst Cassirer calls this the content of meaning. An intuition is radically transformed into the possession of the intellect, handed over to the full sovereignty of intellect, and a fulfilled space-time is created, culminating in *language*, in the time of the tone and the space of the letter. In this construction, in the creative finding (*Er-Findung*) of a sign-world, the intellect proves itself to be the sovereign over signs and over meanings, the free-ruling semantic power that is able to preserve our knowledge and our wisdom, make them endure, and make them communicable. This is the *mnemosyne* that constitutes the formal foundation of history.

As a metaphor for the sign Hegel uses *the pyramid* that Derrida borrowed for the title of an essay (Derrida; see Vieweg, "Das Bildliche").[7] The move from the shaft to the pyramid concludes: "The sign is any immediate intuition that presents a completely different content than what it has for itself—the pyramid in which an alien soul is displaced and preserved" (Hegel, *Enzyklopädie* 10: 270). At a higher level a mind-structure is again attained, in particular, mind-born language that, with its logos-constitution, its inner logic, indicates the transition to a mode of thinking that has its appropriate form in language. The imagination stands between intuition and thought and thus fails to achieve the perfect identity of self-relation and self-determination in the form of thought thinking itself. The true iconoclasm of conceptual thought, as Hegel conceives it, remains beyond the reach of the imagination.[8] But that is another story.

NOTES

This essay was translated from the German by Timothy C. Huson, to whom the author would like to express his appreciation.

1   The first edition of Hegel's *Enzyklopädie*, from the text in volumes 8–10 of the *Werke in zwanzig Bänden*, is cited by volume and page number. The second edition, from 1827, is cited as *Enzyklopädie* (1827) with the page number.

2   Compare this to Schelling's statement "The ego [*Ich*] is in one and the same action formally free and formally compelled or passive" (*System des transzendentalen Idealismus* 533).

3   I would like to thank Mr. Rometsch for allowing me to read his dissertation.

4   Elsewhere, in respect of the ego (*Ich*), Hegel speaks of a receptacle, a container, and shelter for all and sundry: "Every human being is a total world of representations, which are buried in the night of the ego" (*Enzyklopädie* 8: 83). The ego is the universal, in which all particulars are abstracted, but in which at the same time everything lies hidden, the abstract universal and the universality that contains everything in itself.

5   In Christianity, according to Hegel, the reconciliation of the god-human takes place in the past; that of the human in the future; while in the present no reconciliation is possible. See Vieweg, "Religion und absolutes Wissen."

6   For further elaboration of this point, see Vieweg, *Skepsis und Freiheit*.

7   Derrida's essay presents an interesting and incisive attempt at exploring Hegel's theory of imagination, in which Hegel is—correctly—declared to be the modern founder of semiotic theory. To be sure, Derrida's essay neither sufficiently nor persuasively thematizes the transition from representation to concept, to conceptual thought, which is essential for Hegel's position. In short, the relationship between metaphor and concept is not subjected to clarification in Hegel's sense.

8   See Hegel's remarks in the *Phänomenologie*: "In thinking, I am free, because I am not in an other, but remain simply and solely in communion with myself" (156).

WORKS CITED

Busch, Werner, ed. *Landschaftsmalerei*. Vol. 3 of *Geschichte der klassischen Bildgattungen in Quellentexten und Kommentaren*. Darmstadt: Wissenschaftliche Buchgesellschaft, 1997.

Derrida, Jacques. "Der Schacht und die Pyramide. Einführung in die Hegelsche Semiologie." *Randgänge der Philosophie*. Ed. Peter Engelmann. Vienna: Passagen, 1988.

Düsing, Klaus. "Hegels Theorie der Einbildungskraft." *Psychologie und Anthropologie oder Philosophie des Geistes*. Ed. Franz Hespe and Burkhard Tuschling. Stuttgart: Frommann Holzboog, 1991. 298–307.

Fulda, Hans Friedrich. "Vom Gedächtnis zum Denken." *Psychologie und Anthropologie oder Philosophie des Geistes*. Eds. Franz Hespe and Burkhard Tuschling. Stuttgart: Frommann Holzboog, 1991.

Hegel, Georg Wilhelm Friedrich. *Enzyklopädie der philosophischen Wissenschaften*. Vols. 8–10 of Hegel, *Werke in zwanzig Bänden*.

———. *Enzyklopädie der philosophischen Wissenschaften*. Second edition. Heidelberg: Oßwald, 1827.

———. *Phänomenologie des Geistes*. Vol. 3 of Hegel, *Werke in zwanzig Bänden*.

———. *Vorlesungen über die Ästhetik*. Vols. 13–15 of Hegel, *Werke in zwanzig Bänden*.

———. *Vorlesungen über die Geschichte der Philosophie*. Vols. 18–20 of Hegel, *Werke in zwanzig Bänden*.

———. *Werke in zwanzig Bänden: Theorie-Werkausgabe*. Ed. Eva Moldenhauer and Karl Markus Michel. 20 vols. Frankfurt/Main: Suhrkamp, 1970.

———. *Wissenschaft der Logik*. Vols. 5–6 of Hegel, *Werke in zwanzig Bänden*.

Hume, David. *A Treatise of Human Nature*. Ed. Ernest C. Mossner. Harmondsworth: Penguin, 1969.

Kant, Immanuel. *Kritik der reinen Vernunft*. Vol. 3 of *Immanuel Kant: Werkausgabe*. Ed. Wilhelm Weischedel. Frankfurt/Main: Suhrkamp, 1977.

———. *Kritik der Urteilskraft*. Vol. 10 of *Immanuel Kant: Werkausgabe*. Ed. Wilhelm Weischedel. Frankfurt/Main: Suhrkamp, 1977.

Rometsch, Jens. "Hegels Theorie des erkennenden Subjekts." Diss., Universität Heidelberg, 2006.

Schelling, Friedrich Wilhelm Joseph von. *System des transzendentalen Idealismus*. Vol. 1 of *Ausgewählte Schriften*. Ed. Manfred Frank. Frankfurt/Main: Suhrkamp, 1985.

Vieweg, Klaus. "Das Bildliche und der Begriff: Hegel zur Aufhebung der Sprache der Vorstellung in die Sprache des Begriffs." *Hegel und Nietzsche: Eine literarisch-philosophische Begegnung*. Ed. Klaus Vieweg and Richard T. Gray. Weimar: Bauhaus Universität, 2007. 8–28.

———. "Religion und absolutes Wissen—Der Übergang von der Vorstellung in den Begriff." *Hegels Phänomenologie des Geistes*. Ed. Klaus Vieweg and Wolfgang Welsch. Frankfurt/Main: Suhrkamp, 2008. 581–600.

———. *Skepsis und Freiheit—Hegel über den Skeptizismus zwischen Philosophie und Literatur*. Paderborn: Fink, 2007.

Welsch, Wolfgang. *Aisthesis: Grundzüge und Perspektiven der Aristotelischen Sinnenlehre*. Stuttgart: Klett-Cotta, 1987.

8

The Status of Literature in Hegel's *Phenomenology of Spirit*

ON THE LIVES OF CONCEPTS

Robert B. Pippin

MY question is a simple one, and may not be important. Why does Hegel, in a chapter called "Absolute Knowing," end his most exciting and original work, the Jena *Phenomenology of Spirit*, with a quotation, or rather a significant misquotation, of a poet? The poet is Schiller and the poem is his 1782 "Freundschaft" (Friendship). This immediately turns into two questions: Why are the last words *not* Hegel's own, and why *are* they rather a poet's?

I will turn to the details in a moment but, as noted, such an inquiry may not be worth the trouble. Authors, even philosophers (who, with only a few exceptions, are not known for their literary style) like to cite poets and other writers as a way of summarizing a point, a way of concluding an argument with a dramatic flourish, a way of demonstrating their erudition, or simply as a way of relieving the pressure of sustained and difficult analysis. The device could be merely rhetorical. And, in Hegel's day, authors were often so well read in and familiar with important writers that they clearly cited from memory, frequently carelessly and inaccurately. After all, Hegel's citation in the section "Pleasure and Necessity" of four lines from Goethe's so-called 1790 "Faust-Fragment" is also a misquotation, although in that case, too, the alterations are philosophically significant. But perhaps such carelessness is all there is to it.

But one ought to hesitate before dismissing the issue. For one thing, a mere nine years later, in the *Heidelberger Niederschrift* of the "Introduction" to the *Lectures on the History of Philosophy*, Hegel makes it quite clear that he can quote this particular passage with perfect fidelity when that suits his purposes. For another, this is not the first time a literary work is cited, and the citations raise a general, not a particular, question. There are many other such instances in the *Phenomenology* (Goethe, Sophocles, Diderot, and Jacobi, as well as Schiller, are famous instances), and these invocations do not appear merely illustrative or summary. They enter the text as evidence of a certain kind about Hegel's unusual topic—"Spirit's experience of itself." In his discussion of Greek *Sittlichkeit* or "the true Spirit," Sophoclean tragedy is not merely illustrative of some phenomenon of interest to Hegel; it is the phenomenon, and it is hard to imagine Hegel saying what he wants to say about the breakdown in the authority of ethical norms without Attic tragedy at the center of the discussion. (The passages do raise the question, though, of whether there is anything important—as there seems to be—in these being *aesthetic* phenomena, works of the imagination, rather than historical or social events.) For another, this was an extraordinary period in German aesthetics, what with positions by Lessing, Novalis, Schiller, Schlegel, and many others swirling around or about to appear, and it would be unusual if Hegel did not have at least the rudiments of his own theory about the relation between literature (or "die schöne Kunst," fine art in general) and philosophy, and it would be unusual if elements of some view about that relationship were not at work in the treatment of literature in the *Phenomenology*. Of course, much of that account will only be made explicit several years later, in the lectures on aesthetics Hegel gave four times in the 1820s; but some view about the relation is explicit in the *Phenomenology*, and it makes the closing quotation even more mysterious.

I mean, for example, the dramatic remarks made in the Preface about the role of beauty in the work. The passage is so striking that I will take the liberty of quoting it at length.

> The activity of dissolution is the power and work of the Under-standing, the most astonishing and mightiest of powers, or rather the absolute power. The circle that remains self-enclosed and, like substance, holds its moments together, is an immediate relationship, one therefore which has nothing astonishing about it. But that an accident as such, detached from what circumscribes it, what is bound and is actual only in its context with others, should attain an existence of its own and a separate freedom—this is the tremendous power of the negative; it is the energy of thought, of the pure "I." Death, if that is what we want to call this non-actuality, is of all things the most dreadful, and to hold fast what is dead requires the greatest strength. [And the following is the most decisive remark:] *Lacking strength, Beauty hates the Understanding* for asking of her what it cannot do. But the life of Spirit is not the life that shrinks from death and keeps itself untouched by devastation, but rather the life that endures it and maintains itself in it. It wins its truth only when, in utter dismember-ment, it finds itself. (*Phenomenology of Spirit* §32)

This passage would seem consistent with Hegel's deep suspicion and criti-cism of Schlegel's blurring of the lines between philosophy and poetry, and even with Hegel's dismissal of those who get too caught up in what he called the "mythic" dimensions of Platonic dialogues. But considered in the light of the *Phenomenology* as a whole, this passage must be counted an exaggeration, somewhat one-sided. The "cutting" power of the analytic understanding, of what he elsewhere calls reflection, to dissolve harmoni-ous unity, like the harmonious unity of ethical life, indeed to "tear it apart" (*zerrissen*) and kill it, is so highly praised here that, concentrating on such a passage in isolation would make it hard to imagine how Hegel ever acquired the reputation of a *Versöhnungsphilosoph*, a philosopher of reconciliation. He seems like Adorno *avant la lettre*, praising a wholly "negative dialectic." That is, the possibility of re-integration, *Aufhebung*, and affirmation is not as evident in such formulations as it might be. The power of tearing apart the life of *Geist* is ascribed to the understanding (*Verstand*), but we are told nothing here about how *Geist* might find itself "in" what it has also torn apart. It seems clear that ultimately this sort of opposition between beauty (*Schönheit*) and the understanding (*Verstand*) prepares us for the standpoint of reason (*Vernunft*), a point of view wherein the one-sidedness and division of this contrast can be transcended. Clearly the emphasis has been corrected by the time we reach the end of the work, and some great faith might be expressed in the poet's power by giving him "the last word." And then there is also the fact that this extreme contrast is itself portrayed as if it were a psychological drama (that is, portrayed in a beautiful image, poetically) between *Schönheit* and *Verstand*, and in the personified metaphorical claim that beauty "hates" the understanding for expecting of it what it cannot do.

But *what* is it that beauty cannot do? And why would the understanding, as though it were a bullying character in a play, expect beauty to do something that it could not do? What kind of questions are these?

If we simply adopt the language of the image for a while, then what beauty cannot do is apparently "tarry [*verweilen*] with the negative," look it in the face, endure the self-dissolving character of the human experience of the human. (Novalis's claim that Greek art aestheticized and repressed death and "the negative" comes to mind.) These are odd claims, but in the manner typical of Hegel's idealism, this must be because such disintegration and death cannot, from the aesthetic point of view, be properly understood, and so is experienced as a contingent, irreconcilable event, a surd. This thought suggests something that is not surprising, given the prominence of the aesthetic theories of Kant and Schiller: the proper function of works and things of beauty is *resistance* to disintegration and the *creation* of harmony and unity.

On the other hand, and perhaps more importantly, the passage also rather subtly implies some limitation *on the part of an analytic understanding*. Asking *die Schönheit* to do something it cannot do is, after all, a reasonable ground for the indignation of *die Schönheit*, and it points to the limitations of the point of view of *Verstand* that dominate Hegel's other discussions of this faculty in the rest of his corpus—as in his criticisms of modern philosophies of reflection (Locke, Kant) and in his contrast between *Verstand* and *Vernunft*.

These are mere hints about the link between imaginative, aesthetic phenomena, which Hegel connects to some sort of living unity or resistance to disintegration, and the limitations of the analytic understanding. Since beauty is said to be "lacking strength," it (art) will not be the force that unites what has been pulled asunder, but apparently it is well suited to embody and manifest such new living unities when they arise or are otherwise achieved. But the hints are at least suggestive about the place of *die Schönheit* in a philosophical account like Hegel's, and perhaps even about the much stronger claim concerning the impossibility of doing something like what Hegel is attempting without some reliance on literary phenomena.

So what *is* Hegel attempting in the *Phenomenology*? Officially, the *Phenomenology* is the "science of the experience of consciousness," as in its alternate title. Experience, however, cannot be described from a sideways-on or third-person point of view. If it is to be made present to us, it must in a sense be re-enacted, as if from the point of view of the experiencing subject. This already brings us close to our theme. Such a re-enactment must be a kind of dramatic exercise, so it is not for nothing that the *Phenomenology* is often called a *Bildungsroman* (see Royce 147–56). We must be told "what it is like" to be *Geist*, as in one well-known formulation of the subjective viewpoint. But this experience is also said to be developmental. The experience itself counts as the education of a "natural consciousness" burdened with many dualisms (subject and object, self and other, individual and community, inner and outer, human and Divine) up to the standpoint of "absolute knowing," which is absolute precisely by virtue of having reached a way of understanding human experience (and therewith a way of experiencing) that has overcome such dualisms without collapsing them. The "engine" driving forward this development is abstractly described as *das Negative*, the negative, and more poetically is said to be a kind of "violence" that consciousness suffers at its own hands, as it struggles with its most basic issue—its attempt at self-knowledge.

Such familiar characterizations raise a host of interpretive questions, but there is a more general characterization by Hegel of what he is about that brings us closer to the function of literature. Indeed, it is a passage that follows closely upon the extraordinary evocation of beauty's hatred for the understanding that was quoted above.

> The manner of study in ancient times differed from that of the modern age in that the former was the proper and complete formation of the natural consciousness. Putting itself to the test at every point of its existence, and philosophizing about everything it came across, it made itself into a universality that was active through and through. In mod-

ern times, however, the individual finds the abstract form ready-made; the effort to grasp and appropriate it is more the direct driving-forth of what is within and the truncated generation of the universal than it is the emergence of the latter from the concrete variety of existence. Hence the task nowadays consists not so much in purging the individual of an immediate, sensuous mode of apprehension, and making him into a substance that is an object of thought and that thinks, but rather in just the opposite, in freeing determinate thoughts from their fixity so as to give actuality to the universal, and impart to it spiritual life. (*Phenomenology* §33)

This claim about actualizing and especially spiritualizing and enlivening the universal is an extremely valuable hint, and a deep characterization of the *Phenomenology*'s task that has not received the attention it deserves in commentary on the work. The most interesting way to begin to demonstrate this is somewhat risky from a scholarly point of view. It involves reading the early Hegel at least partly and in a preliminary way in the light of the later. I mean the Berlin Hegel of the 1820s and the author of the four lecture series on the fine arts (1820, 1823, 1826, 1828). I have no evidence whatsoever that Hegel had even in a preliminary way worked out during the Jena period the major claims of these lectures, but it is striking that one of the tasks he attributes to philosophy so early on—"enlivening" concepts or norms—plays such a crucial role in those lectures.[1] Perhaps the central conceptual claim throughout about fine art concerns the issue of *Lebendigkeit* (life or enlivening). Understanding that role helps us to clarify the appeal to literature in the *Phenomenology*.

The emphasis on *Lebendigkeit* begins already in the early 1820 lectures, continues throughout, and is quite prominent in the Hotho compilation traditionally used (for all its now well-known problems) as the text of Hegel's theory of fine art. Indeed, one might say that even though Hegel pays homage to Kant for recognizing that the core issue to be grasped in understanding the aesthetic domain is a problem of reflection and of judgment (and not simply "the sensuous" or mere feeling), it is the significance of *Lebendigkeit* that is the right focus in any philosophical aesthetics, not *Zweckmäßigkeit ohne Zweck* (purposefulness without purpose) or harmony as such. A characteristic gloss on the concept of beauty, for example, stresses "the look of independent and total life [*Lebendigkeit*] and freedom which lies at the root of the essence of beauty" (*Aesthetics* 1: 149); and it is not uncommon for him, when discussing the particular arts, especially painting and the lyric, to note that "the life [*Lebendigkeit*] and joy of independent existence in general" can be said to be the true subject matter of art (*Aesthetics* 2: 833). Some of his statements go very far and raise controversial issues both about the arts and about the very structure of Hegel's system.

These passages stress the importance of the mediated point of view on human experience occupied by the fine arts.

> Thereby the sensuous aspect of a work of art, in comparison with the immediate existence of things in general, is elevated to a pure appearance, and the work of art stands in the *middle* [*Mitte*] between immediate sensuousness and ideal thought. It is not yet pure thought, but, despite its sensuousness, is no longer a purely material existent either. (*Aesthetics* 1: 38)

And:

> Therefore the world-view of the Greeks is precisely the milieu [*Mitte*] in which beauty begins its true life and builds its serene kingdom; the milieu [*Mitte*] of free vitality which is not only there naturally and immediately but is generated by spiritual vision and transfigured by art; the milieu [*Mitte*] of a development of reflection and at the same time of that absence of reflection that neither isolates the individual nor can bring back to positive unity and reconciliation his negativity, grief, and misfortune. (*Aesthetics* 1: 437)

Now in the Hegelian universe, the "middle" is not a bad position to occupy (indeed, it seems the "natural" Hegelian position), and Hegel goes so far in praising this capacity of the arts that he gives one pause about what appears to be his official, systematic Encyclopedia architectonic.

> Thinking, however, results in thoughts alone; it evaporates the form of reality into the form of the pure Concept, and even if it grasps and apprehends real things in their particular character and real existence, it nevertheless lifts even this particular sphere into the element of the universal and ideal wherein alone thinking is at home with itself.... Thinking is only a reconciliation between reality and truth

within thinking itself. But poetic creation and formation is a reconciliation in the form of a real phenomenon itself, even if this form be presented only spiritually. (*Aesthetics* 2: 976)

Or consider: "In this way the sensuous aspect of art is spiritualized, since the spirit appears in art as made sensuous" (*Aesthetics* 1: 39).

There are even two passages in the discussion of the lyric that go *very* far indeed in stressing the *indispensability* of the aesthetic dimension *within*, not merely as a preparation or propadeutic, for the proper expression of philosophical science, and they thereby illuminate the corresponding indispensability of the *Phenomenology* itself. That is, the two familiar disputes about the "dispensability" of art in the modern age and the dispensability of the *Phenomenology* for the "system" are deeply linked. In discussing the role of poetry in a prosaic age, burdened with divisions and dualisms (that is, our age, identified as such since the *Differenzschrift* [Treatise on Difference], Hegel notes the following:

> In these circumstances poetry needs a more deliberate energy in order to work its way out of the abstractions in the ordinary way of putting things into the concrete life [of a new mode of expression]. But if it attains its aim, not only is it liberated from that separation between thinking, which is concentrated on the universal, and feeling and vision, which seize on the individual, but it also at the same time frees these latter forms of consciousness and their content and objects from their servitude to thinking and conducts them victoriously to reconciliation with the universality of thought. (*Aesthetics* 2: 1006)

In the other passage, having differentiated in his usual way "the imagination of heart and vision" from that "form of the spirit" that deals with "free self-consciousness in a more decisively universal way and in more necessary connectedness" (*Aesthetics* 2: 1128), that is, philosophy, he goes on to say the following:

> Yet this form, conversely, is burdened with the abstraction of developing solely in the province of thinking, i.e., of purely ideal universality, so that man in the concrete may find himself forced to express the contents and results of his philosophical mind in a concrete way as penetrated by his heart and vision, his imagination and feeling, in

order in this way to have and provide a total expression of his whole inner life. (*Aesthetics* 2: 1128)

I trust that I am not alone in being somewhat taken aback by the phrases "burdened with the abstraction" and "solely in the province of thinking," as if the traditional view of the referent of "absolute knowing"—that the phrase refers to "thought's" self-determinations in the *Science of Logic*—is just in itself already one-sided, incomplete without somehow being thought together with the expression of thought in a "concrete way." The passage suggests that many commentators on Hegel might have been misled a bit by Hegel's claims about the "incompleteness" and partiality of religious and aesthetic representation, as if he meant the picture to look thereby like a simple ascent to what was complete and infinite, leaving behind what was not. Even on the face of it, though, this is a non-dialectical and implausible picture of the "realm" of Absolute Spirit.

Moreover, this is a crucial issue in Hegel that goes back at least to *Glauben und Wissen* (*Faith and Knowledge*) and in essence defines the whole Hegelian project. That is, the issue of how we might understand the indispensability of aesthetic representation in the exposition and demonstration of any truth about what Hegel calls *der Begriff,* the concept, is part and parcel of his early insistence that Kant had strayed from his own greatest insight by abstractly separating the contributions of *Begriff* and *Anschauung* (intuition) in experience. The passages are familiar and justifiably well known. Hegel contrasts his own "organic idea of productive imagination" with what he attributes to Kant as "the mechanical relation of a unity of self-consciousness which stands in antithesis to the empirical manifold, either determining it or reflecting on it" (*Glauben und Wissen* 343; *Faith and Knowledge* 92). And he goes on to note that Kant himself (in the second edition deduction) is led to undermine his own official claims about the strictness of the epistemic separability between conceptions and intuitions in experience.

Hence, the original synthetic unity of apperception is recognized also as the principle of the figurative synthesis; i.e. of the forms of intuition; space and time are themselves conceived as synthetic unities, and spontaneity, the absolute synthetic activity of the productive imagination, is conceived as the principle of the very sensibility which was previously characterized only as receptivity. (*Glauben und Wissen* 327; *Faith and Knowledge* 69–70)

Such remarks, when seen in the light of Hegel's characterizations of the indispensability of aesthetic representation in the expression of philosophical truth, and in the light of his insisting in the *Phenomenology* on the need to spiritualize and enliven (*begeistern* and *beleben*) our *Begriffe*, suggest that understanding Hegel will require understanding the appeals to art and literature as much more than the invocation of rich, vivid examples, and as much different from mere propaedeutics for the eventual abandonment of just such forms of expression. The inherent conceptuality of sensory experience, one different from both a "thought determination" and from any putative sensory immediacy, as well as the way physical, public actions can be said to bear or manifest practical intentions, the "logic" of this relation, all seem at stake. How might the closing words of the *Phenomenology* contribute to this issue?

We need first a few details from the final paragraphs of the last chapter. The main general point to make is that the discussion in these passages continually suggests how misleading it is to understand the *Phenomenology* in terms of the Wittgenstein image that one hears so often invoked in discussions of the book—that it is a ladder to be kicked away once climbed. It is true, of course, that Hegel himself uses this image in Paragraph 26 of the *Phenomenology*: "Science on its part requires that self-consciousness should have raised itself into this Aether in order to be able to live—and [actually] to live. Conversely, the individual has the right to demand that Science should at least provide him with the *ladder* to this standpoint" (§26, 14–15). (We can note here already the problem of being able to live, and of life itself.) The point that is emerging in the passages we have looked at is that it would be precisely the wrong conclusion to draw from this image that such a ladder could be "kicked away." That would result in the standpoint, as it were, of "falling to the ground," of collapsing. Such an error would be the same as thinking that the *Science of Logic* provided something like the conceptual "foundation" or underlying real structure of the world and its appearances.[2] The language in these passages is extremely compressed, but some feeling for what Hegel is getting at can be sensed even in his most abstract formulations. For example,

> For this reason it must be said that nothing is known that is not in experience, or, as it is also expressed, that is not felt to be true, not given as an inwardly revealed eternal verity, as something sacred that it believed. . . . For experience is just this, that the content—which is

Spirit—is in itself substance, and therefore an object of consciousness. But this substance which is Spirit is the process in which Spirit
becomes what it is in itself; and it is only as this process of reflecting
itself into itself that it is in itself truly Spirit. (*Phenomenology* §802)

A more formulaic expression: "Just as Spirit in its existence is not richer
than Science, so too it is not poorer either in content" (*Phenomenology*
§805, 491).

And in a passage stated in almost biblical form: "But the other side of
its [i.e. the Subject's] Becoming, *History*, is a *conscious*, self-*mediating* process—Spirit emptied out into time; but this externalization, this kenosis
[*diese Entäusserung*] is equally an externalization of itself; the negative is
the negative of itself" (*Phenomenology* §808, 492). (I say biblical here because
"*Entäusserung*" is Luther's term in his translation of the Bible for "*kenosis*,"
and Miller, the English translator, actually translates here *Entäusserung*
with the transliterated word, "*kenosis*," alongside "externalization.")[3] The
religious notion too of God's "emptying of himself" into the world, understood not as a loss (in conceptual terms, say, a loss of determinacy) but as a
self-realization, will play a large role in Hegel's poetic ending.

These formulations, together with the remarks on beauty and the
understanding, together with the emphasis on enlivening and spiritualizing, together with the role assigned such an enlivening by the aesthetics
lectures, prepare us then for the closing passage.

Hegel extracts the couplet that ends the *Phenomenology* from Schiller's
1782 poem (in its first version) "Freundschaft." As already noted and as we
shall see in more detail, Hegel misquotes the couplet. He is also quoting
out of context, since the poem as a whole concerns friendship between
two persons, treated in the poem as an example or image of a possible reconciliation between the *Geisterreich*, or "realm of spirit," and the *Körper-
weltgewühle*, or the "throng of the corporeal world," as well as between an
isolated self and an other. Hegel focuses attention only on the divine side
of the issue. One overarching idea in the poem is that friendship is expres-
sive of what we might call a divine logic for the world, one particularly
appealing to Hegel, according to which one knows and loves oneself only in
one's reflection in another ("Nur in dir bestaun' ich mich" [Only in you do I
admire myself] from stanza five), and that this is true of the divine creator's
relation to his creations with the crucial difference that a "world-master"
(*Weltenmeister*) cannot find an equal, a true mirror of himself, and con-

fronts instead a "foaming" infinity. Humans in love *can* enjoy a divine "süssen Sympathie," sweet sympathy, with another. (One of the best couplets is: "Todte Gruppen sind wir—wenn wir hassen / Götter—wenn wir liebend uns umfassen" (We are dead groups when we hate / Gods when we lovingly embrace each other). Here is the original last stanza of Schiller's poem:

> Freundlos war der große Weltenmeister,
> Fühlte *Mangel*—darum schuf er Geister,
>   Selge Speigel *seiner* Seligkeit!—
> Fand das höchste Wesen schon kein gleiches,
> Aus dem Kelch des ganzen Seelenreiches
>   Schäumt *ihm*—die Unendlichkeit. (Schiller 1: 93)
> (Friendless was the great world-master,
> Felt *lack*—and so created spirits
>   Blessed mirrors of *his own* blessedness!—
> The highest essence found no equal,
> From the chalice of the entire realm of souls
>   Foams up to *him*—infinity.)

Hegel however cites only two lines:

> Aus dem Kelche dieses Geistesreiches
> Schäumt ihm seine Unendlichkeit.

These brief phrases represent several alterations of the original, all of which have the effect of making Schiller's work seem like a close expression of Hegel's theory: (1) In the closing sentence of the chapter, immediately before the quotation, Hegel refers to the *Weltenmeister* as a way of alluding to "absolute Geist," and he suggests that such a divine being would be "lifeless and alone" (here is the reference to *Lebendigkeit* again) were it not for the "foaming up" of *his own* infinity, interpreted by Hegel as "the inwardizing [*die Erinnerung*]" of its own actual history, its own "actuality." The two lines that Hegel re-formulates, in other words, suggest a satisfying self-recognition and apparent self-satisfaction in Spirit's products. (2) and (3) "The chalice of the *entire* realm of souls" (Kelch des *ganzen Seelen*reiches) has become "the chalice of *this* realm of *spirits*" (Kelche *dieses Geist*esreiches). And (4) "infinity" (*die* Unendlichkeit) has become "*his own* infinitude" (*seine* Unendlichkeit). Once again, the original suggests that human beings can experience in love and friendship a unity and consolation that any divine being, however divine, also requires. But the Hegelian version shifts the emphasis to the achievement of the perspective of "absolute Spirit" and that subject's experience of *itself* in the infinity of its world. Even though Schiller elsewhere refers to "Zahlenloser Geister" (countless Spirits) in stanza eight, the substitution in the last lines of *Geist* for *Seele* "Hegelianizes" the passage and has it asking about *Geist's* experience of itself in *its own creations*, in the historical achievement of forms of non-alienating practices and institutions, *Geistesreiches*, rather than "the" infinity of the independent or (as in Hegel's *Anthropologie*, natural) "soul" world. And this is not a terminological issue alone. It suggests the answer to the question posed at the beginning of this essay about the unique appropriateness of works of art for Hegel's purposes in the *Phenomenology*. The *Reich des Geistes* is the *Reich* of *Geist's* productions, especially reflective attempts at self-knowledge. *Geist* indeed is itself paradoxically said by Hegel to be "the result of itself." It is whatever it understands itself to be, if it can come to understand itself as expressed in its productions.

The citation and Hegel's alterations introduce several issues, but I want to conclude here by mentioning only two. First, the passage introduces us to the language of Hegel's most frequent characterizations of the core issue in his philosophy. That issue, to sum everything up rather breathlessly, is the problem of freedom or *Geist's* self-determination, and what counts as the true *Verwirklichung*, the "realization" of freedom. In one form, the problem is how to understand how the free activity of making judgments, taking a stand of sorts about how things are (rather than having been caused to be in some doxastic state), could be said to have the required objective purport, the directedness to objects, necessary for such a judging. There is, then, also the question of the normative credentials of such judgments. If "freely" made, not mental events that happen to us, how do we hold ourselves and each other to account in the making of such claims? The interrelation of empirical, non-empirical, aesthetic, and practical judgments are all in play in this issue. Second, the very same issues are involved when Hegel addresses the question of intentional action as well. How should we understand the formation and execution of intentions, which seem matters "internal" to reflective deliberation alone, and its "other," the "outer" movements in public space that seem to issue from such resolutions? In both cases we are responsive to reasons about what to believe and do, and being responsive to reasons just is the exercise of rational and so free agency in the post-Kantian tradition. The problem, of course, is that we are not just or exclusively responsive to reasons. We are also subject to the laws of nature in the exercise of our sensory capacities, and are also so subject in the storms of passions and instincts, and in our movements in space. And in both cases, Hegel suggests frequently, the basic "logical" or conceptual problem is understanding the proper logical or conceptual relation between "inner" and "outer" (what we might call the relation between mind and world in thought and in action), and in both cases he tells us often that the way to understand the issue is not as a duality, but as a kind of speculative identity.

Given these formulations, any summary of Hegel's own position about such a speculative identity sounds just as metaphorical and opaque as this talk of a divine being's experiencing the foaming of its own infinity from a chalice. For he says such things as: concepts and the manifold should not be understood as if either the formation or application of a concept is a matter of such a norm being restricted or constrained or directly and immediately guided by some exogenous "material." Rather the concept "negates" its own separate or logically distinct status and so "negates" itself,[4] or even should be said to "give itself its own content." And these formulations, since they seem to suggest a weird sort of dependence of the world and embodied action on "thought's self-determination," continue to resist interpretations that could allow Hegel to play much of a role in any contemporary discussion of the issues. Indeed, they are so opaque that they cannot even be referred to as dead historical positions. What "positions"?

However, at the very least the relevance of the poetic claim to Hegel's mature position is not hard to establish. Schiller's poem is about friendship and, at one point (stanza 8), love, and that theme is important not only for the practical philosophy of the young Hegel's writings on Christianity, but it plays a profound role in Hegel's attempt to explain the heart of his theoretical philosophy, his *Science of Logic*. One example can establish that. In his *Begriffslogik*, when he is discussing "the universal Concept" and claims that "the universal is therefore *free power*" (*Science of Logic* 603), he hastens to point out that this should not be understood as something like the exercise of the subject's organizing and abstracting power *over* something separate and resistant. (As one might conceive the rule of a divine *Weltenmeister*.) What is "other" than *der Begriff* can itself play its role as other only as so conceptualized. To explain what he means by that, he makes the following extraordinary remark:

> The universal . . . is itself and takes the other within its embrace,
> but without doing violence to it; on the contrary, the universal is, in
> its other, in peaceful communion with itself. We have called it free
> power, but it could also be called *free love* and *boundless blessedness*,
> for it bears itself toward the other as toward its own self; in it, it has
> returned to itself. (*Science of Logic* 603)

In the poetic sense, this is not legislative power sitting on its self-sufficient throne, legislating to the world, or what McDowell might call "frictionless spinning." The suggestion that the logic of the mind-world relation is like the "logic of love" remains a strange and forbidding image, but one gets a glimpse of sorts of how Hegel wants to understand the relations of dependence and independence in human experience when finally understood adequately in Absolute Knowing.

Moreover, in the entire last chapter of the *Phenomenology of Spirit*, Hegel continually reverts to his account of the nature of action in the two most important accounts of action in the *Phenomenology*: section Vc, "Individuality which takes itself to be real in and for itself" (where Hegel tries to show that individuality so conceived, in and for itself, cannot be "real"), and section VIc, "Spirit that is certain of itself. Morality," all in order to explain the position achieved by absolute knowledge. In both the relevant sections of the *Phenomenology*, Hegel tries to exhibit phenomenologically the severe limitations of this position and proposes instead to look not at several distinct, causally initiated phases of an action, but to view actions as evolving and changing expressions of a subject's intentions over an extended time, determinate only in extended confrontation and reaction within what Terry Pinkard has called "social space," and not the causal results of a discrete event. That is, Hegel denies that the right way to fix the determinacy of an action, to determine just what it was that was done, is to look exclusively to a subject's *ex ante* formulated intention. He insists that such putative intentions cannot, if they are to be understood as "actual" intentions, be temporally isolated from their expression in action, that such subjective formulations and reasons change in the course of the deed, and that it is quite possible that persons can be wrong about their actual intentions and motivation, that only as expressed in the deed in this public, social space, is it clear what they are committed to and sometimes clear why. This is a counterintuitive position. It means that a subject can often only "learn from the deed," as Hegel says, what it is he did and what his stake in the deed actually was, and it implies a deep dependence on the reception of the deed in society as helping to fix determinately what in fact was done. But in our context, it becomes intuitively clearer why Hegel is referring so frequently to this position as a way of explaining why there is no strict separation between a concept and its "actualization" or "satisfaction," why the comprehension of conceptual content requires attention to the "fluidity" (*Flüssigkeit*) and "living spirituality" (*lebendige Geistigkeit*) of a norm, what I have identified as the core position of the *Phenomenology of Spirit*. In Hegel's view in the relevant sections of the *Phenomenology*, actually to have an intention *is* to struggle to express that intention in a public and publicly contestable deed, subject to great temporal fluidity and to appropriations and interpretations by others that can greatly alter one's own sense of what one is about.

It is, to use Hegel's term, to "sacrifice" the purity and certainty (and so security) of one's self-understanding and to subject oneself to the reactions, counter-claims, and challenges of others. Were one to remain in the Inner Citadel of Subjective Certainty or cling only to what can be formally definable, one's self-understanding would have to remain suspended in doubt. The question of whether I am actually committed to what I take myself to be, the question of the *Wirklichkeit* of any self-image or any claim about normative propriety, would be left suspended, and because of that could be counted as much a fantasy of resolve or intention or commitment as genuine. Action must be understood as a self-negation in this sense, a negation of the subject's pretension to complete ownership of the nature and import of the deed, and therewith the sharing of such authority with others, or even the sacrifice of philosophy as an ahistorical a priori discipline in the traditional, both Platonic and Kantian, senses. All of this can seem like "the pathway of despair" just in the sense Hegel suggested, "the loss of oneself." But as in many other examples of Hegel's Christian imagery, the experiential *Bildung* can show that by this loss of a false independence and mastery, one has gained true independence, referred to in the *Rechtsphilosophie* as "being oneself in an another" (in diesem Anderen bei sich selbst) (*Philosophy of Right* §7).[5]

What, then, would it mean *not* to think of absolute *Geist* as "der große Weltenmeister" or a self-sufficient but lonely "Wesenlenker," a guide for all creatures? I have been trying to suggest that the closing image of the *Phenomenology* does not refer to a pantheistic metaphysics, or a neo-Platonic view about the underlying "divine mind" or "cosmic spirit" of which everything natural and *geistig* is an expression. He is making use of the imagery of such positions to suggest a radically different view on the relation between free agents and the world in which that agency is embodied and expressed, neither divinely sovereign nor pulled and pushed hither and yon by natural forces. That, I am claiming, is what Hegel's philosophy is simply *about*. The analogy with the logic of action is the issue he constantly returns to, especially in the last chapter, to make this point, and it is very revealing that he does so.

So from an initial, subjectively self-certain point of view, action looks like a self-negation, a violation of the purity and exclusive ownership of the deed thought to be a condition for seeing myself in the deed and so for freedom. But Hegel tries to illuminate the enormous burden carried by such a self-understanding, tries to render experientially plausible the claim that such stubbornness will eventually "break" under such a burden (as in "das Brechen des harten Herzens" in "Moralität"), and that ultimately such a subject will come to understand such a negation of its own pure subjectivity as the true *realization* of such subjectivity. This "burden" is not solely or even mainly a matter of logically incompatible commitments, and this "breaking" is not merely the conceptual resolution of such incompatibilities. To think of it this way would be to perpetuate the one-sidedness, the hold of which the *Phenomenology of Spirit* is trying to break.

But if this is all true, or at least plausible, what does it mean for the status of literature in the *Phenomenology of Spirit*? The analogy we have been constructing would hold that it is a conceptual confusion to regard an agent's deeds as if they were somehow imperfect expressions of what was purely intended, that the true meaning of the action must reside in the pure intending of the agent, as if all the rest, the actual results, should be seen as the result of intervening contingencies. Instead, as the intention unfolds in the deed over time, it could be said to "acquire" the only determinate shape it could have. This is a hard thought for Hegel to convey. It suggests that it is "in" the complex deed, as that deed is subject to the interpretations and reactions of others, that the intention, or the subject's stake in and sense of the deed, "lives," and we are on the contrary deeply wedded to the notion of a "prior" intention being "responsible" for the deed. Likewise, with any question about the determinate content of thought and action-guiding norms—norms like *Freiheit, Recht, Schönheit, Liebe,* or even *Wahrheit*—we should not say, on this account, that the manifestation of such norms in poetry, drama, sculpture, music, painting, and novels (or politics and religion for that matter) are expressions of independently held commitments and so mere illustrations. It is only *in* such representative attempts at self-knowledge (and Hegel's view that *die schöne Kunst* is best understood as such an attempt at self-knowledge is obviously deeply controversial) that the norm can be said to "live."

Hegel's citation of Schiller (already itself a kind of expression of *Freundschaft*) and his alteration thus serve an appropriately double purpose. The *citation* gives evidence for the indispensability of the living, aesthetic dimension of experience for any philosophical account of norms, all on the theory of conceptual and intentional content alluded to above, and the *alteration*, one might say, likewise gives evidence that the completion and *Aufhebung* of aesthetic representation by philosophic reflection is just as indispensable. The last word, in other words, turns out to be neither Schiller's nor Hegel's alone, making a case by its very presence for the indispensability of a reflective and philosophically informed attention to historical and living *geistige Wirklichkeit* for any genuine philosophy worthy of the name.

NOTES

1   I am not claiming that the Berlin lectures can always be used this way. There are also great differences, as in the *Antigone* interpretation, for example. See Speight 52.

2   Again, there is the same error in thinking that, because Hegel claimed in the *Aesthetics* lectures that art could no longer on its own convey Spirit's highest truths about itself, that either art could manifest *no* relevant or important truths, or that philosophy's putatively "higher" truths could be completely and perfectly expressed in conceptual terms alone, without a concept's *Wirklichkeit*, its reality or effectiveness. But this is clearly a different subject.

3   I am grateful to Terry Pinkard for correspondence about this issue. Pinkard's translation of the *Phenomenology* will appear soon.

4   Here is a typical statement about negation from his *Berlin Phenomenology*, as challenging to an interpreter now as it must have sounded then to his first readers: "The I is now this subjectivity, this infinite relation to itself, but therein, namely in this subjectivity, lies its negative relation to itself, diremption, differentiation, judgment. The I judges, and this constitutes it as consciousness; it repels itself from itself; this is a logical determination" (*Berlin Phenomenology* 2).

5   Hegel makes what he would consider a "logical" point about the major events in "both" bibles. The story of creation in the Hebrew Bible represents the insufficiency of a God merely contained with himself, and so the need to "empty"

(*entäussern*) himself in creating the world. There is little doubt that Hegel accepts the Lutheran take on this word—Luther's translation for kenosis—and goes farther, claiming as a meaning for the image that God had to empty or lose or externalize himself in what appeared other than him in order finally to be God. I follow here Terry Pinkard's translation and reading in his forthcoming rendering of the *Phenomenology of Spirit*. And in the New Testament the imagery is even more Hegelian. God the Father had to become his own son, externalized in the world and lost to him (to himself), preparing the way for reconciliation, or *der heilige Geist*, the Holy Spirit. The deeper point here is also, I would argue, ultimately politico-ethical: Christ's iconic status as both Master and Servant, his own father and his own son, at the same time.

WORKS CITED

Hegel, Georg Wilhelm Friedrich. *Aesthetics: Lectures on Fine Art.* 2 vols. Trans. T. M. Knox. Oxford: Clarendon Press, 1975.
———. *The Berlin Phenomenology.* Trans. M. Petry. Dordrecht: Riedel, 1981.
———. *Faith and Knowledge.* Trans. Walter Cerf and H. S. Harris. Albany: SUNY Press, 1977.
———. *Glauben und Wissen.* Vol. 4 of *Gesammelte Werke.* Hamburg: Felix Meiner, 1968.
———. *Phenomenology of Spirit.* Trans. A. V. Miller. Oxford: Oxford University Press, 1977.
———. *Philosophy of Right.* Trans S. W. Dyde. Amherst, NY: Prometheus Books, 1996.
———. *Science of Logic.* Trans. A. V. Miller. London: George Allen & Unwin, 1969.
Royce, Josiah. *Lectures on Modern Idealism.* New Haven: Yale University Press, 1919.
Schiller, Friedrich. *Sämtliche Werke.* 5 vols. Eds. Gerhard Fricke and Herbert G. Göpfert. Munich: Hanser, 1965.
Speight, Allen. *Hegel, Literature and the Problem of Agency.* Cambridge: Cambridge University Press, 2001.

9

Difficult Freedom

HEGEL'S SYMBOLIC ART AND SCHELLING'S
HISTORIOGRAPHY IN *THE AGES OF THE WORLD* (1815)

Tilottama Rajan

CAN Romanticism, which is often linked to organic and teleological models that subtend totalizing political ideologies, be said to invent an imagination that unworks such models? In "The Oldest Systematic Program of German Idealism" (1797), a text in Hegel's handwriting that is also attributed to Schelling and Hölderlin, the communal authors dismiss the state as "mechanical" and unfree. In a language that also reminds us of Friedrich Schlegel, they insist that we must "go beyond the state" to think "ideas [as] aesthetic, i.e., mythological" (161–62). The state here is the anchor of what William Godwin calls "institution," a term he often uses in the singular to denote not just a set of political and civil institutions but also a certain instituting and reifying of ideas that is the invisible result (1: 175–78). But in *The Philosophy of Right* and *The Philosophy of Mind* Hegel revalues the state as organic, and it is civil society, with its "atomistic" and self-interested individualism, that he sees as mechanical (*Philosophy of Mind* 256–57). In contrast to the more complex meaning of the term "organic" (as used by Schelling or Goethe, for instance), Hegel, in trying to sublate Goethe's deeply threatening work on plants, associates the term "organic" with the idea of integrated wholeness, which informs his distinction of the animal from the plant organism. Plants, Hegel writes in *The Philosophy of Nature*, "fall apart" into a "number of individuals." The "plant is thus impotent to hold its members in its power"; indeed, it does not have "true members," only parts that are the same. By contrast, the animal organism is a whole that subsumes its differences, both synchronously and teleologically. To do this it must have differences; thus the whole must be "articulated into parts that are *separate and distinct*," such that each member is "reciprocally end and means" (276, 303). Or, as Hegel writes in the *Aesthetics*, the highest form of organism reconciles "the real differences . . . and specific characteristics" "of all the members" and their "universal ideality," whereas in the plant "every branch is a new plant and not at all . . . just a single member" (1: 120, 137).

In *The Philosophy of Right*, then, the state is the culmination of a freedom that has dialectically worked through the inadequacies of family and civil society as a congeries of parts. In *The Philosophy of History*, moreover, the German nation—hardly a nation at the time—becomes the embodiment of this romanticized, mystical state-to-come, in which individuals are means to an end and yet achieve their ultimate freedom. Aesthetics as it is instituted as a discipline of German Idealism functions both as supplement and substrate for this transcendentalism of the state. To begin with, the "center of art," as Hegel defines it, "is a unification, self-enclosed so as to be a free totality, a unification of the content with its entirely adequate shape" (*Aesthetics* 1: 427). The aesthetic thus conceived takes on the force of a category of understanding. As the totality, unification, and legitimation only of what finds adequate expression, it determines our understanding of history, the political, and the projected course of the world. Coleridge's concept of "constitution" as the maximum "individuation" combined with the maximum "integration" is just such an example of aesthetic ideology, in that it conceives the state and the body politic according to the aesthetic ideal of multiplicity in unity (Coleridge 2: 839). Nor is the aesthetic only a form of cognition. For, as Marc Redfield argues, aesthetics also participates in "processes of mediation and reproduction that we may properly style *technical*" (16): aesthetics yields a technics that produces certain subjects and a certain kind of history. To be sure, the aesthetic in German Idealism is not even necessarily linked to the project of the nation, and in formulations such as the literary absolute may be completely apart from it. But this transcendence of the aesthetic simply veils the biopolitical effects to which Redfield points. As important, even as and precisely as a form of transcendental thinking, the aesthetic models a way of being that, in elevating art above the state and placing thinking spirit outside its materiality, allows the state to be analogously elevated into and aestheticized as spirit.

Schelling's early *Philosophy of Art* in no way departs from this pattern. For Schelling thinks of the aesthetic within Idealism, conceived as what Georges Bataille would call a restricted economy of knowledge, whereas elsewhere and later he rethinks Idealism within the more general economy of Romanticism. This is to say that Schelling's lectures on art develop within the envelope of his transcendental idealism, which synchronizes the real and the ideal so as to allow what seems subject to "endless development" and difference in "appearing nature" to be grasped "as one in the absolute" (*Ideas* 272): grasped aesthetically, according to a principle of teleological judgment. In Schelling's *System of Transcendental Idealism* (1800) this substitution of the ideal for the real allows history to end in a "universal constitution," a universal state that unites freedom and necessity (*System* 199, 203). It is art, thought of in a restricted sense, that allows history to be transformed from a science of the actual into an ideal science. For, as Schelling explains in *Lectures on the Method of Academic Study* (translated as *On University Studies*), art "presents real events and histories in complete form . . . so that they express the highest Ideas" (107). The role played by nature in this process of disciplinary supplementation is to naturalize the prosthesis of aesthetic ordering; thus Schelling describes nature in *The System* as "the unconscious poetry of spirit" (198, 209–10), just as for Hegel it is "the idealism of life" (*Aesthetics* 1: 120), even though Hegel also concedes that nature is "an alien existence," "the negative of itself" (*Philosophy of Nature* 3, 429). In *The System*, then, history, art, and nature are coordinated within a closed pattern of regulated metaphoric transfers that forwards the goals of Idealism as a restricted economy of knowledge. Or, as Odo Marquard puts it, *The System* "takes an aesthetic perspective on existence: it determines philosophy primarily as aesthetics" (13).

Nevertheless we can read between Hegel's *Aesthetics* and Schelling's middle work to discern an aesthetics in Romanticism that is deeply at odds with aesthetic education and aesthetic ideology. Or perhaps not an aesthetics, since to describe it as such is to formalize what is more the symptom of an auto-immunity in the Idealist system, wherein the system's turning on itself is the basis of its speculative energy. For Derrida, who wants to open up philosophy as a restricted economy, "system" implies a whole "architecture of philosophy" that Schelling assumes in his early "system" of transcendental idealism, and that Hegel also tries to construct in his *Encyclopedia* as the "onto- and auto-encyclopedic circle of the State," at least as Derrida sees it (*Points* 212; "Age of Hegel" 148). "System" is the standing together (*systasis*) of an architectonics of related assumptions, such that this invisible interweaving of concepts in aesthetics, language, logic, history, metaphysics, and so on can be unraveled from any point in the structure (*Points* 212). Hence Derrida's claim that deconstruction "has to do with systems" (*Points* 212).

The organism is such a point in Hegel's system. For the subsumption of the geological into the vegetable organism, and the vegetable into the animal—not to mention the inclusion of the human within the animal—leaves remainders that call into question what an organism is and in what its organicity consists. The history of art is another such point. For what is notable here is that art *has* a history in which it always falls short of being what it should be: "the unification of the content with its entirely adequate shape" (*Aesthetics* 1: 431). That art has a history means that philosophy too has a history in which it never gets beyond art. For, as we shall see, in the history of German philosophy that forms a subplot in Hegel's *History of Philosophy*, philosophy begins with Jacob Boehme, who relies on allegory to coordinate matter and spirit, and ends with Schelling, who has still not moved from art to science. Art does not return in Schelling's own corpus as the point at which the ideality of philosophy gives up its "own immunitary protections." But this auto-immunity, which for Derrida is also the vitality of systems (*Rogues* 124, 55), characterizes Schelling's return in his middle work to history, viewed through geology, as a way of revisiting the issue of freedom.

Implicit in this argument is a further assumption, about the state of the knowledges in play in relation to the state. In his *Lectures on Academic Study* Schelling distinguishes between positive sciences and absolute knowledge. Positive sciences are restricted forms of knowledge "that attain to objectivity within the state and in function of it" (78–79), as do theology and law in Kant's *Conflict of the Faculties*. They are in effect technologies. Absolute knowledge, by contrast, is a following of the particular wherever it may lead and thus a pushing of knowledge to its limits. According to Hegel, who makes a related distinction in his *Encyclopedia*, positive sciences are finite; they see themselves as self-contained and exhaustive, whereas in absolute knowledge one sphere of knowledge unfolds into another (54). To be sure, Idealism in its restricted form closes down the speculative potential of this interdisciplinarity by synchronizing the various disciplines it brings under the umbrella of philosophy. Absolute knowledge thus becomes a form of totalization. If not strictly a positive science, it posits itself as science or certain knowledge. It is in this sense of the term absolute knowledge, which was picked up by British Idealists of the Victorian period, that we can see it as correlated with a state that, despite being conceived anti-instrumentally, risks being a form of restricted economy.

Yet, as Jean-Luc Nancy points out, "certain words" in Hegel have a "twofold speculative meaning," "absolute knowledge" being one such term.[1] In what remains I explore the speculative potential, created between Hegel and Schelling, of the unfolding and enfolding of different knowledges by one another, when these knowledges are thought of as being outside the architectonic of Idealism and within the general economy of Romanticism. More specifically, I will read between Hegel's history of art and the unsettling role played by the symbolic in his schema and Schelling's deconstruction, against the grain of his own idealism, of Hegelian history and the logic that supports it. As is well known, Hegel divides the history of art into three stages that involve different relations between "inwardness" and its "externalization," "theme" and "execution," and the "idea" and its "embodiment." Ostensibly this narrato-logic charts a philosophical and cultural progress similar to that of *The Philosophy of History:* from the Orient, through the Classical world, to Europe. But, as I have argued elsewhere, the history of art in Hegel has a curiously concave form, as if the content of the dialectic had been hollowed out and only its shape preserved, or as if the shape of history did not adequately express its inwardness ("Toward a Cultural Idealism" 53–54). For in the *Aesthetics*, unlike *The Philosophy of Right* or *The Philosophy of History*, the moment of synthesis comes in the middle and not the end, as Hegel seems discontent with an end of history. In the earliest or symbolic phase represented by the oriental, art fails to achieve identity with itself because of a deficiency in self-consciousness that results in the Idea still being "indeterminate." Expressing itself in the forms available to it, the Idea assumes an "untrue and bad determinancy" that results in distorted forms such as the monstrous and the grotesque. This problem is overcome in classicism as art becomes "the adequate embodiment of the Idea" in plastic form (*Aesthetics* 1: 76–77). But in the romantic phase, form and content are again separated, this time because of a deficiency in matter that repeats and reverses the problems of the symbolic (1: 79). External forms are insufficient to present an Idea that is now fully developed but that in "the previous shapes . . . can no longer find its adequate reality" (1: 422). The romantic form thus "cancels again the completed unification of the Idea and its reality, and reverts, even if in a higher way, to that difference and opposition of the two sides which in symbolic art remained unconquered" (1:79). "In a higher way," Hegel says. Still, as developed as the Idea is in the romantic, it "still needs an external medium for its expression" and must also be judged defective insofar as it resists an "adequate union with the external," which would, however, compromise its freedom (1: 77–81).

What is notable here is the odd position of the classical. Classical art is the "adequate embodiment of the Idea" through the identity of form and content or inside and outside, and thus the "unity of the artist's subjective activity with his topic and work" (1: 431). The classical has no remainders, it "display[s] in its existence nothing but itself" (1: 431). It is also the very consummation of art, since "this adequate mode of configuration achieves what true art is in its essential nature" (1: 427). Classicism thus cements the identity of art and nation since it teaches us to believe in the adequacy of the outside as the full expression of the inside. It ought, then, to be the end of art's history, the achievement of art's place in the aesthetic education of history. Nevertheless, despite its imagined resolution of the underlying contradictions in the symbolic, the classical is superseded by the romantic, which seems compelled to repeat the difference of idea and shape in the symbolic. For if the classical artist adequately embodies the Idea, this is only because he receives his content "cut and dried" from "national faith and myth." Since this content is "already determined for imagination as settled," the classical artist is then "free" to focus on "shaping the external artistic appearance" and on producing a formal perfection that is the simulacrum of unity and identity (1: 439). By contrast, the symbolic artist "tosses about in a thousand forms," adapting "to the meaning sought the shapes that ever remain alien" (1:438). This "restless fermentation" of forms in the symbolic is part of the "labor" of the negative, wherein consciousness is still "producing its content and making it clear to itself" (1: 438). Implicit in this contrast is a difference at the heart of Hegel's concept of freedom. Classical art is a "free totality," because the classical artist is a "clear-headed man" who "*knows* what he wills," "*can* accomplish" it, and is not "unclear about the meaning and the substantial content which he intends to shape outwardly for contemplation" (1: 438). The freedom in question here is of a particular kind: the freedom of "subjectivity in charge of itself," as Derrida puts it, freedom as a "power, or attribute of a subject" linked to "an intentional or deciding will" (*Rogues* 43–44). By contrast, symbolic art is overdetermined, unfree, because spirit is not yet "clear to itself" (*Aesthetics* 1: 438). It is bound by the materiality of a thought that has not yet become concept. But because nothing in it is determined as settled, symbolic art is also unbound from the constrictions of classical unity. This very different freedom, which Hegel resists by placing the symbolic at the uncouth beginnings of aesthetic history, is one to which he cannot avoid being drawn back when the classical gives way to the romantic as a revisiting of a certain restlessness of the negative in the symbolic.

To be sure, Hegel sees the symbolic as inferior to the classical, not least because it is oriental. But then he also finds the classical a disappointment, which must be superseded by what is less adequate, as if what is less adequate is in some way more adequate. In classical art "the content is determinate and the free shape is determined by the content itself and it belongs to it absolutely," so that the artist only "execute[s] what is already cut and dried on its own account in essence" (*Aesthetics* 1: 439). In effect the classical is mechanical and without imagination, like the state itself in the "Systematic Program." Indeed, the belonging of art to its content resembles the reduction of philosophy to its content that Derrida sees Hegel as insisting on in his letter on education in the Gymnasium. Here "philosophy proper," including metaphysics and the history of philosophy, is "excluded" (as required by the Prussian state), but its "content" is taught in the "prescriptive and normative" forms of ethics, religion, and, most importantly, logic as the road to what Christian Wolff called the "*idea clara.*" Classicism, then, is the Gymnasium of Spirit where "that solid tempered content" is conveyed that can later be given "speculative form." Yet we should not too quickly identify Hegel with the forms of mediation and *Bildung* promoted in the Gymnasium letter, to which, like Kant in *The Conflict of Faculties*, he accedes in order to preserve a space for speculation in the university.[2] For, as Jacques D'Hondt suggests, there are three Hegels: one who is cited in support of the state; one whose work his friends read between the lines; and one who never ceases to negotiate between the philosopher and the state in his daily life (2–3), like Kant, whom Derrida describes as the first to live the aporetic identity of the philosopher who must think his work both inside and outside the institution.

But perhaps this classicism that Hegel reluctantly damns with faint praise is Roman rather than Greek. In *The Philosophy of History*, Hegel is highly critical of Rome, which he associates with a "sterile Understanding" (289). Of Kant's sense of understanding, Karl Jaspers says that reason makes things too big for our understanding while understanding makes them too small for our reason (46). Hegel suggests that Rome appropriated the Greek gods for limited and pragmatic rather than infinite purposes, and represents "an extreme prose of the spirit," "in contrast with that primeval wild poetry and transmutation of the finite, which we observe in the east" (*Philosophy of History* 291–92, 288). This understanding without imagination, in turn, derives from the very structure of Roman society. As an "artificial state" held together by force, Rome requires the sacrifice of the subject to the state and a "harshness in respect to the family relation," as a result of which "the world is sunk in melancholy" (283, 286, 278). In Rome, then, the state is not a "moral, liberal connection," an inward connection, and art is purely "mechanical" (283, 289).

It would seem then that Hegel thinks that there can be a form of classicism, and a form of state, that *is* free and liberal. In *The Philosophy of History* he tells us that the Greeks achieved a "well-balanced freedom" that is not Roman but is also not the "wild poetry" of the symbolic. The condition of possibility for this freedom is adequacy of form, since "free art can arise" only after "the mechanical side has been brought to perfection" (288).[3] Yet Hegel's language is revealing, since it seems to put Greece after Rome: the free art of Greece can arise only "after" art has been formally perfected in Rome. Moreover, even though in the *Aesthetics* Hegel also claims that "the actualization of classical art in history" is to be sought "in the Greeks," Greek art as he describes it is not the humanism he wants but the symbolic embarrassment of its mythology. The Greeks borrow Egyptian gods, as Hegel knew before Nietzsche and Erwin Rohde, and their religion is profoundly linked to animism. These borrowings undergo a "necessary transformation of what . . . belong[s] to the Ideal, though in an unsuitable form at first" (441–43), but Greek art is therefore constituted on the repression of the sedimented traces of the symbolic. Greek art, then, seems to be only the struggle to achieve the classical. But is the classical worth achieving? For it is not Roman but classical art in general that Hegel describes as "cut and dried," as if the inadequacies of the Roman extend to the very concept of the classical, or as if Hegel senses that formal adequacy and freedom are fundamentally at odds. And this in turn is because it is unclear where the freedom of the classical resides. On the one hand, we are told that only once formal perfection has been achieved can the content develop freely, which implies that classical art aims at intellectual freedom. But on the other hand, it is because the content has been pre-arranged that the artist is described as "free" to concentrate on formal perfection (*Aesthetics* 1: 439). According to the authors of the "Systematic Program," only "that which is the object of freedom is the idea" (161). But does classicism in its adequation of form and content achieve freedom only in a mechanical sense? Does it achieve or surrender freedom at the level of the "Idea"?

The same dialectic of discontent with regard to an adequate form of philosophy is played out in Hegel's history of German philosophy. For Hegel begins this history with the mystic Jacob Boehme, whom he interestingly describes as oriental, and whose method is essentially symbolic (Rajan, "How Not To Speak Properly" 127–31). He then ends with Schelling, and with a certain inchoation that returns philosophy to a perpetual Romanticism. For Schelling, Hegel complains, keeps beginning "again from the beginning" (Hegel, *History of Philosophy* 3: 515). This phrase curiously accords with Schelling's own account of history itself in the 1815 *Ages of the World* as a "perpetually advancing and retreating movement," in which "Nature" develops "qualities, aspects, works and talents to their pinnacle, only again to . . . start anew, perhaps in a new species, but certainly only to attain again the same peak" (21). Between Boehme and Schelling are Leibniz, who did not write in German, Christian Wolff, Tschirnhausen, and Christian Thomasius. Wolff represents a classicization of philosophy as clarity, but adopts the viewpoint "of the understanding merely," performing a "pedantic systematization" of Leibniz from which "the speculative interest is quite eliminated" (*History of Philosophy* 3: 349–50). Tschirnhausen and Thomasius cannot even be dignified as classical. On the contrary, they represent a prosaic Germanness of "so-called healthy reason" (3: 349): a *bürgerliche Gesellschaft* like Dutch art in the *Aesthetics*, which, as the "prose of actuality," is the beginning of the end of art (*Aesthetics* 1: 595). These are classical philosophers only in the Roman sense. Together they institute a professionalization of their discipline as part of the formation of the German nation, wherein the "spiritual [*geistige*]" element that emerged in Boehme, "though still in a peculiar and barbarous form," is lost entirely (*History of Philosophy* 3: 350). Their philosophy is what Hegel allows for in the Gymnasium. In fact it is philosophy as a "positive science," in Schelling's terms. Yet Hegel is not drawn to these philosophers and instead ends his history with the friend with whom he had irrevocably broken in 1807. And he does so in a fraught and ambivalent way. For, on the one hand, Schelling's "great merit," Hegel insists, "is to have pointed out in Nature the forms of Spirit; thus electricity, magnetism, &c., are for him only external modes of the Idea." This is to say that Schelling thinks imaginatively and not according to the understanding. And on the other hand, Hegel complains that Schelling "has misconceived the nature of thought; the work of art thus becomes for him the . . . only mode in which the Idea exists for spirit" (3: 542).

Moreover, this art is not classical, but symbolic or romantic, since at the heart of philosophy's failure to become a science is the criterion of adequate embodiment. For in Boehme and Schelling the very failure to embody the Idea has its own adequacy, since, as Hegel says in commenting on what he calls "defectiveness in form," such forms fail only in terms of "beauty," but in terms of adequacy "the specific shape which every content of the Idea gives to itself in the particular forms of art is always adequate to that content" (*Aesthetics* 1: 300). And, as he also concedes, "the clearer and more accurate configuration" may be "incapable . . . of expressing the deeper meaning" (309). Conceived on this model, the *work* of art is not form or hypostasis but "configuration," "the work on form, the deformation of form," as much as it is "formation" (Carroll 29, 39). Whereas classical art is the hypostasis of figure, the settling of form in beauty, symbolic art registers the violence of forcing the unshapable into determinate shapes: its distortion thus returns us to the process of figure, the *work* of art, from which art always begins. Romantic art too withdraws from hypostasis, but is said to return "in a higher way" to "that difference and opposition" of "Idea and shape," which "in symbolic art remained unconquered" (*Aesthetics* 1: 79, 81). In other words, in symbolic art the Idea cannot find expression in the shapes in which it prematurely posits itself, because the Idea is still deficient. But in romantic art it is "perfected in itself as spirit and heart," and outward shapes merely fail to convey it (1: 79–81). The two forms, however, are not opposed but are different formulations of, different attitudes toward, difference. Romantic art, as sensitive plant, beautiful soul, or ineffectual angel, withdraws into the inwardness of pure ideality, while symbolic art does its work at the site of the material. What this means is that symbolic art, in its very positivity, even as and precisely as a "bad and untrue determinacy" (1: 76–77), is involved in history: in the imagining and de-imagining of history.

Of course, as the unshaped that exceeds judgments based on criteria of aesthetic beauty, Hegel prefers the romantic because its formlessness is not unaesthetic. The French Revolution, which for Kant was disturbingly unreadable if potentially sublime, is not romantic, even though it was produced by Romanticism (Kant, *Conflict* 153). As a symbolic event, a particular case that cannot be subsumed under universal rules, the Revolution posed in its time a profound challenge to judgment. If Kant sought to romanticize the symbolic, the romantic for Hegel is an alibi for revisiting the symbolic. In what remains I suggest that this radicality of the symbolic can be recovered from its conflicted place in the *Aesthetics* by reading it through the more difficult freedom theorized by Schelling in *Ages of the World*. Hegel, to be sure, could not have read the *Ages*, which was twice brought to publication in 1811 and 1813, and abandoned on both occasions, only to be completely unworked in the third unpublished version in 1815. But the *Weltalter* project was known to be in process (by Coleridge for instance), and Hegel did read the *Philosophical Investigations into the Essence of Human Freedom* (1809), which is the only work of Schelling's that he praises after their rift in 1807. Of the *Freedom* essay Hegel writes that it is "deeply speculative in character" but remains "isolated and independent," whereas "in Philosophy . . . nothing isolated can be worked out or developed" (*History of Philosophy* 3: 514). Indeed, although the *Ages* brings together human, natural, and psychic history, Schelling did not develop the consequences for the aesthetic domain of a freedom wherein nothing can be "expected from what easily unfolds," and wherein there is no "evolution without the involution that precede[s] it" (107). Still, the *Ages'* focus on history, as the psychoanalysis of Idealist history,[4] lets us develop the implications of symbolic art for historical forms in a way that is not dominated by the force of institution, but by a process of de-imagining.

In the *Stuttgart Seminars* Schelling questions what Godwin calls "institution," when he sees the state as "a doomed attempt to become a whole," a merely "external unity" that cannot be "reconciled with the essence of free beings" (*Stuttgart* 227). Schelling thus takes us back to the "Systematic Program," which had wanted to "go beyond" any containment of "absolute freedom" in the state, and had described the "philosophy of the spirit" as "an aesthetic philosophy." Evoking Kant by referring to "ideas" like "eternal peace" that must be endlessly (de)constructed, the "Systematic Program" had already given art the role of critique (161–62). The reference here is not just to Kant's essay "To Perpetual Peace," but also to the *Critique of Judgment*, where Kant divides ideas into "aesthetical" ideas, which are intuitions of the imagination to which no "definite thought" or "concept" is "adequate," and "rational" ideas, which are concepts that cannot be concretely embodied (Kant, *Critique of Judgment* 157). As alternately rational and aesthetical, the idea is a perpetual difference from itself, which the authors of the "Systematic Program" try to sublimate into a transcendental paradox by making "ideas aesthetic, i.e., mythological" and mythology "reasonable" (162). This literary absolute, however, is still under the sign of a certain aestheticization that Carl Schmitt castigates as "subjectified occasionalism." Such occasionalism, a term Schmitt adapts from Nicholas Malebranche, allows the subject to "shift the intellectual center into itself" so as to assert its own infinite productivity. The point is not to agree with Schmitt, or even with Hegel's similar but more complex critique of Romantic irony, but to recognize that the literary absolute models a freedom linked to a sense of subjective agency that Schelling comes to question in the *Freedom* essay. But what kind of art, then, would withdraw from aesthetic ideology without substituting an occasionalist aestheticism? Or, what kind of art would correspond to the darkening of enlightenment in Schelling's *Ages*, rather than to the enthusiastic plenitude of the "Systematic Program"?

Schelling, as we have said, did not return to the aesthetic after his early period. But symbolic art is the form of imagination that comes closest to his revision of history as a negative dialectic in the third (1815) *Ages*, through a rethinking of freedom itself as the ongoing analysis of its own psychosis. For symbolic art, in its self-contesting turbulence, has much in common with the endless rotary movement of expansive and contractive drives that Schelling sees as the primal scene of history, of the world, and of being itself. On the one hand, Schelling wants to confine this movement to paganism, as he does in the 1811 *Ages'* philosophy of revelation, and as Hegel also does in seeing the symbolic as pre-art, before history. On the other hand, the 1815 version of *Ages* unfolds into a psychoanalysis of how "actual history" as a "series of free actions" never begins (49), because the rotary movement that precedes it cannot be firmly closed off in the past. A psychoanalysis, because one who would grasp "the history of the cosmos," Schelling says, must be able to "write completely the history of their own life." But "most people turn away from what is concealed within themselves just as they turn away from . . . the abysses of that past which are still in one just as much as the present" (3–4).

In the *Stuttgart Seminars*, which provide "the principal link" between the *Freedom* essay and the *Ages* but which Schelling says contain much material that has not been worked out (196), Schelling begins to probe the abyss of freedom. He turns from the state to the church, which also fails because it either "assimilat[es] the external forms of the state" and "eventually" tries "to produce *external* unity by means of the state," or because it becomes restricted to the "inwardness" that Hegel associates with the romantic (228–29). Schelling then turns, in a manner typical of the Romantic artist, to nostalgia, melancholy, and illness. These pathologies profoundly compromise the term "spirit," since in these affects it is "not the body that infects the spirit but vice versa": "hence the spirit cannot be the highest form" (232). Turning to such maladies of the soul, Schelling darkens his own earlier enlightenment in a way that offers no clear path forward. Schelling also insists that "error . . . is something intrinsically positive," that the pathologies he lists are "powers," that the "most profound essence of the human spirit—is *madness*," and that "human beings devoid of all madness have but an empty and barren understanding" (231–33). But Schelling, it seems, does not know how to access the creativity of this madness and error.

Turning back to these abysses in the third version of *Ages*, Schelling reads the history of spirit in the history of nature, using the one to disturb the other rather than synchronizing them. As the title *Ages of the World* suggests, Schelling thus confronts history, which he had described as one of the "ideal" sciences (*University Studies* 103), with its mirror stage in the "real" science of geology, as the site of the sedimented traces of nature's unconscious. As a psychoanalysis of spirit through nature as its "human nature" (*Ages* 46), the 1815 *Ages* challenges both the progressive teleology that Hegel projected onto history and the logic that subtends that progress: a progress Schelling too had assumed in the *System of Transcendental Idealism*. For in Schelling's recasting of dialectical logic in the 1815 *Ages*, the third potency, which should be "outside and above all antithesis," cannot be removed from contention, because "each of the three has an equal right to be that which has being" (36, 19). Thus there is no synthesis that does not negate the right of what resists unification to have being, for synthesis is the opposite, not the transcendence, of difference. This is to say that all syntheses, all imaginary or symbolic resolutions, must be drawn back into the rotation, the endless revolution, of a self-consciousness that is interminable rather than progressive.

At the heart of this turbulence in history and psychic history is the resistance between what "is outpouring and goes forth from itself" and "something inhibiting . . . something conflicting," a "primordial negating force" that "closes itself off": "this Other which, so to speak, should not be and yet is, nay must be . . . this darkening that resists the light" or "obliquity that resists the straight . . . however else one has attempted to express [it] in images" (6–7). In the 1811 *Ages* these two drives, as Schelling calls them— the positive and the negating, or the expansive and the contracting—are linearized in a progressive dialectic rather than being locked within the even more primal "annular drive [*Umtrieb*]" of the 1815 version, through which they endlessly unwork each other (103). In the 1813 version, which interestingly omits all mention of the rotary movement, the repressed trace of this movement is nevertheless closed off through a linguistics that also yields a historiography. For at the very end of this version, Schelling does indeed institute history as a series of free actions by formulating a profoundly logocentric theory of expression wherein the "*expressing* (the essence of the copula) . . . can only be one," although the "expressed" may be "two that are opposed" (127). Both earlier versions of the *Ages* thus fail to build a bridge between the difficult freedom Schelling had theorized in the *Freedom* essay and the "madness" that is the "most profound essence of the human spirit" (235), instead retreating back to the Idealist history sketched at the end of the much earlier *System of Transcendental Idealism*.

But in the 1815 *Ages* the return to the rotary movement is the collapse of this expressing that would allow for a more conventionally Hegelian history. Describing this history, Schelling writes that a "true beginning" would be one "that does not always begin again but persists" so that there is a "steady progression," thus also permitting a "veritable end" that "does not need to retreat from itself back to the beginning" (20). But Schelling cannot constitute the "decisive past" (42) that would allow him to proceed to the future, as he does in relegating the rotary movement to paganism in the 1811 version. Nor is this impossibility of "positing something as past" (44) simply a failure. For, as he says in a passage that seems to have both the French Revolution and the earlier linguistics of "expression" in its background:

If an organic being becomes sick, forces appear that previously lay concealed in it. Or if the copula of the unity dissolves altogether and if the life forces that were previously subjugated by something higher are deserted by the ruling spirit and can freely follow their own inclina-

tions and manners of acting, then something terrible becomes manifest. . . . Which was held down by the magic of life. . . . For when the
abysses of the human heart open up in evil and that terrible thought
comes to the fore that should have been buried eternally in night and
darkness, we first know what lies in the human in accordance with its
possibility and how human nature . . . is actually constituted. (48)

And, as he then continues, deconstructing the enlightenment of an Idealist
history:

If we take into consideration the many terrible things in nature and
the spiritual world and the great many other things that a benevolent
hand seems to cover up from us, then we could not doubt that the
Godhead sits enthroned over a world of terrors. (49)

Recognizing that idealism is "the soul of philosophy" and "realism its
body" (*Philosophical Investigations* 236), Schelling in the 1815 *Ages* restages
Idealism itself as a rotary movement between the Idea's expansion in history and its contraction into its own psychoanalysis. For, as he says, linking history to self-consciousness in what seems a classic German Idealist
formulation, "There is no dawning of consciousness . . . without positing
something as past." But Schelling also insists that there "is no consciousness without something that is at the same time excluded and contracted,"
which he calls "the unconscious": that of which consciousness is "conscious
as not itself." And insofar as it is conscious of this unconscious, consciousness "must again attract it as that of which it is conscious *as itself*, only in a
different form" (*Ages* [1815] 44; emphasis mine). The expressing that is the
beginning of history is thus always drawn back to what is not said in the
expression. Yet this unconscious is after all not excluded entirely; rather it
is "negated and in the dark." It is "contracted" into "something not yet made
good" that "pushes its essence forward," as Jürgen Habermas says in commenting on Schelling's importance to the utopianism of Ernst Bloch (71).
     Because this "something" pushes itself forward in expression, the
expressing can no longer be thought of as "one," as Schelling still conceived
it in the Idealist historiography of the 1813 *Ages*. For in the section on "The
Construction of the Cosmos" in the 1815 version, Schelling discerns a primal scene of imagination at the beginning of nature that is not Coleridge's
"Eternal Sum or I AM" but a "gathering together" of "averse forces" in a

series of "rotary wholes [*rotatorische Ganzen*]" generated in "the most violent revulsion" and "contradiction" (91–92). Symbolic art, I suggest, is the secondary form of this primary imagination in which "each single particular nature commences with the rotation about its own axis" and thus in "a state of inner revulsion" (*Ages* [1815] 92). For in symbolic art the Idea pushes itself forward within a material form that causes it to contract into and away from itself. This contraction and "discontent," Schelling says, is "the poison of life that needs to be overcome," yet if "the negative force's inspiriting could wane in the wholes," life would "sink back into universal being" and non-entity (91, 89, 92). To be sure, this "incessant systole and diastole" (90) does not sound like Hegelian history, the expansion of which is predicated on the contraction of the Symbolic. In his later work Hegel follows the organization of knowledge outlined by the early Schelling in *On University Studies*, where Schelling links history to the "science of right or jurisprudence," describing its goal as a "world order based on law" and the state as "the external organism of a freely achieved harmony between necessity and freedom" (79, 104). But, in fact, the Hegelian dialectic is only seemingly progressive. In *The Philosophy of History*, all world-historical cultures, and not just world history itself, are said to have three periods (281). These often end in dissolution rather than resolution, producing micro-dialectics at odds with the larger dialectic. Thus, in the classical phase, Greek culture dissolves when it comes into contact with Rome: then they can do "nothing but despair of the state of affairs" and "retreat into Philosophy" (277)—a curious comment on Hegel's own melancholy turn to philosophy and away from art at the end of the *Aesthetics*. And in Rome the third period is characterized by "internal distraction" because Roman power "is profoundly ruptured within itself" (288), disclosing an "internal contradiction" already present in the second period in the aridity of the Roman state form (311–12).

But perhaps the dissolution of preceding cultures is dialectically necessary for the emergence of the final stage of *The Philosophy of History*. Yet history has no more reached a resolution in Germany or in Fukuyama's America than has philosophy in *The History of Philosophy*. In fact, the four (rather than three) stages in *The Philosophy of History* could equally well be seen as separate epistemes, marked by what Foucault calls an absolute "discontinuity" and "rupture" (Foucault 217). Each episteme would then be worked through and unworked, such that history would "begin again from the beginning," as Hegel complains of Schelling, whose work "ever pressed on to seek a new form" (Hegel, *History of Philosophy* 3: 515). Or each idea or event, such as the French Revolution or even the Greek *polis*, could be thought of as a "rotary whole" rather than as a free totality, which is to say that the forces "gather[ed] together" become not a synthesis but a fantasy of wholeness that is an "inherent contradiction" (Schelling, *Ages* [1815] 91). As soon as we feel "the common denomination and the conflict of forces," then we also want to "separate" what has been "gathered together" (91), to deconstruct what has been posited. The driving force in history, then, would be not a world-historical "spirit" but rather a "world-soul": an early idea of Schelling's that acquires a new resonance in the 1815 *Ages* as an always embryonic, turbulent form of spirit endlessly engaged in the rotary labor of the negative.[5] In his lectures *On University Studies*, Schelling had seen the unfolding of history toward "a universal constitution" as the task of art, art being a particular way of imagining history that produces a synthesis of "the given and actual with the ideal" (107). What he outlines in the 1815 *Ages*, going back to the primal traumatic creativity at the origin of the world, is a very different way of imagining history and freedom "symbolically" in Hegel's terms: an imagining of history and freedom that departs from aesthetic ideology.

NOTES

1   Nancy further writes, "An economy of remarks seems to double up the economy of logical discourse: an economy of remarks, that is, a subordinated, detached 'dispersed' economy which does not obey the strict progression of the concept" (48).
2   See Derrida, "The Age of Hegel" (146–47 and, more generally, 138–49); Hegel, "To the Royal Ministry" (153–56). Derrida does recognize a "mobile strategy" (144) in Hegel's dealings with the "state" in the Gymnasium letter and *The Philosophy of Right*, but arguably he does not go far enough in reading Hegel's "strategy." Hegel's postponement of speculative thought to the university—under cover of an opening statement that laments that the university is required to admit even ignorant and uneducated youths and that thus makes the Gymnasium sound more important than the university—aims precisely to preserve a space for speculative thinking in the university, as Kant does in a similarly backhanded way in *The Conflict of Faculties*. Indeed, Hegel excludes the history of philosophy from the Gymnasium not because it is dangerous but because "without presupposing the speculative idea," which cannot be taught since the ministry does not allow philosophy proper to be taught, this history "might well become nothing more than a narrative" (Hegel, "To the Royal Ministry," 150–51, 153).

3   Curiously, this would seem to imply that the "free" art of Greece justified and came after Roman formalism. But, of course, it was Rome that succeeded Greece.

4   I discuss this relation between history and psychoanalysis in Schelling's work further in "'The Abyss of the Past': Psychoanalysis in Schelling's *Ages of the World* (1815)."

5   In the 1815 *Ages*, Schelling describes "soul" as the ideal principle that is not yet spirit and dwells in matter, and that can "come out" only if it is "enveloped and retained by the negating force as by a receptacle" (69, 57–58). Even in the early work, the "world-soul" is a complex notion, and not a conventionally organicist concept. Writing from a Deleuzian perspective, Iain Hamilton Grant distinguishes organicism from the notion of "organization" with which it is associated in Raymond Williams's *Keywords* (227–29). Grant argues that the world-soul "*unconditions the subject of the organization*. In other words, infinitely individuated parts never turn back on themselves to be sealed up into *an* organization, but proliferate unrestrictedly, as the 'positive force' of nature. . . . The World Soul cannot be approached as if it were a body" (132–33).

WORKS CITED

Carroll, David. *Paraesthetics: Foucault, Lyotard, Derrida*. New York and London: Methuen, 1987.

Coleridge, Samuel Taylor. *Lectures 1818–1819: On The History of Philosophy*. Ed. J. R. de J. Jackson. 2 Vols. Princeton: Princeton University Press, 2000.

Derrida, Jacques. "The Age of Hegel." *Who's Afraid of Philosophy: Right to Philosophy 1*. Trans. Jan Plug. Stanford: Stanford University Press, 2002. 117–57.

———. *Points . . . Interviews, 1974–1994*. Ed. Elisabeth Weber. Trans. Peggy Kamuf et al. Stanford: Stanford University Press, 1995.

———. *Rogues: Two Essays on Reason*. Trans. Pascale-Anne Brault and Michael Naas. Stanford: Stanford University Press, 2005.

D'Hondt, Jacques. *Hegel in His Time: Berlin, 1818–1831*. Trans. John Burbidge. Peterborough, ON: Broadview Press, 1988.

Foucault, Michel. *The Order of Things: An Archaeology of the Human Sciences*. New York: Vintage, 1973.

Godwin, William. *Enquiry Concerning Political Justice and its Influence on Morals and Happiness*. Ed. F. E. L. Priestley. 3 Vols. Toronto: University of Toronto Press, 1946.

Grant, Iain Hamilton. "'Philosophy Become Generic:' The Physics of the World Soul." *The New Schelling*. Ed. Judith Norman and Alistair Welchman. New York: Continuum, 2004. 128–50.

Habermas, Jürgen. *Philosophical-Political Profiles*. Trans. Frederick G. Lawrence. Cambridge, MA: MIT Press, 1983.

Hegel, Georg Wilhelm Friedrich. *Aesthetics: Lectures on Fine Art*. 2 vols. Trans. T. M. Knox. Oxford: Clarendon Press, 1975.

———. *Encyclopedia of the Philosophical Sciences in Outline*. Trans. Steven A. Taubeneck. In *Encyclopedia of the Philosophical Sciences in Outline and Critical Writings*. Ed. Ernst Behler. New York: Continuum, 1990. 45–264.

———. *Lectures on the History of Philosophy*. Trans. E. S. Haldane and Frances H. Simson. 3 vols. 1892. Lincoln: University of Nebraska Press, 1995.

———. *The Philosophy of History*. Trans. J. Sibree. New York: Dover, 1956.

———. *The Philosophy of Mind*. Trans. William Wallace and A. V. Miller. Oxford: Clarendon, 1971.

———. *Philosophy of Nature*. Trans. A. V. Miller. Oxford: Clarendon, 1970.

———. "To the Royal Ministry of Spiritual, Academic and Medical Affairs." *Who's Afraid of Philosophy: Right to Philosophy 1*. By Jacques Derrida. Trans. Jan Plug. Stanford: Stanford University Press, 2002. 150–57.

Jaspers, Karl. *Kant*. Trans. Ralph Manheim. New York: Harcourt, Brace & World, 1957.

Kant, Immanuel. *The Conflict of the Faculties*. Trans. Mary J. Gregor. Lincoln: University of Nebraska Press, 1992.

———. *Critique of Judgment*. Trans. J. H. Bernard. New York: Hafner Publishing Company, 1974.

Marquard, Odo. "Several Connections Between Aesthetics and Therapeutics in Nineteenth-Century Philosophy." *The New Schelling*. Ed. Judith Norman and Alistair Welchman. New York: Continuum, 2004. 13–29.

Nancy, Jean-Luc. *The Speculative Remark (One of Hegel's Bons Mots)*. Trans. Céline Surprenant. Stanford: Stanford University Press, 2001.

"The Oldest Systematic Program of German Idealism." Trans. Diana Behler. *Philosophy of German Idealism*. Ed. Ernst Behler. New York: Continuum, 1987. 161–63.

Rajan, Tilottama. "'The Abyss of the Past': Psychoanalysis in Schelling's *Ages of the World* (1815)." "Romantic Psyche and Psychoanalysis." Ed. Joel Faflak. *Romantic Circles Praxis*. Dec. 2008. http://www.rc.umd.edu/praxis/psychoanalysis/index.html.

———. "How (Not) To Speak Properly: Writing 'German' Philosophy in Hegel's *Aesthetics* and *History of Philosophy*." *Clio* 33.2 (2004): 119–42.

———. "Toward a Cultural Idealism: Negativity and Freedom in Hegel and Kant." *Idealism Without Absolutes: Philosophy and Romantic Culture*. Ed. Tilottama Rajan and Arkady Plotnitsky. Albany: SUNY Press, 2004. 51–72.

Redfield, Marc. *The Politics of Aesthetics: Nationalism, Gender, Romanticism*. Stanford: Stanford University Press, 2003.

Schelling, Friedrich Wilhelm Joseph von. *Ages of the World* (1813). Trans. Judith Norman. Ed. Slavoj Žižek and F.W.J. Schelling. *The Abyss of Freedom/Ages of the World*. Ann Arbor: University of Michigan Press, 1997. 105–82.

———. *Ages of the World* (1815). Trans. Jason M. Wirth. Albany: SUNY Press, 2000.

———. *Ideas for a Philosophy of Nature* (1797/1803). Trans. Errol E. Harris and Peter Heath. Cambridge: Cambridge University Press, 1988.

———. *On University Studies*. Trans. E. S. Morgan. Athens: University of Ohio Press, 1966.

———. *Philosophical Investigations into the Essence of Human Freedom and Related Matters*. Trans. Priscilla Hayden-Roy. *Philosophy of German Idealism*. Ed. Ernst Behler. New York: Continuum, 1987. 217–84.

———. *Stuttgart Seminars. Idealism and the Endgame of Theory: Three Essays.* Ed. and trans. Thomas Pfau. Albany: SUNY Press, 1994. 195–268.

———. *System of Transcendental Idealism.* Trans. Peter Heath. Charlottesville: University Press of Virginia, 1978.

Schmitt, Carl. *Political Romanticism.* Trans. Guy Oakes. Cambridge, MA: MIT Press, 1986.

Williams, Raymond. *Keywords.* London: Fontana, 1976.

10

From Art to History

SCHELLING'S MODERN MYTHOLOGY
AND THE COMING COMMUNITY

Richard Block

I N an odd but telling letter written to Goethe from Jena in March 1801, Schiller recounts a recent conversation with Schelling in which Schiller challenges Schelling's deduction of the art work in the *System of Transcendental Idealism*. At issue is Schelling's assertion that production of the artwork begins with consciousness and ends without consciousness (*Schillers Briefe* 400). On the one hand, Schiller's objection may result from Schelling's rather overt inversion of the former's formulation, most notably in his *Aesthetic Letters*, to render the beautiful sublime.[1] On the other hand, what might have baffled Schiller was not the inversion itself, but the very shift in Schelling's thought that such an inversion anticipated. Although Schelling asserts that the philosophy of art is "the universal organon of philosophy" and the "keystone of its entire arch" (§349),[2] the product deduced in the final version has an uncertain, almost ambiguous status. In the final version, a series of largely ignored but wholly consistent footnotes reflects a set of revisions that in turn lend the entire text a startling new emphasis. In several instances where Schelling had indicated resolution of the absolute contradiction between conscious and unconscious activities, those passages are either eliminated or replaced by ones that posit the non-sublatibility of that supreme contradiction. The task that Schelling had assigned transcendental philosophy at the outset was to demonstrate absolute identity of the self and nature, and the system could be regarded as complete only "if it revert[ed] back to its own principle" (§629). But in tracing the genesis and history of the self, Schelling no longer seems to have found it possible to revert to that first principle of absolute identity from which the self ostensibly originated. What has been taken apart or severed through consciousness is curiously different upon reassembly. More than leaving the system closed or incomplete, the changed character of the art product signals the abandonment of system for process and history, and thus anticipates the new or modern mythology of *The Philosophy of Art*. Since the mythology of the Greeks cannot be recaptured, what is now called upon to replace it is a new mythology emerging in the "future destinies of the world" and through the collective history of the people acting as "one Poet" (§629). The "dark and powerful idea of totality," which Schiller in the same letter claimed Schelling had discounted, now assumes mythological proportions, determining the form, if not the content, of history.

In this essay the dimensions of that apparent shift in the status of the art product will be assessed. Initial attention will focus on retracing the procedures of transcendental idealism that lead to the deduction of the art product. Discussion will then move to the significance of the footnotes and the startling character of Schelling's revisions. I will then return to a discussion of Schelling's concept of history as presented in the *System* and link it to his call for a new mythology as outlined four years later in the *Philosophy of Art*. The essay will conclude by examining how the changed status of the artwork, offering only an *Abglanz*, or something that reflects (upon) an absence, forms the basis for a community of exiles. Since the philosophy of art serves as the "keystone" of the entire *System of Transcendental Idealism*, Heidegger's so-called thinking dialogue with Hölderlin's poetry will serve as an analogue for understanding the fragile character of this community.

At the outset of the *System*, Schelling states the fundamental task of transcendental idealism: to demonstrate that things outside us in nature exist only by virtue of their identity with the proposition "I exist" (§345). To do so, he shifts into the transcendental mode of apprehension; that is, the transcendental philosopher brings to consciousness what otherwise escapes it: the acts and epochs of self-positing. Transcendental idealism thus begins with what Schelling calls the free imitation of the absolute act of self-positing. Through interruption of the self's evolution, the philosopher projects herself/himself back to the starting point and originates a new series of free acts. "Now philosophical talent does not in fact consist merely in the capacity for freely repeating the series of original acts; it lies chiefly in again becoming aware, in the course of this free repetition, of the original necessity of those acts" (§398). Moreover, what the self strives to bring forward—or what the transcendental philosopher seeks to recover for consciousness—is the identity of self and object, of conscious and unconscious activities.[3]

To begin, the most basic of questions must be posed: what self is the self seeking? The self of empirical consciousness arises as the self attempts to know itself. Having initiated that attempt, the absolute self cannot remain absolute, rather it becomes an intelligence. To arrive at an intuition of itself through the products of its own actions, the self must separate itself from those products. The act whereby the self separates itself from its actions is the transcendental abstraction, and with it arises the concept. Here, Schelling introduces the term "judgment" (*Urteil*; §507) and thereby indicates that what was initially joined is now separated. The condition for judgment is the transcendental abstraction. As intelligence, the subject now becomes aware of an objective manifold, unaware that it is responsible for that manifold. How presentations of objects conform or accommodate the self's concepts is evident in that initially they were one and the same. What is not so evident is the origination of the object; what constitutes the capacity for its production?

Initially, the self must have a notion of being or of substance, an ability to distinguish between what it sees now and what came before. The self must also prepare for the object to stand before it. This presupposes a boundary, a distinction between inner and outer. This boundary is that line at which the self, attempting to push beyond, is contained or pushed back. The feeling of being driven back to a stage to which the self cannot in reality return is the feeling of the present. The boundary as object, as something standing opposed to the self, is the negation, in Schelling's terms, of all intensity; it becomes extensity into space: "Then the self cannot oppose the object to itself without inner and outer intuition not only separating themselves but also becoming, as such, objects" (§516). The transcendental schema, as such, becomes the intermediary between inner and outer sense, which at root is time. Time is not merely inner sense, but a magnitude extended in one direction. The self, in other words, is "activated time," and time is "coeval with being" (Roberts 133).

Still unclear is how after the arrival of consciousness, after the transcendental abstraction, this separation can be overcome in the practical sphere—or how the transcendental schema itself can become an object. The answer is: by willing. In willing, there arises an opposition within freedom or between finitude and infinitude, the latter arising by virtue of the compulsion to direct the will upon an external object. Oscillating between finitude and infinitude is the imagination; and what it produces are ideas (§558). The idea produced in willing is unconditioned by anything empirical, and thus its content is infinite. But insofar as its form is concerned, it is finite. The mediating link, that which joins the idea to a determinant object, is the ideal, "which is for acting precisely what in thinking . . . the schema is for the concepts" (§558). In its striving or willing, the self translates a representative of the object as it should be into an ideal, but the ideal, attempting to realize the infinite dimensions of the idea within finite dimensions, never fully completes its task: "The idea itself, which . . . becomes infinite again in reflecting upon the action, can be realized only in a progression ad infinitum" (§526). Once again, time is the actualizing link. The progressive realization of the idea presupposes succession or time. Freedom, likewise, in its infinite pursuit of realizing itself, is the mediation between present and future. Apparent at this point in the *System* is that what the self strives to bring forward in alteration of the object through idealization and realization of the ideas is nothing other than consciousness of an original identity. But the self, as activated time, is always ahead of itself, extended by necessity along a line of temporality concomitant with its infinite producing. With the first act of self-consciousness, absolute identity is severed; the self is divided against itself along an axis of time, standing in ecstatic relation to itself and destined to intuit itself in a productive activity always temporally beyond it. What is also apparent is that without the feeling of an independent external world there exists no consciousness of finitude and thus no possibility of bringing forth the infinite through finitude. Practical philosophy (freedom) requires this separation or the presence of an objective world to act against. What is now required for the transcendental philosopher is a third activity (the first being the positing of the world, the second, consciousness of that positing in practical philosophy), one that shows the absolute identity of these two activities; that is, not only the form of the object's genesis but also its actual genesis must be brought to consciousness. And this activity, which is none other than the production of the artwork, must occur after nature or the objective world has arisen for consciousness. This activity does not seek the mimesis of an object but rather the mimesis of the free repetition of the self's positing. What the artwork need demonstrate is the "identity of the conscious and unconscious in the self, and consciousness of this identity" (§611).

THE ART OF FORGETTING

Towards the end of the *System* Schelling appears to have demonstrated that identity:

> The ultimate ground of all harmony between subjective and objective could be exhibited in its original identity only through intellectual intuition; and it is precisely this ground, [that], by means of the work of art, has been brought forth entirely from the subjective and rendered wholly objective, in such wise, that we have gradually led our object, the self itself, up to the very point where we ourselves were standing when we began to philosophize. (§629)

He goes on to assert that if this point in production is reached, history ends. Time comes to a standstill, which, paradoxically, would be the end of the self. Its realization would be its death. "It must be impossible for the producer to go on producing, for the condition of all producing is precisely the opposition between conscious and unconscious activity, but here they have absolutely to coincide, and thus within the intelligence all conflict has to be eliminated, all contradiction reconciled" (§614). In his revisions, Schelling strikes that entire paragraph. A few pages later he makes a similar revision in which elimination of that conflict is replaced by recognition of its coincidence in the art product (§622). Still a few pages later Schelling once again makes a critical revision, striking the words "wholly resolved" from the text. And upon finally identifying and explicating that productive power by which the object arises, the transcendental imagination, the word "capacity" becomes the preferred word for what was previously described as a primary potentiality of the poetic self.

Earlier in the *System* Schelling had remarked that self-consciousness was the lamp of the whole system of knowledge, but it cast its light ahead, not behind (§317). Thus, the original act of self-positing, in which the self assumed a dual nature toward itself, in which it was both productive and intuiting, cannot appear in empirical consciousness. What these revisions and deletions begin to suggest is how completely inaccessible that original identity might have been. If we can bring forward no product to exhibit that identity, it remains mere postulate. The philosopher's stone is attempting to recapture for consciousness something that has been (and continues to be) forgotten. Its mythical character derives from the fact that the original unity occurred, if at all, before time.[4] Art is now asked to return the lost relationship between the self and nature by reminding the self of its identity with nature in a transcendental past. It is essentially anamnestic and anticipates the call for a new mythology, since it is mythology that "brings nature back to us in art" (Schelling, *Philosophy of Art* §51).

According to Schelling, the art product begins with an infinite contraction and ends with an infinite finitely displayed (*System of Transcendental Idealism* §619–20). While the product begins in freedom, which necessitates separation of the activities for the possibility of freedom, something unexpected or beyond the conscious intentions of the artist comes into play. This unknown element, which can "never attain to consciousness" (§614), is for the artist what destiny is for the agent. Schelling calls this irresistible urge, this agent of involuntary activity that drives the artist to production, genius. As something that never arrives at consciousness, the urge is tied to that element of necessity attributed to the unconscious. We have thus arrived at the core question of the entire system: if artistic production is involuntary and freedom is voluntary, how are the two reconciled? Schelling emphasizes that the contradiction initiating artistic production is one that strikes at the ultimate core of the artist, and the experience of a contradiction at the core of the artist can only mean the absence of identity. It is thus experience of no identity that engenders an irresistible urge to create it. The artist is driven to remember or recreate an identity, which may never really have ever been, which at the core of her being is revealed as absent: "and the marvel which, had it existed but once only, would necessarily have convinced us of the absolute reality of that event" (§617). Thus, one should not be distracted by the previous assertion: "It is as if in the artist that unalterable identity on which all existence is founded had laid aside the veil wherewith it shrouds itself in others, and just as it is directly affected by things, so it also works upon everything" (§614). Here he is not asserting that an absolute identity is revealed. What is unveiled once the shroud is lifted is the absence of identity and the necessity to conceal that absence by attempting to produce it.[5] What prompts Schelling to characterize the artist as exceptional is the latter's keen recognition of the supreme contradiction at the root of existence (§617). The value to the philosopher is that it reveals the infinite contradiction in a single object instead of in the whole of nature. Through a second intellectual intuition the philosopher witnesses the condition of consciousness, which the first such intuition lacked and which the entirety of nature, lacking some form of limitation, cannot render. The significance of limitation, of an infinite finitely displayed, becomes transparent upon consideration of the artwork, or more specifically, of the sublime and the beautiful.

Once again, Schelling's revisions indicate an important shift. Initially, Schelling argues that the difference between the two lies in the object. In the beautiful, the infinite contradiction is eliminated in the object itself; in the sublime the contradiction is still present in the object and eliminated only in an intuition of that object (§622). In the revision, Schelling writes: "For although sublimity is customarily contrasted with beauty, there is actually no true objective opposition between beauty and sublimity; the truly and absolutely beautiful is invariably also sublime, and the sublime (if it truly is so) is beautiful as well" (§622). A comparison of this passage with a similar one in Schelling's *The Philosophy of Art* is instructive. Initially, Schelling contrasts the two: "sublimity is the informing of the infinite into the finite and beauty the informing of the finite into the infinite" (*Philosophy of Art* §90). In the next paragraph, that relationship is clarified: "there is no sphere in which something can be called beautiful that in a different situation might not also be sublime, and for this reason both qualities appear inextricably interwoven" (§91). In other words, one cannot be thought of without the other. The sublime is the infinite finitely expressed in something real, whose basic characteristic is beauty. The sublime is thus not merely an infinite. On the contrary, it is an infinite contradiction between our finite powers of apprehension and the boundlessness of that which presents itself. It is the supreme contradiction that arises with the birth of consciousness.

Without the limitation that grants the sublime the character of beauty, the sublime is merely "monstrous or adventurous" (§90); that is, not sublime. Although Schelling defines the character of beauty in the *System* as one of "supreme calm and grandeur," of infinite tranquility deriving from the expression of an infinite contradiction (*System of Transcendental Idealism* §620), it is the expression itself, its momentary containment or limitation, that triggers the emotion.

Seen in another light, Schelling is grappling with his own equivalent of the thing-in-itself. Consciousness of the absolute identity of freedom and necessity, its expression in the artwork, would signal apprehension of the self itself, which is visible only in the object or in nature. Such an expression would signal apprehension of the thing-in-itself, or the self as self-consciousness; the system of transcendental idealism would be closed. The sublime, in the form of the beautiful, however, offers only an "Ab-" of the thing-in-itself. The system is open-ended, wherein the sublime becomes the eventual and privileged expression of a progressive series of contradictions, which assume their darkest and most original form in genius. The contradiction constitutive of genius is the absence of identity and the necessity of making conscious an unconscious or absent identity. This announces an ontological reversal, whereby the *Abglanz* (deflection), or what Schelling calls a *Widerschein* (reflection), is prior to an identity it apparently reflects (§351).[6] As the self moves out ahead of itself in time and thus loses or forgets itself, the necessity of catching up with itself is always frustrated. "In seeking itself, it flees from itself" (§628), sending the spirit on a boundless odyssey. And in the spirit's marvelous delusion of seeking, under the "permanent restrictions" of nature, what could exist only within, the self turns to history and the possibility of a new race, a new mythology, and a new age (§629).

A COMING COMMUNITY

In his preface to the *Phenomenology of Mind,* Hegel offers his oft-quoted critique of Schelling: "to give out its Absolute as the night in which, as we say, all cows are black; that is the very naiveté of emptiness and knowledge" (79). Hegel considers Schelling's intellectual intuition, even if it combines within itself the being of substance, "inert and abstract." In contrast to the organized whole of determinate knowledge, Hegel accuses Schelling of expounding reality in "an unreal manner" (80). In one respect, Hegel is completely correct. The intellectual intuition, which is the postulate behind the entire system, "cannot be demonstrated but only demanded" (Schelling, *System of Transcendental Idealism* §370). "It enacts itself prior to and beyond the reach of cognitive awareness; it is largely, in fact unconscious" (Vater xxviii). But if for Hegel, philosophy, like the owl of Minerva, spreads its wings only at dusk, Schelling's system opens up onto the future. The elusiveness of actualizing the intellectual intuition, its presence as mere *Abglanz*, is supplemented by a more complete, and potentially total, substantive expression in history—or what can only be called a mytho-poetic history.[7]

Not surprisingly, this call for a mytho-poetic history corresponds in critical ways to the model of tragedy Schelling presents in *The Philosophy of Art*, whereby the essence of tragedy is the "actual and objective conflict between freedom of the subject, on the one hand, and necessity on the other" (§251). The protagonist expresses his freedom only insofar as he wrestles with fate, but inevitably he succumbs to fate since necessity is irresistible. The sublimity of tragedy lies in the protagonist voluntarily bearing punishment for her or his "unavoidable" transgression in order to "manifest [her or his] freedom precisely in the loss of that very same freedom, and to perish amid a declaration of free will" (§254). The conflict at the heart of tragedy echoes the one that constitutes genius. While the genius or agent begins his activity with consciousness and freedom, he is soon given over to an irrepressible urge that signals the loss of such freedom. This "incomprehensible agent," which works "in opposition to freedom," endows the product of the activity with an objectivity "as if by no help of the agent's own"; "just as the man of destiny does not execute what he wishes or intends" (*System of Transcendental Idealism* §68). Something beyond the conscious intentions of the agent results from his actions. Like the protagonist, genius wrestles with fate, undertaking to re-present or recreate something that the agent cannot locate within himself or that the self can re-present to itself as having been, even once. Fate, as in tragedy, necessarily triumphs, handed over to a project that must necessarily fail. After all, the resolution of the supreme contradiction is unattainable; the agent perishes amid a declaration of free will, freely delivering himself to fate: "That this guiltless guilty person accept punishment voluntarily—this is the sublimity of tragedy; thereby alone does freedom transfigure itself into the highest identity with necessity" (*Philosophy of Art* §132). For genius, sublimity is expressed in the "deep emotion" (*ein Ruehrendes*) that accompanies completion—an obvious echo of the emotion Kant assigned to apprehension of the sublime after an initial instance of displeasure. The notion of necessity translated into a historical context thus extends beyond individual consciousness and becomes the dark, rather unfathomable character—the black cow—of modernity's destiny. The motor of history is the tragic or the successive attempts to realize the unrealizable. Now it is left to the species, acting as one poet, to return the "individual streams of a severed consciousness back to the universal ocean of poetry" (*System of Transcendental Idealism* §629). It is no longer individual genius that is handed over to a tragic fate, but the species as a whole. In fact, it is the common pursuit of that ideal, "whose everlasting sun conceals itself behind its own unclouded light" (§599), that constitutes the species as a species in the first place. As the "invisible root of which all intelligences are but powers" (§599), the ideal in its absence becomes the very condition of consciousness. Seen in this light, freedom is not merely a ruse, whose expression inevitably hands it over to necessity. Rather, freedom becomes the exercise of a consciousness out of which the species acting as one—shall we call this a nation?—embarks on a shared odyssey of the spirit.

Such a nation can be understood only as having lost its way. Or, there is no way back, since the ideal after which the species searches freely to realize was always only absent. The nation, if I may persist in using this term, is always displaced, about to be realized in the free expression of its people as it seeks out the "universal ocean of poetry," only necessarily to be barred from that realization. The shared ground of the species is an absent one. The heroes of the nation are tragic insofar as they forfeit a homeland. They do not bask in the sun; they bask in what I have called its *Abglanz*. Only if what they seek in their odyssey turns away, refuses their appropriation, and leaves them at least somewhat in the dark, can they exist as a people or species. In other words, this mobility founds a community that can never be settled, whose membership is always in flux. It is, as Avital Ronnel remarks in another context, a non-hegemonic mode of connectedness whose ways of coming together are possible only in their undoing.[8] And since this nation is without a fixed place, insofar as the self that grounds the community always supplements sameness with self-produced difference, there is no territory that is not immediately de-territorialized. The nation is realized only in exile, or in a diaspora.

I would now like to recast the terms of my argument by briefly remarking on Heidegger's thinking dialogue with Hölderlin's poetry, specifically on one of the early verses of "Andenken" and Heidegger's attempt to greet the poet, who since Plato's *Republic* has been in exile. Poetry is philosophy's other, and the manner in which they speak or greet each other mirrors in some fashion thinking in exile from itself.[9] I will therefore speak to the tensional holding together and coming apart of these two modalities of the (thinking) self as a reflection, albeit an imperfect one, of Schelling's dirempted self that signals the foundation of a community that resists appropriation of alterity, for every community confirms its associations with some form of greeting.

Already, the fifth verse of Hölderlin's poem reads: "Geh aber nun und grüße" ("But go now and greet"; Hölderlin 2: 196). The greeting is an embarking upon an odyssey to greet what is remembered only as having been on foreign shores. It can be approached but never arrived at, suggesting that the greeting will never be eye to eye. In nearing and distancing itself from its remembered origin, the one who greets comes to himself only by allowing the greeted to approach by virtue of the greeting but also by allowing the greeted one to remain afar, ungraspable in its alterity. Then how does one greet that which has already disappeared or been forgotten, one that in Schelling's terms has been rendered unconscious? The greeting becomes less a means to recover what was lost—how does one recover an originary absence?—and serves more to confirm and insist upon distance and difference as an occasion for greeting and celebrating community. The diffusional character of a greeting that leaves one behind pronounces a farewell in the very moment it would welcome the one greeted. Schelling's species, acting as one poet, is now already two. Moreover, the question that haunts Hölderlin's poem, "Wo aber sind die Freunde" ("But where are the friends"; 2: 196) confirms that the greeting, founded upon a going-away, establishes a community that is always taking leave of itself. There are no friends, or there are friends only insofar as they greet each other as permanent strangers, in eternal anticipation of being greeted in return. Friendship is possible only as the self posits itself and sends itself into exile. In other words, *das Urteil*, or the judgment that announces self-estrangement and the fragmentation of consciousness, disavows friendship only to discover its possibility in otherness. It is the impossible possibility inherent in the act of self-positing. Stated otherwise, the poetic word, the greeting, hovers as it anticipates a response that will never come, establishing in its exile a site, always in transition, for a coming community that issues from an irretrievable past.

The promise of Schelling's mytho-poetic community is thus refused the moment it is proffered. But its fate is less certain once the promise is understood in terms of the politics of friendship as they emerge in the eighteenth century.[10] That is to say, there is every reason to suspect that the nationalism that subtends Hölderlin's poetry is not only related to the phratocentrism of the French Revolution but issues just as conveniently from the self's preoccupation with itself or from German Romantic Idealism.[11] The temptation for the self to found such a self-enclosed or self-affirming community is what leads Schelling to conceive of a second intellectual intuition whereby a self-same unity could be imagined (Schelling, *System of Transcendental Idealism* §624–25); there can be no system if the origin cannot be reproduced for consciousness (§628–29). But fundamental to any system is the potential, if not the capacity, to sublate all heteronomy under, for example, the shibboleth of a universal humanity. Every distance, any extensivity that by virtue of its origin in time frustrates restoration of an original unity is, nonetheless, calculated and calculable. A symmetrical, reciprocal association of egos becomes the ground of what was to have been a community of exiles. The mere positing of an original unity, despite its absence, manages thereby in absentia to lord over a community of dispossessed selves. If, as Derrida insists, a non-phratocentric community must think of relationality through an interruption of sameness in which interval sisters and mothers would be greeted, then any promise or anticipation of self-recognition by virtue of the greeting must be doomed (232–34).[12]

Even Hölderlin's poem, not to mention Heidegger's lecture on it, acknowledges the threat. "Der Nordost wehet / Der liebste unter den Winden / Mir" ("The northeasterly wind blows in / Among the winds my favorite"; 2: 196). The wind that sustains the self's odyssey is potentially always only for the self. How then does the wind not carry the self to distant shores? How does the northeasterly wind not serve to refashion those shores in the self's image and thus colonize them? How, stated otherwise, does that wind prevent a philosophical appropriation of the distant shores upon which alterity is to appear in its poetic splendor? Schelling's *System* requires the poetic word, as references to an odyssey of the spirit or the "holy of holies" indicates. Heidegger, no less so. That which would greet the other has already, if we read with Hölderlin, named that other as "me."

Yet such recognition prompts Hölderlin, at least, to ask, "Wo aber sind die Freunde" ("But where are the friends"), as if the greeting of oneself as friend only confirmed the assertion attributed to Aristotle: "O my friends, there is no friend."[13] To be temporally displaced from oneself comes to dissolve friendship the moment the friend is recognized. The moment recognition violates the very dissymmetry that allowed the greeted one to appear in its poetic splendor, there can be no talk of friends. The self, abandoned at the origins, betrays the friend by positing the friend as a condition of the self. However erratic the odyssey of the self, it cannot escape self-recognition, being called back to the origin or its home. But, if we take Hölderlin's question seriously, then turning toward the self to find in that alienated self a friend means that there are no friends, which may be the only way to speak of friends or to greet friends. That is to say, betrayal is turned back upon itself or betrays itself; the friend is denied.

The more precise mechanism of this double betrayal is evident in Heidegger's reading of the brown women who appear on holidays in Hölderlin's poem ("Am Feiertage gehen / Die braunen Frauen daselbst / Auf seidem Boden" ("On holidays / Brown women walk / The silky ground"; 2: 197; see Heidegger, *Erläuterungen zu Hölderlins Dichtung* 65–67). The significance of a racial and gendered other prompts Heidegger to stall, as Avital Ronell notes, and turn to a more generic discussion of the essence of the holiday (Ronell 24–26). He is stalling not simply because the discussion of holidays forestalls any discussion of dark-skinned women, but also because it turns back the clock to commemorate what Heidegger claims is the ground and essence of history, the festival (Heidegger, *Erläuterungen* 75–77; Ronell 27–28). This digression can only be described as a form of stuttering. Thinking's invitation to poetry finds an emblem of absolute otherness, the brown women, and changes registers. Disoriented, Heidegger tries to reclaim the high ground by denouncing academic readings of poetry as "questionable" and "shameful." Particularly offensive is "operating with passages," which operating is hardly absent in Heidegger's readings (Heidegger, *Hölderlins Hymne "Andenken"* 661).[14] The odyssey of the self sets off on a search for its alienated self that takes it to shores where brown women celebrate the holidays. That stunning discovery forces the self, or in this case, Heidegger, to turn back on himself. He calls himself out. Could it be that the greeting as well as the friendship and the community it grounds can be affirmed only by a stutter? Ronell notes that in other published and edited versions of Heidegger's commentary the paragraphs "inspired by and surrounding the brown women disappear" (Ronell 31).[15] The greeting becomes a gesture of self-erasure, which implicates the one greeting, not the least because the latter is the alienated self of the one erased. Seen in this context, Schelling's attempt to recapture the originary moment of the self's unity through philosophical analysis of the artwork is the equivalent of the philosopher seeking to greet the poet by stuttering. The originary moment is available only as an interruption. And just as time is stalled on a holiday, the greeting that announces the holiday starts.

If this chiasmus between selves in Schelling and the poet (Hölderlin) and the thinker (Heidegger) threatens the poet's voice by subsuming it under the thinker's, it is not merely because of the omnipresence of the "me" or "mir" noted above, but because Hölderlin's voice is equally halting. The reference to "brown women" is nothing if not a platitude, a prosaic interruption, whose alienating and unpoetic quality, according to Heidegger, is common to many of Hölderlin's poems at the time. The poetic word thus loses its character, which is to say it loses itself.[16] The greeting that signals or founds a coming community displaces itself as it greets, which is the only way to greet one that *is* by virtue of an originary displacement or diremption.[17] The loss of self greeted by or through the loss of the philosopher's and the poet's voices means that any friendship between the two celebrates the occasion to commemorate the loss of any possibility of selfhood. Taking leave occasions the greeting.

Schelling's rather poetic language demonstrates just how fragile such a community is, for it depends upon averting the glance, an *Abglanz*, or never looking the friend in the eyes.[18] While the text—especially if we ignore the footnotes and revisions—appears to valorize an underlying unity between nature and self or nature as alienated self (*System of Transcendental Idealism* §615–16), the artwork that is to confirm the unity is nothing but a semblance or *Abglanz* of that unity. And since Schelling identifies nature with poetry, it is the thinking self that would be affirmed by nature. But the artwork essences, to use a Heidegerrian word, as a radiating against (*widerstrahlen*). It can be beheld only by or as *Abglanz*. More precisely, by misty eyes:

> What we speak of as nature is a poem. . . . Yet the riddle [of the poem] could reveal itself, were we to recognize in it the odyssey of the spirit, which, marvelously deluded, seeks itself, and in seeking flees from itself; for through the world of sense there glimmers, as if through

words the meaning, as if through dissolving mists the land of fantasy, of which we are in search. (Schelling, *System of Transcendental Idealism* §628–29)

Only the mist—tears, perhaps, of a commemorative mourning—preserves the poetry that is nature, preserves the interstitial space of friendship. But this is a peculiar poetry, not only because it is the artwork or organon of the entire system, but also because it is a poetry whose meaning is withheld and whose vision is impaired. That is to say, a poetry of friendship.

NOTES

1   See Jähnig (2: 231–40) for a more thorough discussion of these differences.
2   All references to Schelling's *System of Transcendental Idealism* and his *Philosophy of Art* are cited by paragraph numbers, rather than pages, so as to facilitate cross-referencing between the original German and the published English translations, whose wording I follow.
3   Schelling undertakes the project as a means to systematize Fichte's thinking and to complete Kant's three critiques. See in this regard Vater's Introduction (xii–xiv). In the process, Schelling claims later (*Towards a History of Recent Philosophy*) to have come to his own method under the "cloak of Fichtean" thought (*Sämtliche Werke* 10: 96). The *System* thus anticipates his break with Fichte in 1806 but also suggests that this early work may form a bridge with his later work. One of the few to recognize and analyze this break is Findler.
4   Both Krell and Žižek have much to save about a non-recoverable past or pre-history in relation to Schelling's *Stages of Man*. Such a pre-history is already adumbrated in the *System* and accounts for Schelling's assertion, noted above, that during work on this project he discovered not only his own method but a key element of his thought. I share Žižek's attempt to appropriate Schelling's unconscious for political purpose.
5   As Jähnig writes, "Der Schematismus muss als solches bewusst gemacht werden" (The schematism, as such, must be made conscious; 2: 299).
6   My reasons for using the German *Abglanz* as a term to unite Schelling's various uses of reflection or, for example, of *Widerschein* and *widerstrahlen*, will become apparent below. Justification is amply provided throughout all the essays in the volume *Schelling: Zwischen Fichte und Hegel*, edited by Christoph Asmuth et al. See in particular Werner (671).
7   See Haynes for a clear discussion of the evolution of Schelling's notion of history.
8   Much of what follows relies on Ronell's dazzling reading of Heidegger's reading of Hölderlin's poem "Andenken."

9 See Ronell (17–19) for the political implications of such a greeting between modes of thinking. For the manner in which this reading differs from other Heidegger readings of Hölderlin, see Fynsk.

10 To speak of a politics of friendship is not merely to recall Derrida's work of the same title, but also the manner in which friendship was a very real pedagogical and state issue. See Munzel for the relationships between Kant, pedagogy, and the interests of the state.

11 Fichte's *Reden an die deutsche Nation* (Speeches to the German nation, 1808) indicates what is at stake in frustrating the very systemization of thought that was the initial aim of the *System of Transcendental Idealism*. If the *System* were to confirm the origin of things outside the self in the self, it would lead, as it does in these addresses, to an organic, folkish understanding of the community or nation. The (failed) deduction of the art product signals a break not only from Fichte but a betrayal of incipient nationalism.

12 For a discussion of Derrida's understanding of friendship in the context of Kant, see Fenves (141–44).

13 See Derrida (1–48) for the difficulty of confidently attributing the quote to Aristotle.

14 See note 15 below about certain passages being eliminated from certain versions. Thus, among other reasons, both versions have become the focus of commentary, for example by Ronell.

15 As Ronell writes, "However, even in the most whited-out pages that remain, the exegetical language hems and haws, showing signs of alternating anxiety and indifference" (31, note 8).

16 Heidegger is particularly struck by the use of "daselbst" (*Erläuterungen* 81).

17 "Coming community" cannot be invoked without recalling Agamben's book of the same name. The shared concerns are obvious: a belonging that occurs through language but eschews identity and universality. Thus, Heidegger's thinking dialogue with Hölderlin is potentially, but only potentially, exemplary.

18 For the manner in which Kant insists as well on such an asymmetry in friendship, see Derrida's discussion of Kant's "Doctrine of Virtue" (253–67), in which Kant insists that friendship is both an attraction and a repulsion that requires that the parties not become too familiar with each other. A more radical formulation of friendship, and one that suggests that betrayal, as it is for Schelling, is party to the politics of friendship, is to be found in Kleist and those letters in which he describes Ludwig Brockes as a perfect friend precisely because of his non-selfservingness (*Uneigennützigkeit*). Such a friendship depends on being unreliable lest a calculability threaten the friendship. See Schestag (260–77) for a fuller discussion.

WORKS CITED

Agamben, Giorgio. *The Coming Community*. Trans. Michael Hardt. Minneapolis, London: University of Minnesota Press, 1993.

Asmuth, Christoph, Alfred Deuter, and Michael Vater, eds. *Schelling: Zwischen Fichte und Hegel*. Amsterdam: Grüner, 2000.

Derrida, Jacques. *The Politics of Friendship.* Trans. George C. Collins. London: Verso, 2005.

Fenves, Peter. "Politics of Friendship—Once Again." *Eighteenth-Century Studies* 32 (1998–99): 133–55.

Fichte, Johann Gottlieb. *Reden an die deutsche Nation.* Hamburg: Meiner, 1955.

Findler, Richard. "A Sketch of Schelling's Appropriation of the Kantian Imagination in the *System of Transcendental Idealism*: Schelling's Divergence from Fichte." *Schelling: Zwischen Fichte und Hegel.* Eds. Christoph Asmuth, Alfred Denker, and Michael Vater. Amsterdam: B. R. Gruner, 2001. 41–54.

Fynsk, Christopher. *Heidegger: Thought and Historicity.* Ithaca, NY: Cornell University Press, 1986.

Haynes, Paul. *Reason and Existence: Schelling's Philosophy of History.* Leiden: n. p., 1967.

Hegel, Georg Wilhelm Friedrich. *The Phenomenology of Mind.* Trans. J. B. Baille. London: Allen & Unwin, 1966.

Heidegger, Martin. *Erläuterungen zu Hölderlins Dichtung.* Vol. 4 of *Heidegger Gesamtausgabe.* Ed. Friedrich-Wilhelm von Herrmann. Frankfurt/Main: Klostermann, 1975.

———. *Hölderlin's Hymne "Andenken."* Vol. 52 of *Heidegger Gesamtausgabe.* Ed. Curd Ochwadt. Frankfurt/Main: Klostermann, 1982.

Hölderlin, Friedrich. *Sämtliche Werke: Stuttgarter Ausgabe.* Ed. Friedrich Beisner. 8 vols. Stuttgart: Cotta, 1946–85.

Jähnig, Dieter. *Schelling: Die Kunst in der Philosophie.* 2 vols. Pfullingen: Neske, 1969.

Krell, David Farell. "'Das Vergangene wird gewußt, das Gewußte (aber) wird erzählt': Trauma, Forgetting, and Narrative in F. W. J. Schelling's *Die Weltalter.*" *Typologies of Trauma: Essays on the Limits of Knowledge and Memory.* Eds. L. Belau and P. Ramadanovic. New York: Other, 2007. 3–31.

Munzel, G. Felicitas. "*Menschenfreundschaft*: Friendship and Pedagogy in Kant." *Eighteenth-Century Studies* 32 (1998–99): 247–59.

Roberts, Julian. *German Philosophy: An Introduction.* Atlantic, NJ: Highland, Humanities Press, 1988.

Ronell, Avital. "On the Misery of Theory without Poetry: Heidegger's Reading of Hölderlin's 'Andenken.'" *PMLA* 120 (2005): 16–32.

Schelling, Friedrich Wilhelm Joseph von. *The Philosophy of Art.* Ed. and trans. Douglas W. Stott. Minneapolis: University of Minnesota Press, 1989.

———. *Sämtliche Werke: Münchner Jubiläumsdruck.* Ed. Manfred Schröter. 13 vols. Munich: Beck, 1958.

———. *System des transzendentalen Idealismus.* Ed. Ruth-Eva Schulz. Hamburg: Meiner, 1957.

———. *System of Transcendental Idealism.* Trans. Peter Heath. Charolottesville: University Press of Virginia, 1978.

Schestag, Thomas. "Friend . . . Brockes. Heinrich von Kleist in Letter." Trans. A. Adler. *Eighteenth-Century Studies* 32 (1998–99): 261–77.

Schillers Briefe. Ed. Erwin Streitfeld and Viktor Zmegac. Königstein: Athenäum, 1983.

Schiller, Friedrich. *On the Aesthetic Education of Man in a Series of Letters.* Ed. and trans. Elizabeth M. Wilkinson and L. A. Willoughby. Oxford: Clarendon, 1989.

Vater, Michael. Introduction. *System of Transcendental Idealism.* By F. W. J. Schelling. Trans. Peter Heath. Charolottesville: University Press of Virginia, 1978. i-xxxvi.

Werner, Karl. "Theorien in der deutschen Philosophie des 19. Jahrhunderts." *Österreichische Akademie der Wissenschaften.* Vienna: Österreichische Akademie, 1884. 645–91.

Žižek, Slavoj. *The Indivisible Remainder: An Essay on Schelling.* London: Verso, 1996.

11

"To impose is not to discover"

A ROMANTIC-MODERNIST CONTINUITY IN CONTRADICTION

Christoph Bode

INTRODUCTION

THIS essay is about a continuity between Romantic and Modernist poetry and poetics, a continuity with regard to how both movements conceived of the imagination; which means that, out of the two ways to read the title of our volume, *Inventions of the Imagination*, that is, either as *genitivus subjectivus* or as *genetivus objectivus*, I choose the second one: In which particular way is the imagination thought of? How is it conceived? And—although this brings us close to circularity, and close to the other genitive—how is it imagined? My main focus is on whether the imagination is conceived as producing a new reality that was not there before—in a sort of constructivist way—or whether it is thought to discover a reality that existed before it, irrespective of its being perceived, independent of a subjective imaginative act. In other words: Are the structures that the imagination encounters imposed upon the world or are they found? Are the meanings that we come upon already "there," or do we generate them ourselves?

I believe that both Romantics and Modernists are deeply ambivalent and contradictory about this key question. The dichotomy I see is not rigid, nor is it an aporia in the Kantian sense. But nevertheless it is a fundamentally contradictory stance that these poets take on this question, and, as I will argue, it is significant that they are deeply ambivalent about it. One reason I give away this point as early as possible is that I want to gain time so that we can concentrate on the *specific ways* in which this ambivalence, tension, or contradiction is played out. A second reason is that it is not really one of my main points at all. This essay has only *one* major point, and that is a hypothesis about why there is this continuity in contradiction. For obvious reasons, this point will be made only at the very end.

My essay has two parts: the first is about Romanticism, the second about Modernism. My examples in the first part are William Blake, John Keats, and P. B. Shelley; my witnesses in the second are the American Modernists Robert Frost, H. D. (Hilda Doolittle), and Wallace Stevens.

WILLIAM BLAKE

I should like to begin with one of my favorite passages from Blake, "A Memorable Fancy" from *The Marriage of Heaven and Hell*:

> The prophets Isaiah and Ezekiel dined with me, and I asked them how they dared so roundly to assert. that God spake to them; and whether they did not think at the time, that they would be misunderstood, & so be the cause of imposition.
>
> Isaiah answer'd. I saw no God, nor heard any, in a finite organical perception; but my senses discover'd the infinite in every thing, and as I was then perswaded & remain confirm'd; that the voice of honest indignation is the voice of God, I cared not for consequences but wrote.
>
> Then I asked: does a firm perswasion that a thing is so, make it so? He replied. All poets believe that it does, & in ages of imagination

this form of perswasion removed mountains; but many are not capable of a firm perswasion of anything. (*CP* 186)[1]

This is—is it not?—wonderfully ironic: how can *he* so roundly assert that the prophets Isaiah and Ezekiel dined with him? His firm persuasion is, of course, the only basis for his truth claim. This is, it seems, Blake at his most subjectivist, and there are many more passages in his œuvre that could be cited in support of his apparent conviction that realities are subjectively constructed, and cannot be otherwise: "A fool sees not the same tree that a wise man sees" (*CP* 183). "The hours of folly are measur'd by the clock, but of wisdom: no clock can measure" (*CP* 183). There is, of course, a transition between the poles of folly and wisdom: "If the fool would persist in his folly he would become wise" (*CP* 183)—as there is a world-historical trend against the wisdom of the imagination: "What is now proved was once, only imagined" (*CP* 184). All these are "Proverbs of Hell," and Blake experts will detect a heavy irony in this "only."

It is against this trend that Blake, the visionary artist, sets his visionary art: "The Nature of my Work is Visionary or Imaginative it is an Endeavour to Restore what the Ancients calld the Golden Age. . . . Vision, or Imagination, is a Representation of what Eternally Exists, Really and Unchangeably. . . . This world of Imagination is the World of Eternity; . . . This World of Imagination is Infinite & Eternal" (*PP* 554, 555; the order of these quotes from *A Vision of the Last Judgement* is slightly changed). That is, in Blake the imagination reveals a reality that is eternal, infinite, and unchanging, that has been there since the beginning of time:

> To see a World in a Grain of Sand
> And a Heaven in a Wild Flower
> Hold Infinity in the palm of your hand
> And eternity in an hour. (*Auguries of Innocence*; *CP* 506)

Or, to quote from *There Is No Natural Religion*: "He who sees the infinite in all things sees God" (*CP* 76). This Ulterior Reality is certainly not dependent upon its being imagined or perceived—in "visitations," it is revealed to us.

On the other hand, the different visions that different people have are so characteristic *of them* (as Anselm Feuerbach would later put it, they have formed God in their own image) that it would be hard to argue that simply on account of their being so firmly persuaded of the truth of their visions, these must be true.

> The Vision of Christ that thou doest see
> Is my Visions Greatest Enemy
> Thine has a great hook nose like thine
> Mine has a snub nose like to mine
> Thine is the friend of All Mankind
> Mine speake in parables to the Blind
> Thine loves the same world that mine hates
> Thy heaven doors are my Hell Gates.
> (From the *Notebook* sections on *The Everlasting Gospel*, CP 851)

There is a competition of visions, and each is highly indicative of the visionary's specific "being in the world" (it is hard *not* to be reminded of Karl Marx's famous dictum "Das Sein bestimmt das Bewußtsein" ["Being determines consciousness"]):

> Love seeketh not Itself to please,
> Nor for itself hath any care;
> But for another gives its ease,
> And builds a Heaven in Hells despair.
>
> So sang a little Clod of Clay,
> Trodden with the cattles feet:
> But a Pebble of the brook,
> Warbled out these metres meet.
>
> Love seeketh only Self to please,
> To bind another to its delight;
> Joys in anothers loss of ease,
> And builds a hell in Heavens despite.
> ("The Clod and the Pebble," *CP* 118–19)

Of course, the problem is that of the legitimacy and the authorization of the visionary's or the prophet's speech act: what entitles or empowers me or anyone to speak an eternal truth, to reveal a higher reality in an imaginative act? This is, of course, a general problem of self-legitimizing, self-authorizing foundational discourse, as has been discussed in such an exemplary way by Jacques Derrida in his "Force of Law: The Mystical Foundation of Authority."

How can one counter the charge that this is a merely subjective projection? Evidently, one cannot. The only thing one *can* do is indicate that any rendition of the unconditional in any kind of mediality can only point to its own inadequacy—a gesture commonly known as *romantische Ironie*. We have this right at the beginning of *Songs of Innocence*:

> Piper sit thee down and write
> In a book that all may read—
> So he vanish'd from my sight.
> And I pluck'd a hollow reed. (*CP* 104)

Mediality is tantamount to loss of im-mediacy (that is a pleonasm), which is why visionary art can never transport the vision itself but only an inter-subjective representation of a subjective experience, or of an experience that defies the subject-object dichotomy. By definition, the absolute cannot be represented, and Blake knows this. Blake's art is highly media-conscious, and, contrary to his firmly held beliefs, it is an art that continually signals an awareness of its own limitations and systematic inadequacy (systematic, because this inadequancy is a general condition and not due to a personal failing).

The same can be said about Blake's epic attempts at narrating what cannot be narrated, such as the beginning of all, in *The Book of Urizen*, *The Book of Los*, and *Europe*:

> Times on times he divided, & measur'd
> Space by space in his ninefold darkness
> Unseen, unknown. (*Urizen*; *CP* 242)

This narration perpetually negates the grounds of its own possibility and thereby parades the fact that it is, of course, nothing but a fiction and that it could not be otherwise. But then, as Blake writes in his *Notebook*:

> Do what you will this Lifes a Fiction
> And is made up of Contradiction. (*CP* 857, see Bode 126–27)

In William Blake, the imagination is radically subjective, productive, and indicative of its agent, *and* it is at one and the same time revelatory of an Ulterior Reality, which is eternal, infinite, unchangeable, *not* subject to the understanding or reason—a Reality that, for fundamental reasons, cannot be represented in any medium.

JOHN KEATS

One of the key passages of John Keats's epistolary poetics can be found in his letter to Benjamin Bailey of 22 November 1817—it is the so-called Adam's dream passage:

> I am certain of nothing but of the holiness of the Heart's affections and the truth of Imagination—What the imagination seizes as Beauty must be truth—whether it existed before or not. . . . The Imagination may be compared to Adam's dream [the reference is to *Paradise Lost*, Book 8, 452–90]—he awoke and found it truth. (Keats 102)

"Whether it existed before or not" that is exactly the question. Unless we doubt Keats's religious orthodoxy in this matter, it was not really Adam's dream that created Eve, but God. Adam's dream was but a presentiment of something of which he certainly was not the creator.

The other passage for which Keats is justly famous is, of course, the one about *Negative Capability* as the prime prerequisite for greatness, especially in literature: "that is when a man is capable of being in uncertainties, Mysteries, doubts, without any irritable reaching after fact & reason" (letter to George and Thomas Keats, 21 and 27 December 1817; Keats 109). And, in turn, the basic prerequisite for this is that the real poet has no identity of his own but is perpetually filled by what is around him (see, for example, the filling of Apollo in *Hyperion*: "Knowledge enormous makes a God of me!"; 495). The relevant passage can be found in a letter to Richard Woodhouse (27 October 1818):

> As to the poetical character itself, it is not itself—it has no self—it is everything and nothing—It has no character. . . . A Poet is the most unpoetical of any thing in existence; because he has no Identity—he is continually in for—and filling some other Body . . . the poet has . . . no identity—he is certainly the most unpoetical of all God's creatures.

If then he has no self, and if I am a Poet, where is the Wonder that I should say I would write no more? . . . It is a wretched thing to confess, but is a very fact that no tone word I ever utter can be taken for granted as an opinion growing out of my identical nature—how can it, when I have no nature? (294–95)

In consequence, this means that John Keats's poetics is a poetics of the momentary, of the fleeting, of impressions—here is a fine passage, from the Adam's dream letter again:

I scarcely remember counting upon any Happiness—I look not for it if it be not in the present hour—nothing startles me beyond the Moment [O for a Life of Sensations rather than of Thoughts!, interpolated]—The setting sun will always set me to rights—or if a sparrow come before my Window I take part in its existence and pick about the Gravel. (103)

To be sure, this identificatory sensuousness, not to say sensuality (consider the pleasure thermometer in *Endymion*), which holds that the world is accessible only aesthetically, through our senses, and in a radically subjective way, is somewhat at odds with a poetics that tries to make any claims about objective reality, about truth in the traditional sense. In a letter to John Hamilton Reynolds (3 May 1818), Keats speaks of the "grand march of intellect" that allows Wordsworth to look deeper into "those dark Passages" than Milton did, and of "the general and gregarious advance of intellect" (245). But at the same time Keats knows that, given his poetics, it is impossible to articulate such an insight from *inside* his poetry, because there is simply no speaker's position from which such a truth could be formulated without self-contradiction.

This is borne out by Keats's abortive *Hyperion* project: one of the main reasons Keats broke off at the moment he did was that he saw the narratological impossibility of telling the story of the fall of the Titans from an *epical, auctorial* point of view—it would flatly contradict his subjective poetics, as articulated in the same epic! This is why *The Fall of Hyperion: A Dream*, his second take on the same material, is radically subjectivized and told from a first-person point of view, but remains a fragment as well: from such a point of view, which for Keats is the only possible and only modern one, no serious claims can be made about the history of mankind as such. Or even more pointedly: he may have a credible point of view now, but it does not allow him to articulate anything that would be meaningful—all the poet *can* produce, and that is surely more than enough, is *images* that have the potential to provoke us to grope for some meaning, to trigger some processes of meaning-construction in us. To put this even more pointedly: either you have a Truth but no point from which it could be credibly articulated, or you have that point but no truth that could be *spoken*—at the most, it can be implied. Therefore, to give another concrete example, the unresolved ending of *Ode to a Nightgale* is of a necessary undecideability:

> Was it a vision, or a waking dream?
> Fled is that music:—Do I wake or sleep? (460)

For a subject that hands itself over to the truth of the moment, there is no place from which it could distinguish between illusion and reality, or to tell truth from delusion. You may enjoy Eve, but you might live under the delusion that it was you who created her, and you would be the last person to be able to see through that delusion. Although it is more commonly the other way round: we do *not* see that "Eve" is our construct, which is the problematics negotiated in Keats's *Lamia* and in *La Belle Dame Sans Merci*.

"[A]xioms in philosophy," says Keats, "are not axioms until they are proved upon our pulses" (letter to J. H. Reynolds, 3 May 1820; 244). But then, one's pulses might prove all sorts of axioms, and they would not necessarily be axioms of philosophy. Keats is certainly no mystic like Blake, but he is caught in a comparable fix: from inside his poetry and poetics it is impossible to show that his truths are anything more than just fleeting impressions and subjective momentary gropings, however much he wished they were more.

P. B. SHELLEY

In the first paragraph of his *Defence of Poetry*, Shelley opposes reason, with its principle of analysis, to the imagination, with its principle of synthesis. He then goes on to argue that poetry, being the expression of the imagination, is "connate with the origin of man." Interestingly enough, Shelley's definition of the role of poets in society is very close to the formalist aesthetics of Viktor Sklovskij, as formulated in "Art as Device" (1914). Here is Shelley:

Their language is vitaly metaphorical; that is, it marks the before unapprehended relations of things, and perpetuates their apprehension,
until the words which represent them, become through time signs for
portions or classes of thoughts instead of pictures of integral thoughts;
and then if no new poets should arise to create afresh the associations
which have been thus disorganized, language will be dead to all the
nobler purposes of human intercourse. (Shelley 512)

A couple of pages later, this "unapprehended" is picked up again, with the
same implication, namely that the world exists "out there," but that our perception of it is, as it were, disastrously blunted through the cliché-ridden
and "automatic" (Sklovskij) use of everyday language:

[Poetry] awakens and enlarges the mind itself by rendering it the
receptacle of a thousand unapprehended combinations of thought.
Poetry lifts the veil from the hidden beauty of the world, and makes
familiar objects be as if they were not familiar; it reproduces all that
it represents, and the impersonations clothed in its Elysian light stand
thenceforward in the minds of those who have once contemplated
them, as memorials of that gentle and exalted content which extends
itself over all thoughts and actions with which it coexists. (517)

Language has this special power to either blunt or sharpen our experience of the world because, differing from the materials of other arts, it is
more closely related to thought, to the "actions and passions of our internal
being." Here is Shelley again:

And this springs from the nature itself of language, which is a more
direct representation of the actions and passions of our internal
being, and is susceptible of more various and delicate combinations,
than colour, form, or motion, and is more plastic or obedient to the
controul of that faculty of which it is the creation. For language is
arbitrarily produced by the Imagination and has relation to thoughts
alone. (513)

This idea that "language is arbitrarily produced by the Imagination and has
relation to thoughts alone," and not to objects, is an intriguing one, but it
also complicates Shelley's familiar claim that poetry

strips the veil of familiarity from the world, and lays bare the naked
and sleeping beauty which is the spirit of its forms. . . . [I]t purges from
our inward sight the film of familiarity which obscures from us the
wonder of our being. It compels us to feel that which we perceive, and
to imagine that which we know. It creates anew the universe after it
has been annihilated in our minds by the recurrence of impressions
blunted by reiteration. (533)

This "purging" is a bit like Blake's cleansing of the doors of perception, after
which every thing will appear as it is, infinite. But here the relationship
between language, thought, and world is a highly tricky one: language has
relation to thought alone, and yet its use is said to have a direct bearing on
the way we see the world. This can only be if language, and poetry in particular, as systems, structurally reproduce "the common universe of which
we are portions and percipients" (533). One can call this Shelley's idealis-
tic/linguistic turn: "All things exist as they are perceived," and perception
is a function of language. In a way, this is logically compelling, but what
about those "unapprehended relations"? Do they exist, really, before they
are apprehended? If not, how can we speak of a re-discovery of the world? If
they do, how can we say that all things exist as they are perceived, and that
language has relation to thought alone?

Similarly to Keats, Shelley believes that poetry records moments of
unusual intensity—"Poetry is the record of the best and happiest moments
of the happiest and best minds"—and thus gives permanence to "the visitations of the divinity in man" (532). But Shelley wants to ignore, or so it
seems, that once locked in the prisonhouse of language, it is a bit difficult
for human beings to say anything about the world outside, the world prior
to language, the world as such. In what I think is one of Shelley's most
thought-provoking pieces, the essay "On Life," he draws the most radical
conclusions from this linguistic turn:

Nothing exists but as it is perceived. The difference is merely nomi-
nal between those two classes of thought which are vulgarly distinguished by the names of ideas and of external objects. Pursuing the
same thread of reasoning, the existence of distinct individual minds
similar to that which is employed in now questioning its own nature,
is likewise found to be a delusion. The words, *I, you, they*, are not signs
of any actual difference subsisting between the assemblage of thoughts

thus indicated, but are merely marks employed to denote the different modifications of the one mind. . . . The words *I*, and *you* and *they* are grammatical devices invented simply for arrangement and totally devoid of the intense and exclusive sense usually attached to them. It is difficult to find terms adequately to express so subtle a conception as that to which the intellectual philosophy has conducted us. We are on that verge where words abandon us, and what wonder if we grow dizzy to look down the dark abyss of—how little we know. (508)

There is a contradiction in Shelley's philosophy, in his poetics and poetry, in that he holds, on the one hand, that we can experience the world only through the grid of our language and thought—that is not only the way in which it is *accessible* to us, it is also the only way in which it *exists*—and that, on the other hand, there is still a beyond, though we cannot conceive of it.

This contradiction between the view that the imagination constructs the world in its own image (so that, since our thinking has a grammatical structure, the world is ultimately a function of grammar), and the opposite view that there is a world out there that has patterns, structures, and relations all by itself, which we may apprehend or not, depending on whether the veil is lifted or not, shows itself in most interesting ways in innumerous of Shelley's poems. Three brief examples must suffice:

1) In his poem "To a Sky-Lark," the lyrical voice states that, "What thou art we know not; / What is most like thee?" and then circles the "blithe Spirit! Bird thou never wert—" (305) in a series of similes: the ultimate reality of the sky-lark, its essence, if you will, cannot be reached. What we get instead is a series of approximations to something that, by definition, can never be brought into the realm of the sayable, into human discourse.

2) In "Ozymandias," a prime example of Romantic irony, one of the messages seems to be that the meaning of any writing crucially depends on its context, and that these varying contexts, given enough time, can change radically and thereby change the message radically. This insight is presented in writing, so that any act of reading of this sonnet must necessarily pay attention to the very precariousness of what it has just identified as "the meaning" of that writing.

3) In "The Triumph of Life" we encounter the impossibility for any first-person narrator to make coherent sense of what he sees (in this respect the poem is reminiscent of Keats's *The Fall of Hyperion: A Dream*). As the narrative torch is passed on to the shade of Rousseau, we become aware (because of the similarity of what is described) that it is no longer possible to distinguish between the qualitatively and hierarchically different narrative levels. When the question of the meaning of it all is asked for the fourth and last time— "Then, what is Life?" (500)— and is left without an answer, we have finally understood that this is no longer a "Vision" whose meaning is self-evident, though a bit difficult to report. If it is true that we can understand only what we have made ourselves, then certainly the meaning of "life in general" is something about which we cannot, and therefore should not, speak (Wittgenstein).

More seriously: Shelley's advanced poetics does not allow him to speak about things beyond language. That seems a reasonable restraint. Sadly, this is exactly what he would love to do most of all and most of the time. So he endeavors to widen the realm of what is sayable and thinkable. He lifts veil after veil, and is forever "purg[ing] from our inward sight the film of familiarity," all the time *never* knowing whether he got it right this time, because there is no "right" this side of language. The rest, of course, is silence.

ROBERT FROST

Robert Frost once famously defined the figure a poem makes as "a momentary stay against confusion" (*Norton Anthology of American Literature* 1175). A poetry derived from such an outlook is not necessarily affirmative about the universe, or at least it is less so than most people think. Like his Romantic predecessors, Frost negotiates the question whether the world as it presents itself is a meaningful one or whether it is "just us" projecting meaning onto a world that is essentially mute, meaningless, chaotic, and indifferent to man.

In his disconcerting poem entitled "Design," Front explores this problem of whether there is a "design" out there in creation and whether, if there is, this is a good thing or not. All one has to know before reading the poem is that normally the flower called heal-all is blue, so that the flower in the poem has mutated—it is a chance mutation in a flower that normally is not white:

I found a dimpled spider, fat and white,
On a white heal-all, holding up a moth
Like a white piece of rigid satin cloth—
Assorted characters of death and blight
Mixed ready to begin the morning right,
Like the ingredients of a witches' broth—
A snow-drop spider, a flower like a froth,
And dead wings carried like a paper kite.

What had that flower to do with being white,
The wayside blue and innocent heal-all?
What brought the kindred spider to that height,
Then steered the white moth thither in the night?
What but design of darkness to appall?—
If design govern in a thing so small. (Frost 302)

Sharing the existentialist skepticism behind so much of Frost's poetry, "Design" questions the coincidence of three: spider, flower, and moth. Is it governed by laws of necessity and nature? Is it governed by mere chance? Is there a coherent and purposeful pattern, as opposed to chaos? Bringing in intentionality, could there be a plan, a scheme, an intent, a plot? Could it be that, going far beyond indifference, this universe is openly hostile and malevolent? The alternative seems to be: either everything, even "things so small," is governed by necessity (this would be at odds with our idea of freedom of the will and personal accountability), or everything is just chance, coincidence, and contingency (this would be at odds with our idea of human dignity and with assumptions about the meaning of life). Either way, the sight is not too pleasing for humanity—it is an insult to our presumptions, whichever way you look at it.

The form of this poem is, of course, a sonnet, a perfectly composed one at that. There is a design that sets patterns against the randomness of the universe, or against its dark designs. That is what art is about: to pattern structures that *look* as if they were meaningful (and most probably *are* because they are *man-made* and because there is an intelligence and a design behind them). In Frost, we encounter the possibility that, no matter whether there is a design in creation or not, man-made patterns are a necessity. They are not just a minor, somewhat deficient, small-scale version of meaning production, but are *the very thing itself.* Man-made patterns form a necessary stay against the confusion that is reality, against the non-human, indifferent, impersonally hostile design that we can make out. But characteristically, the question of whether there is design in creation is answered ambiguously. The only objective design or pattern we can definitely discern here is the sonnet, nothing else.

H. D.

Next to Ezra Pound's "In a Station of the Metro," H. D.'s "Oread" is arguably the most famous imagist poem of the twentieth century. It reads:

> Whirl up, sea—
> Whirl your pointed pines,
> splash your great pines
> on our rocks,
> hurl your green over us,
> cover us with your pools of fir.
>   (*Norton Anthology of American Literature* 1305)

What is fascinating about this poem is that it is organized in such a way that it is impossible to say what is the tenor and what is the vehicle of the suggested metaphorical operation: are we to see the sea in terms of a forest of pine trees, or are we invited to imagine a forest of pine trees as an agitated sea? Surely both.

What makes this double metaphorical suggestion possible—to see x in terms of y, and y in terms of x—is, of course, a similarity *in reality*: the wind creates similar patterns in water and trees. This is an important point, but one that is often forgotten, even in handbooks and encyclopedias: metaphorical substitution does not depend upon a similarity in the *signs* (be they written or spoken), but upon a similarity in the *objects*, the *referents*. (Shelley would have to explain how, if language has reference to thought alone, metaphorical substitution is possible at all. In what way could one say that thoughts, in the sense of *signifiés* or concepts, are similar to each other?)

Aristotle was very clear about this when he defined, in his *Poetics*, a good metaphor as one that was at once clear *and* unusual, and the capability to coin one as a true mark of genius: "The greatest thing by far is to be a master of metaphor. It is the one thing that cannot be learnt from others; and it is also a sign of genius, since a good metaphor implies an intuitive perception of the similarity in dissimilars" (22). Do these similarities exist in reality, and are they only *discovered*? Or are they *created* by the metaphorical suggestion? Do metaphors simply draw our attention to and recreate an analogy that exists before them? Or do they *produce* knowledge, *create* structure, pattern, design, meaning?

I am very much in sympathy with Paul Ricœur's reading of Aristotle (in *La métaphore vive*), which is crucially based on a passage in Aristotle's *Rhetoric* (1411b 24–25) and emphasizes the creative and innovative potential of metaphors, their "heuristic function" and their capability to reveal and transform. But that is the decisive point: even Ricœur subscribes to a referential theory of language. It is not reality "as such" that is transformed by metaphor, but our perception of it (which is no mean thing). However, it seems to me significant that at a time when the French *symbolistes* and T. S. Eliot had already discovered *la métaphore absolue*, H. D. still clung to a substitutional idea of metaphor, which anchors poetic language much more firmly to outside reality. It is significant because of H. D.'s further development as a poet and the systematic use she made of myth and symbol systems such as kabbala and tarot, as well as mysticism and the occult, and psychological concepts derived from Freud and, more importantly, from C. G. Jung.

For example, H. D.'s "Helen in Egypt" (1961), which offers a female perspective on the Trojan War, and her long poems written during World War II, such as "The Walls Do Not Fall" (1944), which thematizes the London *Blitz*, display a typical merging of the personal, the historical, and the mythical. In that regard, these works are comparable to Pound and Eliot. The difference, however, is that H. D. seems to have believed in the reality of these similarities and patterns. In H. D., the private becomes political and universal, whereas for Eliot, myth was only a pattern, a scaffold to arrange his materials on (as it was for Joyce; see Eliot's review of *Ulysses* in 1923, "*Ulysses*, Order, and Myth"). For Eliot and Joyce, myth is only a *method*; for H. D., it is increasingly a *reality*. In this respect, H. D. may be closest to W. B. Yeats, who also believed in the objective reality of such patterns.

This is an interesting variation on the pattern that has been established so far: H. D. and Yeats, differing from Joyce and Eliot, but also from Keats and Shelley (though not unlike Blake), believe in the objective reality of meanings and patterns that the human imagination *discovers* but certainly does not create *ex nihilo*. The problem, of course, is that the truth of these mystical or psychological systems can only be believed; it cannot be proven logically.

WALLACE STEVENS

The case of Wallace Stevens is arguably the most complicated in my series, but since the pattern, with its variants, has already been established, I can restrict myself to a few essential observations. On the one hand, we find in Wallace Stevens the firm conviction that it is the human imagination that transcends empirical reality, as we perceive it through the senses. To quote from "The Snow Man":

> One must have a mind of winter
> To regard the frost and the boughs
> Of the pine-trees crusted with snow;
>
> And have been cold a long time
> To behold the junipers shagged with ice,
> The spruces rough in the distant glitter
>
> Of the January sun; and not to think
> Of any misery in the sound of the wind,
> In the sound of a few leaves,
>
> Which is the sound of the land
> Full of the same wind
> That is blowing in the same bare place
>
> For the listener, who listens in the snow,
> And, nothing himself, beholds
> Nothing that is not there and the nothing that is. (Stevens 9–10)

The imagination (if one does not have a mind of winter) makes one hear the misery in the wind, but makes one also behold the nothingness and realize the fact that reality is more than what we perceive through the senses: the nothing that is (there) is the reality of the imgaination that transcends empirical reality.

Stevens is also the great poet of point of view, of subjective projection and innovative metaphorical proposals, as evidenced in "Thirteen Ways of Looking at a Blackbird" (92–95), which can be compared with Hokusai's series of woodcuts *Thirty-six Views of Mount Fuji*, and displays a koan-like quality in its mini stanzas. Sometimes these "ways of looking at" are easily decipherable (especially when an optical phenomenon is alluded to, for example, in IX and XII); sometimes they look like a bold metaphysical conceit (see I). But the implication is always that whatever the blackbird may be, its meaning depends on the way we look at it.

Meaning is imposed upon the world as we confront it. That seems also to be the central message, if one can be abstracted from a poem, of Stevens's "The Idea of Order at Key West":

> She was the single artificer of the world
> In which she sang. And when she sang, the sea,
> Whatever self it had, became the self
> That was her song, for she was the maker. Then we,
> As we beheld her striding there alone,
> Knew that there never was a world for her
> Except the one she sang and, singing, made. (129–30)

The maker's "rage for order" (130) creates the only world she will ever inhabit—a world of her own making, meaningfully opposed to "the grinding water and the gasping wind" (129), which, *as part of her discourse only*, become part of her world, and thereby meaningful.

To generalize: It is the task of the poet, the artist, the composer, to impose order upon the world, and thereby to change it, to transform it into something different. To quote stanzas 1 and 2 from Stevens's "The Man with the Blue Guitar":

> I
> The man bent over his guitar,
> A shearsman of sorts. The day was green.
>
> They said, "You have a blue guitar,
> You do not play things as they are."
>
> The man replied, "Things as they are
> Are changed upon the blue guitar."
>
> And they said then, "But play, you must,
> A tune beyond us, yet ourselves,

A tune upon the blue guitar
Of things exactly as they are."

                    II
I cannot bring a world quite round,
Although I patch it as I can.

I sing a hero's head, large eye
And bearded bronze, but not a man,

Although I patch him as I can
And reach through him almost to man.

If to serenade almost to man
Is to miss, by that, things as they are,

Say that it is the serenade
Of a man that plays a blue guitar. (165–66)

And yet, on the other hand, this view of the relationship between the imagination and reality stands in marked opposition to a view that was also held by Wallace Stevens and which is programmatically summed up in his poem "Not Ideas About the Thing But the Thing Itself," strategically placed at the very end of his *Collected Poetry*.

Can one write a *poem* about a thing that is not at the same time an *idea* about that thing? Is that not in glaring contradiction to Stevens's insight that one cannot have the thing "as such," the thing as *not* perceived by a human subject (see "Thirteen Ways" and "The Idea of Order at Key West")? Within that paradigm and discourse one can, of course, try to be open to the "thing itself," not to impose too much upon it. But against what would this "too much" have to be gauged or measured? It is the same problem that we have already encountered in Shelley.

In an essay from 1942, Stevens argues that poetry has to create order, but that it also must confront reality time and again in order to remain a living force. In *Adagia* (1957) he writes: "The relation of art to life is of the first importance especially in a skeptical age since, in the absence of a belief in God, the mind turns to its own creations and examines them, not alone from the aesthetic point of view, but for what they reveal, for what they validate and invalidate, for the support they give" (*Dictionary of Literary Biography* 3). In the poem "Of Modern Poetry" he speaks of "The poem of the mind in the act of finding / What will suffice. . . . The Poem of the act of the mind" (Stevens 239, 240).

My final quote from a Stevens poem is taken from "Notes Toward a Supreme Fiction":

> But to impose is not
> To discover. To discover an order as of
> A season, to discover summer and know it,
>
> To discover winter and know it well, to find,
> Not to impose, not to have reasoned at all,
> Out of nothing to have come on major weather,
>
> It is possible, possible, possible. It must
> Be possible. (403–04)

That is exactly the problem: to try and get to the thing itself, to present it in its concreteness—revelation, epiphany, the sublime—but to be communicated, it has to be put in language. The thing itself cannot be mediated. What remains? "The final belief," says Wallace Stevens in one of his "Adagia," "is to believe in a fiction, which you know to be a fiction, there being nothing else. The exquisite truth is to know that it is a fiction and that you believe in it willingly" (*Dictionary of Literary Biography* 16).

CODA

To sum up: we find in these Romantic and Modernist poets a certain contradiction with regard to their ideas about the relationship between the imagination and reality. On the one hand, they seem to hold that the patterns and structures we discern in reality are imposed upon it by the imagination. In consequence, meaning is man-made, necessarily constricted by a medium once you try to communicate it; it is subjective, relative, subject to change. On the other hand, these poets seem to hold that the imagination can discover or reveal an ultimate reality, an ultimate truth, a purer, richer, and more adequate view of the world. Obviously, these latter claims cannot possibly be supported if one subscribes to the first set of ideas. The continuity between Romanticism and Modernism is, among other things, the continuity of that contradiction and the continuity of attempts to negotiate it, both in poetry and poetics.

Why do we find this continuity? Generally speaking, with the advent of a fully fledged, functionally differentiated society in the eighteenth century (see Niklas Luhmann), literature is formally freed from any obligation to transport a coherent worldview or ideology that would be binding for any subsystem of society, let alone for society at large. This liberation is accompanied by the devising of the first absolute or autonomous poetics and aesthetics (of which P. B. Shelley's *A Defence of Poetry* is a very fine example). Both in theory and practice, this sea change coincides with an increased awareness of the co-extension of language and thinking, of the restraints of mediality, and of the fluidity of verbal signs. The concept of Romantic irony is a prime indicator of an acute awareness of the whole cluster of conditions under which poetry is composed in modernity. Nevertheless, the gesture with which much of this poetry and the accompanying poetics are presented remains that of the prophet, seer, or purveyor of a higher truth, as if the poet were still functioning in the hierarchically stratified society of pre-modern times. Even if the poems draw attention to their own necessary limitations, this is ultimately done to point to an absolute that, regrettably, can only be hinted at, but cannot be spoken about. The truth claim remains an extraordinary one—especially in these cases, especially when an unspeakable "beyond" is indicated.

Readers who are less familiar with systems theory may perhaps wonder why it is possible, in a historical period characterized by a freeing of literature from any obligation to transport extra-literary ideologies, that poets should still strike the pose of seer or *vates*, of purveyor of a higher truth. But maybe this puzzlement is due only to a confusion on the reader's part of how a historical situation is described in Luhmannian terms with how poets see themselves. The two points of view do not necessarily coincide— as in the history of art, when an art historian describes how, for example, a Mondrian "works" and how abstract art evolves out of Impressionism, this account is bound to be curiously at odds with Mondrian's own theosophic explanation of why he practices non-objective art. In other words (and going back to literature again): within the paradigm of a subsystem of literature that is no longer subservient to any outside authority, it is, of course, perfectly possible for poets to act as if they were prophets. Or party spokespersons. Or nobody in particular. They don't have to. But they can.

Still, the contradiction mentioned above is striking, but then it is an inevitable contradiction: there is only one attitude that is adequate to reading an absolute, modern poem (Arthur Rimbaud: *Il faut être absolument moderne!* [It is necessary to be absolutely modern!]), and that is to treat it as an absolute structure that contains and produces its own meaning, its own patterns, and, more dynamically, its trajectory of meaning. The task for the modern reader is to read the poem *as if* it were a world (if not *the* world). The presupposition must be that it has a meaning—why else read it? Barred from making authoritative statements about God, the universe, and everything, Romantic and Modernist poets present miniature textual worlds. The poems are worlds—subjective constructs, to be sure, but to be engaged with, to be deciphered *as if* they spoke of more than just themselves. And of course they do, inevitably. To the same degree that they thematize their ways of meaning production, they allegorically thematize our own ways of making sense of the world and of our lives. Liberated from the task of conveying meanings produced elsewhere, poems become instantiations of their own meanings, which can be unravelled only if they are scrutinized in their own right.

In other words, it is exactly this contradictory idea of the imagination that defines poetry in this specific historical phase and prepares the way for an adequate aesthetics of reading: the imagination is seen as creative, as productive of the meanings and patterns poetry communicates, and at the same time it is claimed that it is "not just that," that there is more to it, that the meanings and patterns evoked by this poetry are "really" there and not just a subjective projection. And of course, they are *really* there because the poem is there, as an object, to be studied in its own right (the pattern of Frost's sonnet is undeniable). Sometimes the power of the subjective imagination seems something to glory in, sometimes something to make apologies for. It all depends on which section of the argumentative circle you happen to be in at the moment. Modern physicists tell us that sometimes light behaves as if it were waves, sometimes as if it were corpuscles. And yet, it is always light.

The dichotomy of an imagination that *creates* reality and of an imagination that *discovers* reality seems to be irresolvable and characteristic of modern society. Maybe the best way to approach the autonomous structure of poetry characteristic of a functionally differentiated society with an autonomous subsystem of "literature" is to practice "poetic faith," which Samuel Taylor Coleridge defined as a "willing suspension of disbelief for the moment" (Coleridge 490), *and* to act *as if* this poetry were not "just" a subjective construction, but also something that is *objectively* there (which it is) and that makes not only great claims, but also places huge demands on us.

Romanticism and Modernism share a contradiction. It is this shared contradiction that points to the possibility that these two phases in the history of an autonomous literature have more in common than is traditionally assumed.[2] For these truths and meanings can only be suggested and *experienced*, which is why the aesthetic experience becomes analogous to a revelatory or visionary experience. The best way is to believe in the fiction, and have it both ways. Sometimes, to impose *can be* to discover.

NOTES

1   I cite Blake's works with the abbreviations *CP* for *The Complete Poems* and *PP* for *The Complete Poetry and Prose*.

2   One may wonder whether the continuity pointed out in this essay extends through Postmodernism as well. But that would be the topic of an entirely different essay. Suffice it here to say that from the point of view of systems theory we are, of course, still in the period of functional differentiation, or Modernity, which indicates a basic continuity of conditions for the production of literature. On the other hand, it would be unsophisticated not to differentiate within this historical phase and not to acknowledge that interesting changes occur between Modernist and Postmodernist poetry. One of these changes could be exactly that this role of the seer can no longer be assumed in earnest.

WORKS CITED

Aristotle. *The Works of Aristotle.* Vol. 2. Chicago: Encyclopedia Britannica, 1987.

Blake, William. *The Complete Poems* [*CP*]. Ed. Alicia Ostriker. London: Penguin, 1977.

Blake, William. *The Complete Poetry and Prose of William Blake* [*PP*]. Newly revised edition. Ed. David V. Erdman. New York: Doubleday, 1988.

Bode, Christoph. "Huxley and Blake: The Meeting of the Parallels." *The Perennial Satirist: Essays in Honour of Bernfried Nugel.* Ed. Hermann J. Real and Peter E. Firchow. Münster: LIT, 2005. 123–40.

Coleridge, Samuel Taylor. *Coleridge's Poetry and Prose: Authoritative Texts, Criticism.* Ed. Nicholas Halmi, Paul Magnuson, and Raimonda Modiano. New York: Norton, 2004.

Derrida, Jacques. "Force of Law: The Mystical Foundation of Authority." *Deconstruction and the Possibility of Justice*. Ed. Drucilla Cornell, Michael Rosenfeld, and David Gray Carlson. New York: Routledge, 1999. 3–67.

Dictionary of Literary Biography, Volume 54: American Poets, 1880–1945. Third Series. Detroit: Gale, 1987, s.v. "Wallace Stevens," 471–505, here accessed through *Literature Resource Centre*, http://galenet.galegroup.com/servlet/LitRC, 11/27/2006.

Eliot, T. S. "*Ulysses*, Order, and Myth." *Selected Prose of T. S. Eliot*. New York: Harcourt, 1975. 175–78.

Frost, Robert. *The Poetry of Robert Frost: The Collected Poems, Complete and Unabridged*. Ed. Edward Connery Lathem. New York: Holt, Rinehart and Winston, 1969, 1979.

Keats, John. *Keats's Poetry and Prose: Authoritative Texts, Criticism*. Ed. Jeffrey N. Cox. New York: Norton, 2009.

Luhmann, Niklas. *Soziale Systeme: Grundriß einer allgemeinen Theorie*. 2nd ed. Frankfurt/Main: Suhrkamp, 1988.

The Norton Anthology of American Literature. Sixth Edition, Volume D. New York: Norton, 2003.

Ricœur, Paul. *La métaphore vive*. Paris: Editions du Seuil, 1975.

Shelley, Percy Bysshe. *Shelley's Poetry and Prose: Authoritative Texts, Criticism*. 2nd ed. Ed. Donald H. Reiman and Neil Fraistat. New York: Norton, 2002.

Stevens, Wallace. *The Collected Poems*. New York: Vintage, 1990.

Biographies of Editors
and Contributors

HAZARD ADAMS is Professor Emeritus of Comparative Literature at the University of Washington. He is the author of numerous works on Blake, Yeats, Joyce Cary, Lady Gregory, and literary theory, as well as four novels and a book of poems. With Leroy Searle, he is co-editor of the third edition of *Critical Theory since Plato* (2004). He was the founding Chair in 1964 of the Department of English and Comparative Literature at the University of California, Irvine, where he also served as Dean of Humanities and Vice Chancellor. His *The Offense of Poetry* was published in 2007, *Academic Child: A Memoir* in 2008, *Blake's Margins* in 2009, and *William Blake on His Poetry and Painting* in 2010.

RICHARD BLOCK is Associate Professor of Germanics at the University of Washington, a Board member of the European Studies Program, and he teaches in the Jewish Studies Program. He is the author of *The Spell of Italy: Vacation, Magic and the Attraction of Goethe* (2006) and essays on the rebirth of modern literary Zionism, post-Marxist readings of Hegel, and Walter Benjamin's relationship with the George Circle. His current book project investigates the emergence of same-sex desire in the early nineteenth century and how it disables any history of sexuality.

CHRISTOPH BODE is Full Professor and Chair of English Literature at Ludwig-Maximilians-Universität in Munich and Fellow of LMU's Center for Advanced Studies. His major fields are Romanticism, twentieth-century English and American literature, critical theory, and travel writing. He is President of the German Society for English Romanticism and serves on the Advisory Boards of *European Romantic Review* and the *North American Society for Study of Romanticism*, NASSR. In 2006 he was elected Centenary Fellow of the English Association, and in 2007 he became Christensen Fellow at St. Catherine's, Oxford. Bode was awarded the Anglistentagspreis 1988 for *The Aesthetics of Ambiguity* (1988). His recent work includes *The Novel* (forthcoming, 2011) and co-editing *British and European Romanticisms* (2007), *Re-mapping Romanticism: Gender, Texts, Contexts* (2001), and *Historicizing/Contemporizing Shakespeare* (2000).

GEORG BRAUNGART is Professor of Modern German Literature at the University of Tübingen. He has published widely on various topics in German literature and culture. His books include *Leibhafter Sinn* (1993), which examines the tradition of embodied meaning in German literary and philosophical culture from the Enlightenment to Modernism, and *Hofberedsamkeit* (1986), a study of political discourse in the German courts during the period of absolutism. He received a grant from the Volkswagen-Foundation in 2010, and he is currently working on a book project dealing with the repercussions of geological discoveries on German literature of the eighteenth and nineteenth centuries.

MICHAEL N. FORSTER is Glen A. Lloyd Distinguished Service Professor of Philosophy at the University of Chicago, where he served as Chair for ten years. He works mainly in German philosophy, but also has interests in ancient philosophy. His thematic emphasis is on issues in epistemology and the philosophy of language. He is the author of six books: *After Herder: Philosophy of Language in the German Tradition* (2010), *Kant and Skepticism* (2008), *Wittgenstein on the Arbitrariness of Grammar* (2004*)*, *Herder: Philosophical Writings* (2002), *Hegel's Idea of a Phenomenology of Spirit* (1998), and *Hegel and Skepticism* (1989). He also has three books forthcoming: *German Philosophy of Language from Schlegel to Hegel and Beyond*, *Herder's Philosophy*, and *After Wittgenstein: Essays on Modern Philosophy of Language*.

RICHARD T. GRAY is Byron W. and Alice L. Lockwood Professor in the Humanities in the Department of Germanics at the University of Washington. He is the author of several books, including *About Face: German Physiognomic Thought from Lavater to Auschwitz* (2004), *Stations of the Divided Subject: Contestation and Ideological Legitimation in German Bourgeois Literature, 1770–1912* (1995), and *Constructive Destruction: Kafka's Aphorisms* (1987). His most recent book is *Money Matters: Economics and the German Cultural Imagination, 1770–1850* (2008). Gray is also the general editor of the series "Literary Conjugations," which publishes books in the broad field of literary studies for the University of Washington Press.

NICHOLAS HALMI is University Lecturer in English Literature of the Romantic Period at Oxford University and the author of *The Genealogy of the Romantic Symbol* (2007), editor of *Fearful Symmetry: A Study of William Blake by Northrop Frye* (2004), and co-editor of the Norton critical edition of *Coleridge's Poetry and Prose* (2003) and a volume in *The Collected Works of Samuel Taylor Coleridge: Opus Maximum* (2002).

GARY J. HANDWERK is Professor of English and Comparative Literature and Chair of the Department of English at the University of Washington. His scholarly work focuses on modern European narrative and narrative theory, with particular interest in narrative ethics and the relation between political philosophy and fiction. His recent publications engage Romantic-era texts and include critical editions of William Godwin's *Caleb Williams* (2000) and *Fleetwood* (2000) as well as essays on several of Godwin's novels and Jean-Jacques Rousseau's *Emile*. He is the translator and editor of *Human, All Too Human*, in *The Complete Works of Friedrich Nietzsche* (2000), and author of an article on Romantic irony in the *Cambridge History of Literary Criticism, Volume V: Romanticism* (2000).

BETH LORD is Lecturer in Philosophy in the School of Humanities at the University of Dundee, Scotland. Her work focuses on seventeenth- and eighteenth-century philosophy and its connections to contemporary European thought. She is the author of *Kant and Spinozism: Transcendental Idealism and Immanence from Jacobi to Deleuze* (2010), and *Spinoza's Ethics: An Edinburgh Philosophical Guide* (2010). She is co-editor of the *Continuum Companion to Continental Philosophy* (2009) and director of the UK-based Spinoza Research Network.

ROBERT B. PIPPIN is the Evelyn Stefansson Nef Distinguished Service Professor in the Committee on Social Thought and the Department of Philosophy at the University of Chicago. He is the author of several books on German idealism, including *Modernism as a Philosophical Problem: On the Dissatisfactions of European High Culture* (1991), *Hegel's Idealism: The Satisfactions of Self-Consciousness* (1989), and *Idealism as Modernism: Hegelian Variations* (1997). His latest books are *The Persistence of Subjectivity: On the Kantian Aftermath* (2005); *Hegel's Practical Philosophy: Rational Agency as Ethical Life* (2009); *Hollywood Westerns and American Myth: The Importance of Howard Hawks and John Ford for Political Philosophy* (2010), and *Nietzsche, Psychology, First Philosophy* (2010). He is a past winner of the Mellon Distinguished Achievement Award in the Humanities and is a fellow of the American Academy of Arts and Sciences and the American Philosophical Society.

TILOTTAMA RAJAN is Canada Research Chair in English and Theory at the University of Western Ontario, where she was Director of the Centre for Theory Criticism from 1995–2001. She is the author of *Romantic Narrative: Shelley, Hays, Godwin, Wollstonecraft* (2010), *Deconstruction and the Remainders of Phenomenology: Sartre, Derrida, Foucault, Baudrillard* (2002), *The Supplement of Reading: Figures of Understanding in Romantic Theory and Practice* (1990), and *Dark Interpreter: The Discourse of Romanticism* (1980). She has also edited five books, most recently *Idealism Without Absolutes: Philosophy and Romantic Culture* (2004). She is currently working on a book on encyclopedic thought and the organization of knowledge from German idealism to deconstruction.

MICHAEL A. ROSENTHAL is Associate Professor of Philosophy and a member of the Jewish Studies Program at the University of Washington. He is the author of numerous articles on Spinoza and early modern philosophy, which have appeared in journals including *Archiv für Geschichte der Philosophie*, *Journal of the History of Philosophy*, and *Journal of Political Philosophy*. He is the co-editor of *Spinoza's Theological-Political Treatise: A Critical Guide* (2010), and he is currently working on a book on Spinoza's political philosophy.

KLAUS VIEWEG is Professor of Philosophy at the Friedrich Schiller University of Jena. His research focuses on German Idealism, especially Hegel, and Skepticism. He is the author of *Philosophie des Remis—Der junge Hegel und das Gespenst des Skeptizismus* (1999), *Freiheit und Skepsis—Hegel über den Skeptizismus zwischen Philosophie und Literatur* (2007), *Il pensiero della libertà—Hegel e lo scetticismo pirroniano* (2007) and *La idea de la libertad* (2009), editor of *Friedrich Schlegel und Friedrich Nietzsche—Transzendentalpoesie oder Dichtkunst mit Begriffen* (2009), *Hegel: Die Philosophie der Geschichte* (2005), and co-editor of *Hegels Phänomenologie des Geistes* (2008), *Das Interesse des Denkens: Hegel aus heutiger Sicht* (2003), *Hegel und Nietzsche: Eine literarisch-philosophische Begegnung* (2007), and *Skepsis und literarische Imagination* (2004). Currently he is working on a book entitled *Das Denken der Freiheit: Hegels Grundlinien der Philosophie des Rechts*.

WILHELM VOSSKAMP is Professor of German Studies at the University of Cologne. His diverse publications present historical perspectives back to the seventeenth century, considering classicism and the Enlightenment periods, the nineteenth century, and modern media studies. He specializes in the genres of poetry and the novel, spanning the breadth of literary theory and science, from Weimar classicism to contemporary literature. He edits the book series *Communicatio*, and he has recently published *Der Roman des Lebens* (2009).

WOLFGANG WELSCH is Professor of Theoretical Philosophy at Friedrich Schiller University of Jena. In 1992 he was awarded the Max-Planck Research Prize. His main areas of research are epistemology and anthropology, philosophical aesthetics and art theory, cultural philosophy, and contemporary philosophy. He is currently working on a strictly evolutionary conception of the human, including both biological and cultural evolution. His major book publications are *Vernunft: Die zeitgenössische Vernunftkritik und das Konzept der transversalen Vernunft* (4th edition, 2007), *Ästhetisches Denken* (6th edition, 2003), *Unsere postmoderne Moderne* (7th edition, 2008), and *Undoing Aesthetics* (1997).

INDEX